Praise for *Holding the H*

'*Holding the Hope* charts the way to fertile ground thı shock, overwhelm, paralysis and despair. These essays, written by trailblazers in climate psychology and related domains of existential coaching, psychotherapy and philosophy, will validate, strengthen and inspire those looking to help others on this path. A gritty gift for these times.'
Britt Wray, PhD, author of *Generation Dread* and Planetary Health Fellow, Stanford University School of Medicine

'Climate change is a crisis confronting us all, clients and therapists alike. This innovative and important collection of chapters can help us meet this challenge with hope and with a sense of possibility for overcoming inactivity, resignation and despair. An essential read for therapists who want to face the reality of our world in crisis with their eyes open.'
Mick Cooper, Professor of Counselling Psychology, University of Roehampton, and author of *Psychology at the Heart of Social Change*

'The rich contributions here provide prophetic clarion calls for (bio) diverse transformation and engagement, simultaneously synthesising the environmental, political and personal. The chapters are strung together on a thread of hope, with hope itself critiqued rigorously. The reader is left in no doubt that mindless optimism has no space here; rather, what is needed is the radical hope of Jonathan Lear, reflected on deeply in Hetty Einzig's chapter, or what Nick Totton calls for – a releasing of hope, out of our control and into the wild, to make its own way. There is nourishment here, too, for our clinical practices – not fast food, but substantial slow cooking. I am deeply grateful for the work of so many behind this essential curation.'
Judith Anderson, Chair, Climate Psychology Alliance

'Hope dies, action begins. These words helped us to set the tone for Extinction Rebellion back in 2018. I know that where we are headed we will need therapeutic relationships and practices. So this is a timely contribution to the world we find ourselves in, and with excellent breadth and depth. This enriching compilation will be very helpful if it will assist people to find courage after despair and reckon with the responsibility we now shoulder to make hope possible through engagement, care and action. For, in these times, we must earn our hope.'
Clare Farrell, co-founder of Extinction Rebellion, fashion designer and lecturer

'This beautifully curated and intelligent collection reminds us of the interconnectedness that is our birth right and the wisdom that lies in accessing diversity of voices and cultures. Not a comfortable read, given the territory – ecological emergency – but also the authors choose depth, authenticity and courage over cheerleading and false hope. Yet the overarching sense is that there is hope. A vibrant and vital read for all helping professionals.'
Liz Hall, editor of *Coaching at Work*, leadership coach, mindfulness teacher and author of *Mindful Coaching*

'The editors have brought together practitioners from around the world to share insights, examples and pragmatic processes that can help us all – personally and professionally. This book makes significant contributions to reintegrating the natural environment back into our professional and cultural paradigms, helping us all through the emotions of letting in such a disturbing current reality. This book is a powerful call to reconceive the individualistic foundations of our notions of health and therapy.'
Dr Josie McLean, co-founder of Climate Coaching Alliance, coach, leadership and organisational developer and past President of ICF Australasia

'Mild concerns about climate change only a couple of decades ago have now shifted to intense fears of an impending climate crisis and disaster. This book is a call to action for coaches and counsellors and their professional bodies to face up to the challenges of the climate catastrophe while remaining hopeful that it can be addressed. Instead of just becoming overwhelmed by the current situation, practitioners will find this book helpful to stay focused and motivated.'
Professor Stephen Palmer, Director, International Centre for Ecopsychology, Fellow of the Royal Society of Biology and editor of the *Journal of Ecopsychology*

'The global ecological challenge requires humanity to fundamentally change the way we think and how we understand and engage with the world around and beyond us. This book provides so many helpful different perspectives on how we can undertake the transformation the Earth is requiring of us in our personal and professional lives, to move from overwhelm to hope in order to co-create a radical new future in the relationship between humans and the more-than-human world.'
Professor Peter Hawkins, Chairman of Renewal Associates, author and global thought leader on ecology, leadership, systemic coaching and societal change

'This book is full of love and intensely moving, drawing as it does on the insights of practitioners worldwide, with different experiences and perspectives. I found it insightful and relatable personally and professionally. This is a book of breadth and depth that puts climate change in a wider social context. And the section on children and young people wasn't just enlightening, it really gave a sense of their perspective. Please do read this book.'
Eve Turner, co-founder of Climate Coaching Alliance, coach, supervisor, researcher and author of *Ecological and Climate-Conscious Coaching*

'Every word of this text spoke to not only my mind but my heart and soul as well. It brings courage and compassion, wisdom and humility – and it honours the idea that the climate crisis is a human, emotional crisis. All of the helping professionals – and every industry and society – faces a crucial adaptation ahead, and this collection is a key text on what we can think, feel and do about it. I loved the variety of thought, backgrounds and approaches of the different contributors. I will be recommending this book widely for years to come.'
George Warren, coach, supervisor and mentor coach, faculty member of the Academy of Executive coaching Association

Holding
the
hope

REVIVING PSYCHOLOGICAL & SPIRITUAL AGENCY IN THE FACE OF CLIMATE CHANGE

EDITED BY
LINDA ASPEY, CATHERINE JACKSON
& DIANE PARKER

First published 2023

PCCS Books Ltd
Wyastone Business Park
Wyastone Leys
Monmouth
NP25 3SR
contact@pccs-books.co.uk
www.pccs-books.co.uk

Holding the Hope:
Reviving psychological and spiritual agency in the face of climate change

British Library Cataloguing in Publication data: a catalogue record for this book is
available from the British Library.

ISBN Paperback 978 1 915220 27 1
ePub 978 1 915220 28 8

Cover design by Jason Anscomb
Typeset in-house by PCCS Books using Minion Pro
Printed in the UK by Short Run Press, Exeter

Contents

Dedication

To everyone and everything, human, non-human and more than human, on Earth that is being impacted by the devastation of climate change, and to the children and adults who are courageously challenging this ecocide in the face of indifference, denial, greed and hostility.

About the editors

Linda Aspey is a leadership coach, facilitator, psychotherapeutic counsellor, BACP Fellow and activist. She works with people and organisations to support them in engaging and acting on climate, environmental and social crises.

Catherine Jackson is commissioning editor with PCCS Books. Previously she was editor of the BACP magazine *Therapy Today*, and before that edited and worked on several magazines and journals in the healthcare, counselling and mental health fields.

Diane Parker is a coach, group facilitator and creative movement therapist with a background in dance and performance. She is also an experienced freelance writer and editor, and she has edited the BACP journal *Coaching Today* since its launch in January 2012.

Acknowledgements

With grateful thanks to all those who have made this book happen: the people who have generously contributed their ideas and work in its chapters; Sally Weintrobe, for her wonderful foreword; the more-than generous endorsers, for their kind words of support, and all the organisations and other groupings of people whose work has fed into these pages. We stand on the shoulders of giants.

Foreword

Sally Weintrobe

It is a privilege to be asked to write the foreword to *Holding the Hope*. Perhaps what struck me most when reading this rich collection of papers and essays is the way in which the voices of individual authors stand out as vivid and distinct, as well as melding into a group intelligence to forge a powerful new consciousness. This melding of I and we reminded me of the moment in Martin Luther King's famous speech when, egged on by someone with him on the platform ('Tell them about your dream, Martin'), and departing from his prepared text, he launched the words, 'I have a dream...' As he said them, the vast crowd began to murmur with him. People recognised his dream as their dream, now amplified with a preacher's passion. The dream was in the air as King and the crowd inched each other forwards.

To me, the dream inspiring this great book is that, together, people will find the courage and the sense of lively entitlement to transform them/ourselves sufficiently to confront the climate and environmental emergency. Realising this dream requires keeping faith with a belief in moral progress and in goodness, and resisting cynicism and nihilism within and without. Realising this dream also requires undertaking deep working through, within and between us. Chapter after chapter shows us facets of this working through, with authors feeling thoroughly uprooted and exposed to a profound unsettlement, no longer knowing who are I, who is we, and asking, 'Am I we?' They also report feeling bereft of words as they realise how many of the words we habitually reach for are steeped in what Eduardo Viveiros de Castro (2014) called 'modernity's vicious dichotomies'. Working through involves working to undo deep hierarchical splitting and disassociation in a current climate that is so often hostile to care, to association and to love, whenever love threatens vested interests of the powerful.

Working through so often means swimming against the present dominant culture of uncare; also facing our collusion with and seduction by that culture and the loss of moral compass it involves. This can leave us face down on the ground, weeping tears into the soil beneath us. The sense of unsettlement found in these chapters is profound: the place we thought was – in a collective psychic sense – home, safe, reliable, to be trusted, is revealed as a mirage, a climate bubble built on lies. We are left shocked, unsheltered, unseated, as we understand that tolerating an unsettled state is a requirement for sanity these days. Working through also alerts us to the need to shoulder rising trauma that is personal, cumulative and intergenerational.

Working through reveals how broken and dismembered we are and how corrupted and damaged are our minds when we succumb to the culture of uncare – one that promotes the kind of isms that keep splitting in place. It opens our eyes to the genocidal violence and colossal ecocidal damage this splitting leads to.

Yet this working through also leads us to reach solid ground, common ground, the ground of connection and cooperation in the search for what is true. As we undo destructive splitting, we find we also regain lost capacities – we discover we have also split off the good, the capable, the creative, the wild, the responsible, the indigenous within. This ground we can stand on, spread our barefoot toes on and press them in. It can bear our weight, heavy as we are with life and promise. Finding this ground can bring relief and joy. On this ground, we acknowledge our traumatised state, wear wounds openly and treat each other kindly.

Finding this common ground, I believe, requires us to recognise and own destructiveness within us, as well as to perceive it in others. Working through needs to be deep enough to reach that destructiveness. One way it shows is in how we relate to non-human life. I profoundly believe we will not make the needed transition, not make it as a species, unless we reach deep enough to seriously address our hubristic and cruel ways of treating the non-human. Learning from indigenous cultures – as highlighted by several of the contributors – can us help regain respect for all of life and life's ways.

The chapters show a transformation already underway, already happening. Some of it is noisy and played out in public argument. Some is quiet and inwards. This quiet, inner work is a vital part of the struggle and needs recognising as such. Bion (1948) called attention to the way a whole people can become psychiatrically disinherited. *Holding the Hope* shows people claiming their rightful inheritance to mind. This mind acknowledges profound differences and inequities between groups. It eschews any casual reference to a generic 'we'. And yet it also makes space for an emerging understanding of mind as a vastly complex system, as human – and non-human – intelligence shared; mind as collective intelligence, escaping and transcending the boundaries of all our theorising.

I am wary of hope these days. I ward it off and direct it to stay in the corner where I can keep a beady eye on it. I certainly don't want to be infected by it. I believe this response is healthy and lively, given how much hope has been exploited and played with. We are in great danger of getting caught up in predatory delay when we entertain hope. I find it useful to remind myself that not struggling with hope has its pitfalls – it can lead to cynicism, bitterness and a lack of curiosity. The contributors and editors have, in bringing this book together, invited us to stay curious.

I hope you the reader will find this book as fascinating as I have, and I am confident you will learn from it. It is a significant contribution to the serious work of change and transformation now needed.

Sally Weintrobe
Psychoanalyst and author, Fellow of the British Psychoanalytical Society and Chair of the International Psychoanalytical Association's Climate Committee

References

Bion, W. R. (1948). Psychiatry at a time of crisis. *British Journal of Medical Psychology, 21*(2), 181–189.

Viveiros de Castro, E. (2014). *Cannibal metaphysics*. University of Minnesota Press.

Introduction

A collection of writings about psychological and spiritual responses to the possible extinction of the human species – indeed, of all living things, human, non-human and more than human – on Earth might seem, frankly, irrelevant. If there are no humans to deliver and receive therapy, and there is nothing therapy – not even CBT – can do to avert it or, it seems, persuade humans to stop doing what we are doing in order to avert it, then what is the point? Are we not simply perpetrating and perpetuating the collusion that many of the contributors here gently point out is currently happening, both in everyday life and in conversations in countries where the inhabitants are not threatened with imminent displacement due either to rising waters or to raging fires? Aren't we just sidling onto the overloaded bandwagon of commentators constantly writing and talking about the climate crisis and, in doing so, acculturating people to the notion that it has become part of the furniture, so to speak?

Well, yes, arguably, and no, we hope. Alongside this steadily escalating hum of acute anxiety emanating from climate scientists, like the sound of bees sensing an approaching threat, there is a growing number of activists who are persistently disrupting our comfort with discomfort by targeted acts of protest, aimed at stinging into action not just national leaders and politicians but all of humanity. It is our hope that this book will similarly disrupt, dismay and sting members of the psy-professions into action and, most importantly, also inspire them (us, indeed, as two of us are practitioners and one an ally) by demonstrating there is something useful we can do. And there surely is – by understanding and explaining why we are so frozen with fatalistic doom that we seem unable to act and, in our therapy rooms and in our communities and outreach/education work, we can work to free ourselves and others to act. Specifically we can hold the hopes and fears of children and young people who, along with the scientists, like canaries in a coal mine, can metaphorically smell the gas (perhaps because they aren't too busy smelling the skinny latte to notice), and are being shut down and ignored by the self-styled grown-ups.

Diane Parker: The seeds of this book were sown for me back in 2019. For the previous seven years, I had been editing a quarterly journal for coaches and therapists, on behalf of members of the BACP Coaching Division, publishing articles on key contemporary issues of coach-counselling practice.

That summer of 2019, I was becoming increasingly alarmed by media reports of the growing climate emergency and feeling helpless and overwhelmed in the face of all I was hearing. I volunteered as a performer with a faction of Extinction Rebellion, which staged regular performances in public spaces to highlight the urgency of the crisis. I knew very little of the science of the climate emergency, and offered myself simply as an experienced performer, improviser, dancer and concerned citizen of our planet. Our role as a performance group was to 'disrupt' the everyday passage of bodies through space, to entertain, to provoke, to draw attention to the issues and to inform our audience. Although my time with the group was brief, it ignited something in me that had previously lain dormant.

Back at my desk, in my role as editor of *Coaching Today*, I wondered why more of us practitioners weren't talking about what was going on. At the time, I was running movement therapy groups in community mental health with women who had experienced sexual violence and abuse, and the #MeToo movement was at its peak. I was beginning to see a connection between the systemic rape, abuse and exploitation of women, children and minority groups and the ill-treatment of animals and other-than-human life, and our rape, abuse and exploitation of the planet and the natural world.

As a female body-oriented creative therapist working with women, I became curious about our relationship with Gaia, the feminine, and the ways in which Western society and culture are structured in such a way as to sever women from the sources of their feminine power. I recalled my experiences as a coach and therapist working in forensic mental health communities and prisons and the work I had conducted with young men in custody, and realised that these patriarchal structures that were responsible for severing us from our feminine power – the very same structures that privileged capitalism and consumerism over community – were not only damaging women but all life on Earth.

My enquiries led me to Linda, with whom I had worked previously, when she initiated and led the BACP Coaching Division and the *Coaching Today* journal was launched. Linda was now deeply involved in climate activism and vociferous in her demand for some response from the counselling and coaching professions to the growing emergency. I interviewed Linda about her activities and concerns, and our conversation appeared as the lead article in the January 2020 edition of *Coaching Today* (Aspey, 2020).

I already knew Catherine through my work for BACP journals, and we had worked together as writers and editors for several years. Catherine and I began to explore the idea for a broad anthology of essays, looking at how practitioners from across the fields of counselling, therapy and coaching and related areas are devising and adapting their work in order to hold hope and revitalise agency in the face of uncertainty, volatility and the threat of species extinction and collapse.

However, neither of us had many links into the world of climate-change psy-activists, and we wanted a book that didn't draw on the same set of committed folk who were already publishing. We also wanted to reach people who came from or were influenced by different cultures, philosophies and belief systems. So we got in touch with Linda, who could bring all those contacts and more than we could accommodate in one volume.

Linda Aspey: For several years I had been aware of a growing sense of unease and, at times, hopelessness about the state of the natural world and the suffering that our consumer-driven society was causing. I had engaged in low-level activism – mostly environmental campaigning, such as writing to political leaders and CEOs of polluting companies – and had increasingly tried to live in a way that trod gently on the Earth. Yet I had never really allowed myself to stay with the difficult feelings until early 2019, when I had a deep, traumatic 'climate awakening' in response to a radio programme about insect population and species decline. I'd heard some of it before and I had heard about a new organisation – Extinction Rebellion – but it hadn't felt relevant to me. I had not really allowed reality to sink in. But the statistics they gave on that day were so shocking, they hit me hard. From that point on, I could no longer turn away. I walked around in various states of numbness, grief, anger, guilt, and sometimes deep depression, and then I knew it was time to properly engage with Extinction Rebellion.

For the first time in ages, I felt a sense of hope, directing my energies and focusing on training people to protest non-violently, communicating to the public about climate change, and getting to grips with understanding the underlying causes of the state of our planet and our conscious and unconscious responses to it. And I noticed that the coaching and therapy professions were, as a whole, as silent on it as the mainstream media, with some exceptions. So, with two coaching colleagues – Alison Whybrow (who sadly passed away in February 2022) and Zoe Cohen – I issued a public call to the coaching profession to acknowledge that we are in a climate emergency. Our call rippled out and contributed to the launching of the Climate and Environmental Emergency Coaching Alliance.[1]

I had also joined the Climate Psychology Alliance[2] and was heartened to find that actually there were practitioners concerned about it and writing, researching and campaigning – small in number but incredibly passionate. Their calls to action had been ignored for many years and I am grateful we have some of those voices here in this book. I wrote letters to the UK-oriented professional counselling, psychotherapy and coaching bodies and journals, urging them to notice, and to bring into the open, the massive social injustices happening as result of climate change and environmental decline caused by underlying systemic exploitation of people and resources. I wanted them to encourage their members to prepare themselves personally and professionally for what lies ahead and to see what was already happening in other parts of the world and learn from that. Diane and Catherine had both interviewed me and published my letters and articles on the subject, so I gladly accepted their invitation to join as

---

1. www.climatecoachingalliance.org
2. www.climatepsychologyalliance.org

co-editor. I hope that together we have created a book that informs, galvanises, and creates a sense of agency. Because what we all do now matters.

Catherine Jackson: A book on the climate crisis had long been on our list of priorities at PCCS Books. I feel as though I've been anticipating the end of the world all my life, starting with an early-teenage meltdown about nuclear extinction. That we are, effectively, broiling to death ourselves and everything else on this Earth in a sauté dish of our own making induces in me the kind of passive fatalism that contributors to this book warn so urgently against.

I wanted, I needed the book to be about doing, not talking, 'feeling' or 'sitting with' the screaming terror of it all. I was discovering through my role with *Therapy Today* that there were people in the psy-professions doing important work and I wanted PCCS Books to help get their messages out there more widely.

When Diane and I met up and realised we were both wanting to create a book, the same kind of book, I felt it was a start. Now there were two of us. When Linda joined us, with her urgency, passion and insider knowledge and contacts, the project grew... and grew... and grew... to this.

I have to say, working on the book has been hard – very hard. Reading and rereading these brilliant chapters, often in a block, has forced me out of my fatalistic comfort zone and compelled me, impelled me, into facing and feeling that screaming terror. Yes, I have gone on anyway, but differently, I hope; as Linda has said, treading more lightly, trying to share the Earth more equally with our fellow species, and with a new urgency of awareness of its and our fragility and that every little thing counts.

Spring is a time when toads make their annual pilgrimage back to their ponds of origin to breed. Driving along a local road well-known for being a popular crossing place (and usually walled in the spring for much of its length with plastic sheeting, in a bid to block the annual mass extermination), I saw a leaping toad briefly in my headlights and swerved. If I didn't kill it, the car behind certainly did. I wept the whole way home – for the leaping toad, for my crushing of its instinctive hopefulness, for humanity and for the Earth. Doing can be a distraction device, an avoidance tactic, but I hope the 'doing' of this book will make a positive difference: that people whose profession and understanding of the human mind and soul puts them in a very significant position of influence will read it and put into their practice what they learn.

The chapters

The focus of the book was important. We didn't want simply to be commenting on what was (and was not) happening now; we wanted this book to be written for there being a future. The theme came quickly: 'Holding the hope'. How can the psychotherapy, counselling and coaching professions revive and keep alive the flame of hope that keeps people trying to make change happen against seemingly implacable resistance? If psy-professionals can't overcome resistance, inner and outer, then frankly, who can? How can we help maintain the belief, not just of exhausted activists and distressed and despairing children and young people, but of all ordinary folk the world over, that this is not an end game?

And here is the result: the work of some truly inspiring thinkers, writers and therapists, who have each awed and overwhelmed us with what they have brought to the book and the breadth of their knowledge and understanding of the issues.

The book is divided into four sections, although of course the main themes run through them all. This is a book about interconnection; the compartmentalising is purely to help readers digest the contents and create their own patterns of interconnection.

The first section is titled 'We Are All Nature'. It contains chapters that are principally about our relationship with nature, our essential embeddedness in the Earth's ecosystem and the ancient cultural belief systems that inform ways of living well within it.

Opening the section, **Roger Duncan** invites those of us living in Western cultures to radically reimagine the relationship between humans and nature and how we might reconnect human thinking with the ecosystems of the Earth. We desperately need to 'reclaim Western culture's lost and stolen indigenous relationship with nature', he writes, and repair the deep damage of cultural epistemicide – the wholesale destruction of all knowledge systems other than white, Westernised ways of being in the world. His chapter explores the difference between 'human *semantic narratives* and nature's *imaginal narratives* – the difference between the world created by [the] mechanistic Western view and the natural world that emerges out of systemic complexity'. Duncan draws on the work of Donna Haraway and her concept of 'tentacular thinking' – the recognition that everything is 'entangled, systemic and non-linear'. He draws too on polyvagal theory and trauma-informed approaches to advocate a way of thinking about ourselves in the world that makes it impossible for us to separate off, objectify and destroy that without which we cannot survive – the whole of the rest of the natural world.

Bayo Akomolafe's chapter brings a unique African perspective to our thinking about the essential interconnectedness of humanity with each other and all living organisms around us. Bayo draws on ancient Nigerian myths and rituals, as well as modern science, to argue that we can never achieve psychological, spiritual or physical wellness in an unwell world. We are 'becomings not beings', he writes; we are 'diasporic, ecological and atmospheric'. How is this relevant to the climate crisis and the response of the therapist, you may wonder? His is a call to move beyond 'just a patronising stewarding of ecologies. We must think of ourselves as always entangled with the world at large'.

From New Zealand, **Niki Harré** proposes a 'sacred framework for our time' that will, she hopes, enable us to come together, as races, faiths, nations, peoples, communities, to take accumulative action to stop this slide to self-and-other destruction. It is a three-part process, starting with the application of science to understand to our best capacity the 'material reality' of the world around us. Next, we need to identify the 'infinite' values we share – those of belonging (or relationship), expression (learning, creativity), and the natural world and spirituality, which include both faith and love. Finally, we need to respect the 'particularities' of our own time and place and those of others. As nations squabble over reparations and who should bear the greatest cost and responsibility for the Earth's destruction, Harré makes a powerful appeal for acknowledgement that we have the same core interests at heart, 'from which conversation, relationship-building and decision-making can begin'. She has put this framework into action within her local community in Auckland. The results have included the mundane and the exotic, the personal and the political: from creating neighbourhood composting facilities and promoting walking and cycling to taking part in consultations on proposed government legislation. She concludes, 'When I see tales of joy in action – people getting on with life-enhancing solution making alongside others, and doing so with humility and care – everything seems possible.'

Robin Shohet reaches back to a concept he developed back in the 1970s when pollution was the main concern among 'green' activists, and we were yet to take on board the implications of the poisons we were emitting into the Earth's atmosphere. He is concerned with how we unlock the self-induced paralysis induced by nations playing the blame game. He quotes the US cartoonist Pogo, from an eco-activist poster dating back to the 1970s: 'We have met the enemy and he is us.' Shohet explores how fear-based thinking, or 'inner pollution', as he calls it, is preventing us taking action against climate change. He goes on to link this with our need to separate and fight, rather than love. For him, the solution at both individual intra-family level and, by extension, among the global family of nations, is forgiveness – specifically the Hawaiian tradition called *ho'oponopono*. Our mistake, he argues, is that we believe that in order to have an 'us', we need to create a 'them': 'The climate movement takes us too easily and quickly into polarity, into othering others, or otherness, so even if we agree about the necessity of taking action, we are unable to work together to agree what we should do.' He urges us to stop belching fumes of recrimination and resentment, and instead take responsibility for our inner polluter by forgiving the other, regardless of their responsibility, and come together to agree ways to go forward to ensure we have a world that is fit for us all to inhabit. It's simple; it's idealistic, but is it impossible?

Part 2 of the book comprises contributions that explore 'hope' and its place in the psychology of responses to climate crisis.

Hetty Einzig opens with her wide-ranging essay exploring the concept of 'radical hope', where radical means rooted, far-reaching, fundamental, but also disruptive, and 'hope' is, in the words of Czech dissident Vaclav Havel, 'not the conviction that something will turn out well, but the certainty that something makes sense, regardless of how it turns out… an ability to work for something because it is good, not just because it stands a chance to succeed'. Einzig also links radical hope with rootedness in the natural world, and with *iwigara* – a concept that extends beyond soul to include the way 'language, identity, spirit and actions are enmeshed in a continuous co-creative flow'. In this way she takes us outside the restrictions of Western, individualised thinking and into the realms of indigenous beliefs where humans are only a part of a much greater whole. She asks: 'Can we find the courage to sublimate our individual goals and desires to the good of the whole, of the wider planetary project? Can we move from destructive modes of being to regenerative ones? These surely are key to what is being asked of us now.'

Nick Totton does not subscribe to the notion of seeking to 'hold hope'. A pioneer in the theory and practice of wild therapy, for him what is more important is making a space for the client to express and experience the intensity of their despair, grief and anger first. Then it may be possible to revisit hope and reconnect with it in a more grounded way. Get real, he says: 'Given the interlocked catastrophes that face us, we must accept the impossibility of tracing any path from the doomed present to the desired future. This is not to say that such a path will not come into existence – rather that, under the pitch-dark sky of our times, only a wild and grievous hope can offer us any star to navigate by.' He argues that insisting on maintaining hope and perpetuating the belief that it is possible to avert climate catastrophe 'may have become an enormous and unhelpful burden… that we need to find a way of releasing… so that it and we can float free'. In the 'empty invocation of hope', what such people are really saying is: 'I *have* to believe – because in truth I don't, but I cannot bear the truth.' If we can quieten ourselves and drop our defences, we may move into a state of what Donna Haraway calls 'staying with the trouble' – 'a point of inner balance from which we can fight hard to stop something happening while at the same time accepting that, if it *does* happen, it will be as part of a bigger picture, and the overall richness of the cosmos will not be lessened.' But first we need that space to acknowledge the losses and to grieve. That process of breaking the heart open in order to rebuild it with a greater capacity for continuing is the future work of therapists, he says.

Dance movement psychotherapist **Caroline Frizell** reminds us of the filigrees of life that connect us with all living beings and the Earth itself. She brings us back down from visions of global cataclysm to a small spot on a grassy verge inhabited by numerous striped caterpillars that were feasting on the vegetation precisely where she had planned to hold an outdoor workshop. The caterpillars and their food would have been crushed beneath the feet of a group of humans gathered to explore the impact of their own ecological footprints. 'Like adolescents struggling to free ourselves from the sticky web of our dependency on our parents, we have succumbed to an antisocial, anti-environmental tendency, trashing the family home (aka Earth) with a hedonistic house party of economic progress and productivity,' she writes. She finds hope in post-human eco-feminism and the power of individuals to effect change through chains of solidarity, sometimes running thousands of miles across oceans and continents. She reaches out to 'kinship' as a means to 'interrupt existing norms and create new agendas of ethical solidarity and care'. Thus we can, she argues, better 'face the vulnerability of hopelessness and discover a renewed energy through the wisdom of compassion and ethical care'.

This sentiment is echoed by **Emma Palmer** when she cites Sally Weintrobe's description of how community and relationship have been eroded in a culture of 'neoliberal exceptionalism and the culture of uncare' (2021). Palmer writes very personally about embodiment of emotion and the impact on her own bodily sense as she articulates the words 'I' and 'we'. 'I listen to what is happening in my body: "I" constellates around my core, drawing me in and upwards; a few more breaths and "we" encourages my shoulders open, awareness drawn to the expansiveness of my energy field, with subtle heart opening. Loved ones come to mind.' She turns to the reader: 'What happens for you? Who's part of your "we"?' Because, in the face of climate change, 'individual action isn't enough, is it?' Palmer reaches across the space between her words and us, the reader, and drags us out of our cosy detachment from the emotions she describes. Like Totton, she talks too of 'opening our hearts': 'How do we turn towards climate emergency and actively engage, so it does not become "other"?' For her, as for Frizell, it comes back to the 'we': the conversations we have 'within us, between us, in large groups, in and beyond therapy' and, echoing Totton, 'the emergence of grief. Participating in collective grief work – as well as the practice of hope'. And what are the roles of therapists? Her chapter has many suggestions, both for individual and personal therapy work and for wider work within our professional and communities. And, referencing Nick Totton's other writings, she suggests there may be the case for 'meaningfreeness' and 'boundlessness', which for her links with the Buddhist concept of 'holding to nothing whatever'. Perhaps 'holding to' is what has brought us to this impasse where we can't afford to continue what we have been doing but we cannot bear to let go of what we have, even though we stand to lose it if we go on as we are.

The third section, 'From Theory to Practice', brings the focus down more closely to actual practice, whether this is one-to-one in our therapy rooms or in and with wider communities of belief and action. The section starts with **Chris Johnstone's** chapter on Active Hope Training. This is a widely recognised model that seeks to ignite people's capacity to free themselves from the frozen fear or torpor induced by the enormity of the climate crisis threat and begin to move towards action. It sparks motivation and the belief that we can do something to make a difference, however small. Active Hope Training views hope as something we do, not something we have or hold. This shifts our thinking from outcome to process; from our destination to the steps we take to get there. It provides a forum for us to voice and share our fears and helplessness, which in turn helps us mobilise. It 'nourishes our sense of possibility' so we feel empowered to act, Johnstone writes. And it promotes a sense of 'collectiveness': 'When we actively support our hopes for our collective future, it is as though we are finding our place within the larger team of life.'

Maggie Turp takes a different slant on how we may be enabled to overcome disavowal and denial. She explores the power of fiction, in the form of the 'cli-fi' genre. Stories, she argues, can achieve what psychoanalysis seeks to do: it can give people 'words with which to weave a skin around experiences'; they can move 'what was previously "unthinkable" – exiled from consciousness by stringent defences – to something "thinkable", something storied into a narrative and available to be thought through'. She looks in detail at two novels to demonstrate her argument. Putting ourselves in the position of characters in stories opens the door to our exploring what we would do in similar situations. 'The hope is that, in a situation where many of us find ourselves struggling with despair or immobilised by uncertainty and anxiety, we may nevertheless find a way to remain engaged.' This chapter suggests that fiction, by permitting us to visit, if only briefly and in the safety of the pages of a book, situations that we flinch from considering head on, may enable us to stay engaged with what we find distressing and threatening and act on what we see.

Pedro Oliveira writes about his own therapeutic practice with individuals who come to him with 'eco-anxiety', using a case study to illustrate this. 'Sandra' has ceased to be able to live in a state of disavowal about climate crisis but is paralysed, like so many, by fear and guilt, in particular in relation to her child. As an integrative practitioner, Oliveira draws on a breadth of models to help Sandra become unstuck, in a process he calls 'eco-integration': psychoanalysis for helping Sandra to map her defences around the crisis, exploring and understanding her emotions at both conscious and unconscious levels; Gestalt for a psychoanalytical integration in a multi-disciplinary therapy frame; systemic psychotherapy to help her make sense of her relationship network and how that network is operating a socially constructed silence, and third-wave cognitive models like acceptance and commitment therapy (ACT) for helping her move beyond her emotional avoidance and define who she wants to be in relation to the crisis. He also discusses the role of therapist disclosure and the imperative that the practitioner has done their own work and is able to sit with the extremes of emotion or repression they will encounter in the therapy room. Here is the therapist at the gateway, making it possible for the client to move forward into the action that embodies the state of hope. For Sandra, this is about breaking through the silence that her family and friendship network is maintaining around climate crisis and ultimately engaging with others to do something to challenge the greater silence at international government levels. Oliveira reminds us of the notion of tipping points: 'We may only need a significant percentage of society to change for a tipping point to happen… [and] a tipping point in the therapeutic professions is urgently required'.

Deep adaptation, a term coined by Jem Bendell, is the point where we accept that it is too late to stop climate crisis and start learning how to lessen the harm, save what we can, and work towards creating possibilities for future survival. **Matthew Painton** is a 'deep adaptation coach' and his chapter describes how he helps his clients to do that. With great honesty, he describes his own journey to that state of recognition, sparked by the death of his father and his overwhelming sense of grief. He works with 'people who are no longer willing or able to compartmentalise, separate, externalise and defer, and so are suffering intense larger-than-me reality distress in their personal lives and every aspect of their being'. What he describes is very similar to Totton's concept of the heart being broken open in order to rebuild and go on: 'Crossing the "collapse Rubicon" from "avoidable future nightmare" to "unavoidable present reality" was by far the hardest thing I have ever done, and I do not suppose the process will ever be complete… I have to consistently practise my coaching vocation and co-regulate my distress with others, to avoid falling back into futility, despair or runaway reactivity,' he admits. The framework he explains theorises a fundamental truth to which every contributor to this book also subscribes: 'My clients are struggling with epic and highly distressing uncertainty, doubt, futility, wishful thinking, acceptance, resistance and hope. So too am I…Two people doing it together is infinitely easier than one person doing it alone, and groups are often much better than both.'

Yasmin Kapadia has a simple message that will go right to the heart of most readers and chimes with this theme of togetherness, kinship and connection: 'We are our relationships,' she writes. She quotes ecological storyteller Sophie Strand: 'I am not a noun on an empty page. I do nothing alone.' Reaching across the pages to Caroline Frizell's chapter, Kapadia reminds us: 'The dances we dance, the ways we relate, have consequences that ripple outwards.' Kapadia draws an important distinction that Donna Haraway and Anna Tsing, among others, have proposed: we live in the 'Plantationocene', not the 'Anthropocene'. 'It is not "humanity" as a whole that has precipitated our modern-day climate and ecological crises, but rather parts of humanity, who have abused both the other-than-human world *and* other humans.' She reminds us, 'The planetary crisis is a racist crisis… which the black, indigenous and people of colour (BIPoC) global majority has done the least to cause, and yet who are impacted most.' What is needed from the therapy community is 'deep adaptation' on a level equivalent to that which ecological collapse will require of us all, she argues: 'Deep adaptation includes preparing *myself*, as a therapist, to be emotionally and psychologically ready for the conversations that are needed in order to lean into difficult truths with clients and colleagues.' For her, every individual encounter in the counselling room is interwoven with and inextricable from the wider universe, on all levels – societal, ecological and cosmic. What she calls 're-membering' – taking our place once more within the interdependent, Earth-wide mesh of living things – breaks down Westernised ideas about 'me' and 'not me'. 'Therapy can be a space within which this re-membering can be cultivated, explicitly through nature connection and embodiment exercises, and also implicitly, through the internalisation of a therapeutic relationship that embodies it.'

Fred Ehresmann is a self-styled 'jobbing' mental health nurse, working within the medical model. He has seen people's genuine and fully justified fears labelled and pathologised as 'eco-anxiety' and then measured with a scale to assess how acute the feelings are and by how much any 'treatment' reduces them. It is good, he writes, that no pharmaceutical pill has yet been developed and marketed as a cure, but the notion that anyone could or should be 'treated' by any means for their fears is concerning; in the context of the mental health services, a term like eco-anxiety 'gives an air of familiarity to an unfamiliar emerging phenomenon' and encourages the practitioner to think there is something they can do to cure their 'environmental despair'. Referencing Joanna Macy, he argues that this state is 'a sign of healthy awakening to, and empathy for, the distress and suffering of a world – human and non-human – that is in freefall destruction'. Ehresmann is also a solution-focused therapist confronted by an issue where a focus on solutions might seem singularly inappropriate. Solution-focused therapy does not, however, work by the therapist proposing the solutions; instead, they ask questions that, they hope, may open the gate to the client finding their own solutions. He offers a case study to illustrate how that might be helpful. Widowed mother of three Mae comes to him seeking relief from her fears about impending climate calamity. She can't sleep, her GP says she is depressed, she doesn't want pills… Yet, at the end of the first session, she appears to do a sudden body swerve – an abrupt switch from confronting despair into disavowal. She ends the session early, declaring that what she really needs is to take the neglected dog for a walk. And it turns out that she has indeed found her own solution – although she does return for five further sessions. As Ehresmann points out, by privileging the client's own resourcefulness, creativity, agency and expertise, a solution-focused approach puts the solution in the client's own hands. The practitioner needs to be able to stay present, not know, not suggest answers and 'listen carefully for the seeds of the next question that lie in what the person has just said.' For Ehresmann, it was the words of his eight-year-old daughter, when she announced to him that the planet was dying and she feared she would not live to experience adolescence and adulthood that prompted a deep psychological crisis in his own life, that has ensured he would never utter to anyone the words, 'Don't worry, everything will be fine.'

What if the person before you, filled with all this dread and grief, is a child or young person – members of the human race who are seeing their future brought to a dead end by the actions of others over which they have no influence? For parents and grandparents there is a double grief: they grieve for themselves, but they grieve also for their immortality, if you like, through future generations of their family. The contributors to our final section, 'Holding Hope for Children and Young People', are all facing that crisis, personally and professionally. They write movingly of the frustration and despair they see in children and young people whose parents offer palliative words of reassurance that the young person knows are exactly that. Able to face the truth but unable to do anything to change it, these young people are thrust perhaps more deeply and calamitously into a state of frozen terror or inarticulate fury.

Caroline Hickman has worked with children and young people for many years and in many countries, researching their experiences, attitudes and beliefs and supporting them through innovative groupwork to articulate those feelings and turn them into protest, challenge and campaigns. Her chapter explores both practical and imaginal ways to listen to the experiences of children and young people and support them through their emotional reactions, using a form of 'Fisher's curve' – a model of transition and change. It is, she says, less of a curve and more like a 'slinky' – or, indeed, a rollercoaster track – and is based on her own research. It starts with a steep descent from blissful ignorance to acute anxiety, disbelief and terror. It continues through loss of control, utter powerlessness, disillusion with adults and the sense of betrayal by trusted figures. It hits hit rock bottom, in depression, hopelessness, collapse and despair. Here there are two pathways: inwards to internalised anger, self-blame, shame and guilt, or outwards, to externalised anger, then grief, understanding and compassion. Sometimes there is oscillation, of course – because if we know anything, we know the dangers of such binary thinking and rigid models of human feeling and behaviour. And finally, there is a state of acceptance, realism, radical hope and even imagined futures, leading to empowerment, agency, action resilience and wisdom. Like many others in this book, she argues: 'This very descent, depression and experience of grief and loss is what gives meaning to the experience of waking up to the climate crisis. This is where emotional resilience is shaped and nurtured. It an important journey if we are to get under the surface of the feelings and make a space where eco-anxiety and fear can move into relationship with agency and action… Transformation involves making space for and being able to tolerate vulnerability and uncertainty as a healthy part of life.'

Jo McAndrews returns us to the notion of collectivity. She starts her chapter with the very simple message: 'We cannot protect our children and young people from the impact of the climate crisis, but we can protect them from being alone with it.' It is a terrible thing when an adult silences a child and dismisses their fears because they just don't know what to say and have no answers themselves. She cites interpersonal neurobiologist Daniel Siegel, who argues that the most dangerous idea in the history of humanity is that people are individuals. Neuroscience can now give us scientific evidence that we grow and function though connection with others. McAndrews calls it 'interbeing': a truth 'that has been held in cultures around the world who still live in indigenous relationship with the land… and the heart of what it is to be fully human.' Her chapter sets out to explain how adults can reconnect with 'our needs for human and planetary health in order to take meaningful action in the face of the climate crisis and grow a generation of adults who are better equipped to face the changed world they have inherited'. We need to 'come home to our bodies' and attend to our body's experience; grow our resilience to bearing powerful emotions, rather than rationalising or defending against them; use our imagination to envisage a better world where there is respect for difference, diversity and all other forms of life, and, perhaps most importantly, change how we raise our children. 'Contrary to what we have been told, children don't learn to manage their behaviour through adult control. Distressed behaviour is not a choice, it is a survival instinct.' It won't be an easy ride, but it is essential if we are to step up to the plate, she warns: 'My strongest call to adults is to face what is happening in the world and step up to accompany our young people with deep empathy, care and clear action so that they no longer feel abandoned.'

Canadian coach **Andy Miller** works primarily with parents and their teenage children, trying to restore the relationship bond between them that has been frayed by 'the many ills of capitalism', including climate change. His chapter is built around a fictionalised case study where the teenager and parent each write a 'letter to self' that poignantly illustrates the gap between them: the teenager's expression of despair, rage and frustration; the parent's struggle to open themselves to the concerns, fears and preoccupations of their child: 'We could have been outside playing. But we were inside a hot, stuffy, stagnant house, with this negative doom dripping down the walls like sticky oil. Kids shouldn't be burdened like this.' Parents 'must learn how to talk about these issues openly and honestly with those we love most – our kids,' Miller argues. He has developed a model of 'emotion coaching' – a process that seeks not to rid the self of the troubling emotions but to 'honour them and use them for a force for good, instead of paralysis', drawing on nature and imagery to help them articulate their feelings. 'Emotions show themselves in many ways: pain, colour, shapes, facial and postural expression, feeling, voice, dance, acting and role-playing, and through a plethora of other creative arts,' he writes. 'Indirectly tapping into emotion can be a more user friendly and safer way to increase intensity of awareness of emotional experience.' Moreover, 'once our darkest emotions are repeatedly aroused and explored with gentle curiosity and love, they self-regulate… Our bodies seem to know what to do. We need to re-train ourselves to trust our emotions, after centuries of analytical left-brain programming that started in ancient Greece and culminated in the industrial revolution.' As have others in this book, Miller has found that focusing on the somatic emotional aspect of 'Being' releases the person into 'Doing': it provides 'a solid emotional foundation enabling re-imaginative mindset shift.' He has chosen to work with parents, rather than with the child, because parents are often in the greatest denial about climate change and their activist children are too exhausted to engage with coaching. '[Children] need love first… they need to be listened to. They need sensitive reciprocal communications to feel trusting security. And that is the work of the parent.' Once the parent is open to provide this security, they can be of real value to their own child. And he works with families because they are 'our tribe' and healing disconnection within families in order to rebuild the tribe is part of the process of breaking through the socially constructed silence around climate crisis. We are us.

This is a book of interconnected, interwoven, complementary themes. Essentially, it seeks to demonstrate that psychological thinking about the climate crisis can make necessary and useful contributions to challenging global inactivity and paralysis. The therapist may be the first person a client meets at the gate when they begin to understand the enormity of climate crisis and are overwhelmed by a flood of immensely powerful emotions. The therapist's supportive holding of the individual in therapy may be important in enabling them to move beyond that turmoil of emotion or frozen passivity to explore and find meaningful ways to act in whatever way they can. The therapist has a place at the gate between awakened awareness and action, enabling people to pass through and join with others in a growing collective response, powered by wisdom and self-knowledge, not terror and avoidance.

We hope you find much that is inspiring and are motivated to explore these issues further in the many texts mentioned by contributors. We hope too that you take care of yourself when reading the book. These are deeply distressing issues; these are very real threats. You may wish to remind yourself who you have around you who will talk with you about the emotions these chapters stir for you and help you take your stand at the gate, helping others, while drawing on the collective strength beyond.

Linda Aspey
Catherine Jackson
Diane Parker

References

Aspey, L. (2020). Coaching with the Earth in mind. *Coaching Today*, January(33), 8–13.

Weintrobe, S. (2021). *Psychological roots of the climate crisis: Neoliberal exceptionalism and the culture of uncare*. Bloomsbury.

PART 1

We are all nature

1 What your biology teacher didn't teach you: Reclaiming a Western indigenous relationship with nature for a post-mechanistic world

Roger Duncan

When my alarm clock went off this morning, it seemed the sunlight was different. I dozed for another hour, and then woke up more fully and looked at the time. That can't be right. My body felt strangely out of sorts, and I wondered what had happened yesterday to make me feel this way. Nothing of significance. Other than waking up today as a father, and now grandfather, in a world that has lost its mind, at a time when it feels like we have been hurtling towards the abyss of ecological catastrophe in a bus that is out of control, where the driver is asleep at the wheel.

Then I remembered: today we are now in official British Summer; the clocks have 'gone forward'; the start of my working day has been brought an hour closer to my natural waking time, and I have less time to listen in to my body through my morning yoga and meditation practice. My body does not automatically reset itself, as my electronic devices do. There is a dissonance between clock time and the reality of my body's attunement to the world. This dissonance, which we may barely notice, is an example of the difference between how Western, educated, industrialised, rich and democratic worlds think and how nature actually works (Bateson, 2010; Diamond, 2012).

Belief in clock time is a human phenomenon – a mechanist solution that subjugates our felt senses and marginalises systemic patterns of natural order, such as the sleep of babies and new mothers, the dawn chorus, and even our experience of the cycles of the sun. This way of thinking also marginalises all other ancient and contemporary cultures that do not operate on clock time. It smuggles in an implicit colonial view of the world. The South African professor Morgan Ndlovu describes how colonial thinking creeps into our minds with the assumption that the world cannot manage 'without the thinking of a Western subject' (Ndlovu, 2014). My day will be organised by my clock, not by the experience of my body. To move beyond this colonisation of the imagination requires what Professor Nelson Maldonado-Torres describes as a 'decolonial turn' (Maldonado-Torres, 2004).

Narrative collapse

The latest Intergovernmental Panel on Climate Change (IPCC) report describes the most devastating picture of the climate and ecological emergency to date: the catastrophic current state of the world and the fact that the climate crisis is now inevitable, unpredictable and irreversible (IPCC, 2022). The emergency of the climate crisis has been almost impossible to grasp and has been subsumed by other crises that are more concrete and easier to understand and worry about: the global coronavirus pandemic and now the unfolding conflict and ensuing humanitarian crisis in Ukraine. We are facing not only an ecological crisis but also a narrative collapse: a breakdown in our capacity for sense-making (Schmachtenberger, 2020). I would argue that the world is now too complex to be understood from a mechanistic or teleological perspective. We need to update our way of understanding.

This state of the world cannot be separated from the implicit stories about nature that we have been taught in the Western education system: the notion that we can learn about the world by dividing it into different subjects – maths, geography, history, chemistry, physics and biology. Contrary to the narrative of school physicists, the world is not made of atoms; it's made of stories (Rukeyser, 1968), and the ancient and complex stories of the relationship between humans and nature cannot be reduced to mere biology. Both Carl Jung and James Hillman believed that it has been the use of reason and 'directed thinking' that has led Western culture into this process of separation from nature. It has allowed we humans to regard the non-human world as a collection of raw materials and commodities, and societies and cultures as merely groups of mindless consumers (Cheetham, 2015, p.65).

The story that currently organises our biological understanding of nature, and also our destructive ecological practices, is based, not on our relationship with nature but on rationalism. The 'modern synthesis' of biology has reduced the field to a mathematical framework: a taxonomic process of identifying species and benchmarking their ecological advantage or fitness against Darwinian theories of evolution; one that is embedded in linear cause-and-effect thinking (Dawkins, 2006). Darwinian evolution is premised on a belief that the creative drive for survival is the highest contest marker of any relationship in nature; that evolution is a game of winners and losers – an idea that Darwin borrowed from Victorian social norms (Barad, 2007, p.496); an idea that nature is part of an objective reality 'out there', a complicated mechanism that can be captured and explained by human thinking.

In Western culture, children are taught to develop emotional connections with animals through stuffed toys and cartoons. Popular culture and children's films are populated by talking animals, often presented in the form of caricatures with human expressions and character traits, with little resemblance to the real animals. Most biology teaching is totally divorced from direct, embodied experience of nature; rather, it is an implicit communication of stories about how we should think nature works. And, crucially, this way of describing nature, despite the massive popularity of David Attenborough's TV documentaries, has done nothing to halt the ecological destruction of the Earth, with its consequent detrimental impact on human mental health.

Systemic complexity

The Western economic model of Darwinian competition and continuous growth that drives our destruction of nature only makes sense if nature is understood purely mechanistically. But nature is not only more complex than we think; *it is more complex than we can think* (Bateson, 1979). Our world leaders and the individuals driving continuous economic growth are very likely only ever to have been taught a mechanistic story of nature, where nature can be manipulated and controlled. The current desperate state of the world has followed directly from this modernist narrative that refuses to acknowledge any other story as plausible.

I want to explore here the difference between human *semantic narratives* and nature's *imaginal narratives* – the difference between the world created by this mechanistic Western view and the natural world that emerges out of systemic complexity.

As a systemic psychotherapist, I have been working with young people with complex development trauma for more than 10 years. During this time, our understanding of trauma has progressed rapidly, from seeing it as a mental health problem, a disorder of the mind, to recognising it as a chronic state of stress affecting the whole body. The American psychiatrist Bessel van der Kolk, along with other body-based psychotherapists, has described how trauma is best approached through the body and the 'bottom-up' approach, in contrast to the usual approach in psychotherapy of working with the mind, 'the top-down' approach (van der Kolk, 2014; Dana, 2018; Ogden & Minton, 2006). The title of van der Kolk's influential book, *The Body Keeps the Score* (2014), says it all.

When working systemically with families who have experienced trauma, it is essential to look beyond their stories and see them as semantic narratives that the family uses to make sense of complex difficult and overwhelming emotional issues. Deb Dana (2018) describes how these stories are organised by the internal state of individuals who have suffered from trauma, so the story follows from the state.

The stories or narratives we tell ourselves about the world reflect not the reality of the world but our own inner feelings, of which we are largely unaware. Children and adults who have experienced unsafety or aggression will tend to see the world as unsafe and potentially threatening, mirroring their unconscious inner state. In this way, trauma, if unprocessed, can determine who we think we are and how we behave. Research indicates that a tendency towards offending behaviour, self-harm, addiction and drug use can almost always be traced back to early childhood trauma and loss of a sense of psychological belonging (Alexander, 1996; Felitti et al., 1998).

Trauma psychotherapist Resmaa Menakem has explored the legacy of racial trauma in the body (Menakem, 2020). Menakem explains how trauma in a person, when it is decontextualised over time, comes to look like personality – an idea that might be unsettling to people who have not trained in or experienced psychotherapy. Likewise, he proposes, trauma in a family, decontextualised over time, looks like family traits – entrenched, unconscious patterns of behaviour. And trauma in a people, decontextualised over time, looks like culture.

This observation opens a whole new perspective: cultures, as well as individuals and families, can also be psychologically unwell, and Menakem suggests that this understanding might help us perceive and challenge the legacy of colonialism. He describes how the roots of colonisation might lie in historic trauma and the deep legacy of systemic broken attachment and oppression, dating back to the Roman times in Europe. Mac Macartney (2018) describes how the Romans overcame the indigenous Celtic peoples in Britain by severing their sense of belonging and, thereby, their culture. The invaders' first strategic strike was the destruction of the ancient mystery school at Mona (today's Anglesey), symbol of the sacred attachment of the people to the land. This deliberate act of severance of indigenous people from their sacred connection with the land, combined with the cultural epistemicide of indigenous world views and languages, has been used by subsequent colonising forces throughout the world to the same end.

Tentacular thinking

In her book *Staying with the Trouble*, feminist biologist and philosopher Donna Haraway describes how the cultural and ecological problems we now face cannot be solved or even addressed simply by gathering more information (Haraway, 2016). She believes it is not helpful to allow ourselves to be drawn into apocalyptic despair and dissociative flights of fancy about technological fixes and escape. Both these responses keep us firmly embedded in teleological Darwinian thinking about failure and success.

Haraway argues that we need to think in a way that is 'tentacular' – entangled, systemic and non-linear; we need to 'think with' rather than 'think about' nature. Tentacular thinking reaches into deeper issues. When we pick up an item from the supermarket shelf, it appears to be a discrete object but, like an octopus, it has tentacles attached to multiple complex imaginal narratives. A food product has tentacles into farming practice and soil health, agricultural wage structures, petrochemical food miles, oil extraction and world politics. The packaging may have tentacles into open-cast bauxite mining, indigenous land rights, recycling processes, landfill and oceanic plastic pollution. The idea that the world can be compartmentalised into separate, autonomous entities is an illusion. The tentacular aspect of the ecological crisis connects us with and entangles us in issues that involve not only nature but also culture and ways of knowing or not knowing that are woven into the fabric of our Western cultures and ideas.

Haraway's story of the First Nations Black Mesa Navaho women weavers illustrates the difference between rational, semantic narrative and imaginal narratives (Haraway, 2016). Although the women of the Navaho nation had been weaving blankets since the 16th century, when the Navaho-Churro sheep were introduced by the Spanish, Navaho blankets only became identified and commodified by settlers as objects of commercial value in the early 1930s. The blankets then became highly sought after and were sold by weight, like animal skins or raw wool. But the objectification of the blankets as a resource or commercial product also objectified the invisible imaginal narratives connected with them: the lives of the Navaho woman weavers, the ancient craft, the sheep, and the Navaho nation's perception of the complex interaction between their culture and the environment.

This objectification and commodification is what drives the social and ecological destruction wreaked by global capitalism to this day: the idea that nature can be objectified, extracted and exploited as a means to gain wealth. From this way of seeing, the woven blanket is just wool, trees are just wood, whales are just meat, mountains are just minerals – there for the taking, processing and selling. This ontology has subjugated and eradicated almost all other ways of experiencing the world through the systemic process of Western education and colonial epistemicide – the killing of languages and ways of describing the world that do not fit the paradigm of the Western world view. It is a process that privileges the rational and the known over the emergent, the imaginal and the tentacular.

The Navaho women weavers were not engaged solely in the production of saleable commodities. The attention of the Navaho weavers was not on the production of the blanket, but the on the relationships and connections between people, patterns and fibres, family lineages, sheep husbandry and landscape. These blankets were the physical expression of a myriad complex tentacular imaginal narratives and the connections between them. Haraway terms the weaving a 'situated worlding' – a daily ceremonial practice of cosmological significance; a process of 'material semiotics', making sense of a complex world through engaging in skilled practical work (Haraway, 2016, p.91). From this perspective, the weaving can be seen as an embodied process of sense making; a way of engaging in nature as an ontological classroom. Animals, culture and human activities become manifestations of imaginal processes and relationships that can teach us to understand the world in new ways (Duncan, 2021).

Embodied learning

Indigenous cultural learning has always been a deeply social and embodied process, embedded in the systemic complexity of cultural and natural ecosystems. I am defining an indigenous relationship with nature as a relationship where cultural 'sense making' is based on *direct experiences* of nature, rather than just human *thinking about* nature; where nature is seen as a gateway into a deeper reality (Shepard, 1998).

Both Jared Diamond (2012) and Robert Bringhurst (2009) describe how children in indigenous cultures often had unrestricted access to natural experiences, such as tools, fire and animals, and also to the wider community of adults and elders, and to a relationship with ancestors who, although they were no longer alive, were understood to have a powerful influence on living generations. These children's learning acknowledged the complexity of emergent inner and outer wildness and was supported by narratives from ancient stories that could be understood at multiple levels at the same time.

Stories might describe familiar activities like fishing or hunting, but would also draw on complex social patterns of relationships, deep ecological knowledge, animal and human migrations, ancient geological events, and the activities of the ancestors in the spirit world. Robert Bringhurst (2009, p.42) writes of how the First Nations poet Skaay, from the Haida Gwaii islands off present-day British Columbia, described humans as 'plain ordinary surface birds'. This was to contrast us with creatures with more power, such as killer whales, loons, grebes and sea lions, who had the capacity to dive, not only below the surface of the water but also below the surface of perceived reality. Humans could be invited by the animals to learn how to dive and to go with them below the surface of things and to enter the world of the mythic, to encounter the cross-species communication with the natural world and come back speaking poetry.

European settlers heard similar stories from indigenous Australian cultures of this dive below the surface of reality to encounter the source of all nature. They named this world the 'dream time', which Aboriginal scholar and artist Tyson Yunkaporta has re-translated as a 'superrational interdimensional ontology' (Yunkaporta, 2020, p.19).

Learning about the complex multi-dimensionality of nature does not come from biology textbooks; it comes through a long, slow process of transgenerational mutual exchange. It is a process that cannot be understood by the mind alone; it requires experiential learning through doing and making (Yunkaporta, 2020) – the embodied, the haptic, the material and the semiotic. This way of learning has sustained the dynamic cultural stability of indigenous people over millennia – in the case of the Aboriginal Australians, for between 40,000 and 160,000 years (Lawlor, 1992). The common factor in these cultures is a close and sophisticated reading of nature as a teacher, through embodied participation with nature, where the whole environment is encountered subjectively and where plants and animals are understood to be elements of a message requiring symbolic interpretation (Duncan, 2018; Shepard, 1998).

Our current social support structures – mental health services, social care and education – are not adequate to facilitate future generations of children and young people to become the generative, altruistic and ecologically integrated adults required to face the social and ecological challenges of the future.

The current environmental destruction and climate change denial in Western culture may well have resulted from the culmination of centuries of alienation from nature. The accumulated grief of these overwhelming losses has had the effect of closing down our innate sophisticated emotional intelligence in favour of an objectified intellectualism and dissociative detachment from feeling. This is a way of relating that we recognise in psychotherapy to be linked to trauma. This trauma is now so endemic in Western culture that it is difficult to recognise and has become obscured by the myth of technological progress. Seen from this perspective, the crisis in adolescent mental health in the Western world today could be understood as deeply entangled with developmental and transgenerational trauma.

Does the idea of individual mental health still make any sense in a world that has lost its mind?

What can psychotherapy do?

What your biology teacher taught you was not really about nature at all; it was a story to justify and manage the trauma of hundreds of years of the human soul living in exile, an outcast in our modern material world, cut off from its true home in the imaginal world (Cheetham, 2015). The creative evolution of both nature and the human mind predates human thinking, and both emerged from the same matrix of systemic intelligence that still communicates with us, using a curious language of the imaginal world that 'has no things in it but only differences and relationships' (Bateson & Bateson, 2004, p.191). This comes from an older understanding that both nature and human mental wellbeing are two entangled aspects of the *animus mundi*, the soul of the world.

Systemic family therapists may be familiar with the process of searching within people's narratives to find the underlying, hidden, systemic patterns, acknowledgement of which can allow healing and insight to emerge. It is a practice similar to that of the Navaho weavers – one of simultaneously observing what is in the present while weaving yet-to-be-born worlds into existence through a type of deep listening (Duncan, 2021). It is a process that calls forth new pattens from the unknown – a process that Nora Bateson terms *aphanipoiesis* (Bateson, 2020).

It can be difficult to think about what the role of psychotherapy might be in these troubling times. How might we make a difference? It is probably impossible to change or repair existing social structures that have grown out of the legacy of colonial thinking. But perhaps the role of psychotherapists is to understand and reclaim ways to reinstate transformative European indigenous healing ecosystemic practices within the hollow shells of the old cultural structures. We were all once indigenous peoples, and it may be possible to learn how to reclaim this indigenous perspective and a post-mechanistic world view. The emerging fields of ecopsychology, ecopsychotherapy and ecosystemic psychotherapy may have the potential to reconnect the siloed and separate fields of ecology and psychology as a route to the reclaiming of a subjugated indigenous relationship that will be necessary for this ecosystemic return (Duncan, 2021; Rust, 2020; Fisher, 2019).

We now face the unbearable hopelessness of the heart-breaking realisation that Western culture has failed to respond to the climate crisis and that current generations will likely witness some form of catastrophic ecological collapse and the implosion of many of the established structures of Western modernity.

However, our understanding of the neuroscience and the polyvagal system provide ways of identifying and healing trauma through the body and preventing this trauma being passed on to subsequent generations (van der Kolk, 2014; Dana, 2018). The healing of body-based trauma can free us, and future generations, from limiting and destructive thoughts, emotions and behaviour and allow for a more sophisticated and complex ecosystemic understanding of ourselves and nature. Emotional healing opens up the possibility of changing our way of engaging with the world from merely the pursuit of intellectual knowledge to the experience of gnosis, a heart-knowing that transforms the knowing subject. This is the process that is at the core of the work of Carl Jung, James Hillman and Gregory Bateson (Cheetham, 2015; Duncan, 2018).

The healing of trauma and the openness to insights from gnosis are two essential prerequisites for the ancient cultural healing practice of soul-centric initiation. This is a process of facilitating communication between the systemic intelligence of nature and the human soul within the imaginal world. Contemporary nature-based rites of passage and soul initiation practices can be found in the work of soul-craft guides such as Bill Plotkin, who explores ways to connect with the imaginal in nature (Plotkin, 2021). Developing research and practice also suggests psychedelic psychotherapy offers a way to connect the imaginal with the human soul (Razvi & Elfrink, 2020; Strassman, 2001; Carhart-Harris et al., 2014).

To summarise

It is now becoming increasingly clear that the contemporary Western lifestyle not only has a negative impact on the ecosystems of the Earth but also a detrimental effect on human health and psychological wellbeing. It is also an unarguable fact that climate change is the consequence of human influence and that addressing these issues will require 'rapid and far-reaching unprecedented changes in all aspects of society' (IPCC, 2022). I have argued the need to abandon our current mechanistic thinking and reconnect with systemic and heart-based ways of knowing through the adoption of ecosystemic cultural practices, re-engagement with ancient indigenous systemic ways of understanding nature and the development of psychotechnologies that can facilitate this, through connecting with the imaginal. I am, in short, inviting the Westernised reader to radically reimagine how we might reconnect human thinking with the ecosystems of the Earth and in so doing reclaim our lost and stolen indigenous relationship with nature.

For the psychotherapy profession, the emerging fields of ecopsychotherapy and psychedelic psychotherapy may offer ways to break the Western cultural addiction to seeking solutions within rational, semantic narratives and their hollow ghosts in social media. This article is an invitation to reclaim subjugated indigenous practices, social structures and psychotechnologies that facilitate the ancient process of listening and communicating with superrational and interdimensional imaginal narratives as a way of healing the alienation between the human soul and the soul of the world.

References

Alexander, D. (1996). *The roots of addiction in the free market society.* Canadian Centre for Policy Alternatives. www.cfdp.ca/roots.pdf

Barad, K. (2007). *Meeting the universe halfway: Quantum physics and the entanglement of matter and meaning.* Duke University Press.

Bateson, G. (1979). *Mind and nature: A necessary unity.* Wildwood.

Bateson, G. & Bateson, M.C. (2004). *Angel's fear: Towards an epistemology of the sacred.* Hampton Press.

Bateson, N. (Dir.). (2010). *An ecology of mind: A daughter's portrait of Gregory Bateson.* Impact Media Group. www.anecologyofmind.com

Bateson, N. (2020, March 20). *Preparing for a confusing future: Complexity, warm data and education.* [Blog.] Nora Bateson. https://norabateson.wordpress.com/2020/03/20/preparing-for-a-confusing-future-complexity-warm-data-and-education

Bringhurst, R. (2009). *The tree of meaning: Language, mind and ecology.* Counterpoint.

Carhart-Harris, R.L., Leech R., Hellyer P.J., Shanahan, M., Feilding, A., Tagliazucchi, E., Chialvo, D.R. & Nutt, D. (2014). The entropic brain: A theory of conscious states informed by neuroimaging research with psychedelic drugs. *Frontiers of Human Neuroscience, 8*(20). https://doi.org/10.3389/fnhum.2014.00020

Cheetham, T. (2015). *Imaginal love: The meaning of imagination in Henry Corbin and James Hillman.* Spring Publications.

Dana, D. (2018). *The polyvagal theory in therapy: Engaging the rhythm of regulation.* W.W. Norton & Co.

Dawkins, R. (2006). *The blind watch maker*. Penguin Books.

Diamond, J. (2012). *The world until yesterday*. Penguin Books.

Duncan, R. (2018). *Nature in mind: Systemic thinking and imagination in ecopsychology and mental health*. Routledge.

Duncan, R. (2021). Deep Donkey and Dadirri: Asking Creatura out to play. *Murmurations: Journal of transformative systemic practice, 4*(1), 32–47. https://doi.org/10.28963/4.1.4

Felitti, V.J., Anda, R.F., Nordenberg, D., Williamson, D.F., Spitz, A.M., Koss, M.P. & Marks, J.S. (1998). Relationship of childhood abuse and household dysfunction to many of the leading causes of death in adults: The Adverse Childhood Experiences (ACE) study. *American Journal of Preventive Medicine, 14*(4), 245–258.

Fisher, A. (2019). Ecopsychology as decolonial praxis. *Ecopsychology, 8*(3). https://doi.org/10.1089/eco.2019.0008

Haraway, D. (2016). *Staying with the trouble: Making kin in the Chthulucene*. Duke University Press.

Intergovernmental Panel on Climate Change (IPCC). (2022). *Climate change 2022: Impacts, adaptation and vulnerability. Sixth assessment report*. IPCC. www.ipcc.ch/report/ar6/wg2

Lawlor, R. (1992). *Voices of the first day: Awaking in the Aboriginal dream time*. Inner Traditions.

Macartney, M. (2018). *The children's fire: Heart song of a people*. Practical Inspiration Publishing.

Maldonado-Torres, N. (2004). The topology of being and the geopolitics of knowledge. *City: Analysis of urban trends, culture, theory, policy, action, 8*(1), 29–56.

Menakem, R. (2020, June 4). *Notice the rage; notice the silence*. [Podcast.] On being with Krista Tippet. https://onbeing.org/programs/resmaa-menakem-notice-the-rage-notice-the-silence

Ndlovu, M. (2014). Why indigenous knowledges in the 21st century? A decolonial turn. *Yesterday and Today, 11*, 84–98.

Ogden, P. & Minton, K. (2006). *Trauma and the body: A sensorimotor approach to psychotherapy*. W.W. Norton & Co.

Plotkin, B. (2021). *The journey of soul initiation: A field guide for visionaries, evolutionaries, and revolutionaries*. New World Library.

Razvi, S. & Elfrink, S. (2020). The PSIP model: An introduction to a novel method of therapy: Psychedelic somatic interactional psychotherapy. *The Journal of Psychedelic Psychiatry, 2*(3).

Rukeyser, M. (1968). *The speed of darkness*. Random House.

Rust, M.-J. (2020) *Towards an ecopsychotherapy*. Confer Books.

Schmachtenberger, D. (2020). *War on sensemaking V*. [Video.] Rebel Wisdom. www.youtube.com/watch?v=0v5RiMdSqwk

Shepard, P. (1998). *Coming home to the Pleistocene*. Island Press.

Strassman, R. (2001). *DMT: The spirit molecule: A doctors' revolutionary research into the biology of near-death and mystical experience*. Park Street Press.

Van der Kolk, B. (2014). *The body keeps the score: Brain, mind and the body in the healing of trauma*. Viking Books.

Yunkaporta, T. (2020). *Sand talk: How indigenous wisdom can save the world*. Harper Collins.

2 | What does it mean to be well in unwell times?[1]

Bayo Akomolafe

Along with the captured (and yet not fully capturable) bodies of Africans, shackled to the imperatives of an emerging global order, smuggled into slave ships, this chapter leaves behind (without abandoning) the continent and peoples of my birth, the Yorùbá people, and pushes out into the rippling blue, situating itself between West Africa and the so-called New World – somewhere in the Atlantic middle, if you will. Why take these fluid grounds? Why leave the comfort of the familiar? It is because I feel that healing must now be reframed as exile. We must recalibrate healing as exiling our bodies from a colonial imperialistic project that situates the body/mind within an atomic/autonomous *fixed* self.

At the heart of my chapter is this question: '*What does it mean to be well in unwell times?*'

‚What does it mean to be well in unwell times? My aim here is to address this question, stay with the trouble of it and see where that might lead us. I reckon we will end up with more questions than answers, but that's just as well in times of uncertainty.

Emotions as emissions

I'll start with a story. Some years ago, an Englishman, Jonathan Williams, decided to rig the Cinestar, a giant cinema in Mainz, Germany, with capacity for up to 2,700 people, to 'explode'. No, this wasn't a terrorist attack – it wasn't an explosion of that sort. Jonathan Williams and his team rigged the theatre to explode with *feelings*. Their experiment sought to find out if feelings left chemical traces in the air. Williams, an atmospheric chemist and head of the Max Planck Institute for Chemistry, proposed that the air might be thick with emotions.

---

1. This is an edited version of a talk given by Dr Akomolafe titled 'Let us make sanctuary: The outlines of an intra-active psychology and the implications of "the material turn" for mental health', at the Confer event 'Separation Sickness in a Post-Industrial World', held online on 26 March, 2021. www.confer.uk.com/on-demand-events/sickness.html

The Planck research group's study into what they'd later designate the 'volatolome' began with the observation that their 'finely calibrated machines'[2] – designed to measure organic compounds in the atmosphere – tended to go out of joint anytime humans moved close to them. Williams had the first inkling of a research direction: given that humans are gaseous bodies, emitting gases (like carbon dioxide) as a consequence of being embodied, could the mereness of breathing out be contributing to global warming? Measuring these emissions in the Mainz stadium during a football match brought the team to a seeming dead end: there weren't enough emissions from human physiology to compare significantly with human industrial activity.

There is no comparison between what we are emitting just by breathing and what is in the atmosphere – what cars and ships and industries and factories are emitting. However, a second more interesting question came out of the husk of the first. It was evident to the research team that the wild variety of emotions displayed by the crowd at the football match correlated with fluctuating readings on the atmospheric spectrometer. They asked: 'Do people emit gases as a function of their emotions?' What if the air is alive with emotions – with depression and joy and anxiety and suspense? What if all these things are alive, in the air? What if the atmosphere is thick with strange concoctions of errant feelings in their trace-like becomings that are not 'ours'?

To materialise their new obsession, Williams' team took over the Mainz cinema and 'rigged' one room that could seat 250 cinema-goers. They linked their machinery to its air conditioning outflow vent and measured the chemical-affective outcomes in the emissions from viewers as they watched carefully curated scenes from their favourite movies, teasing out the new chemicals that were now in the air as a result. From studying 9,500 film-goers observing 16 movies, they noticed that a predictable mix of chemicals were obtained when specific scenes (marked for the emotions they instigated) were shown. For instance, working with the movie *The Hunger Games: Catching Fire* – I haven't watched any of it – our intrepid researchers found that, in the scenes where the protagonist, played by Jennifer Lawrence, is experiencing danger, the levels of carbon dioxide, isoprene and acetone emitted by the audience rose, and the levels increased with the levels of danger, just as predicted. Different chemicals at different levels were also emitted in humorous, tender and other highly emotive scenes. So, those chemical signals were corresponding with the emotions in the room.

Of course, this is all highly speculative; Williams and his team did not mean to suggest that depression floats in the air as a freely objectifiable compound, for example. What their intriguing study suggests is that it is now almost possible to imagine emotions – affective states – as public events, instead of matters of the exotically impenetrable interiority of the modern subject.

Emotions as territorial realities. A volatolome of nomadic interiorities. The Planck team thinks of the volatolome as an atmosphere that is populated by organic and inorganic compounds and volatile metabolites that are emitted from an organism and

---

2. For more on this research, I urge you to read these two reports: Hamblin, J. (2016, May). Emotions seem to be detectable in air. *The Atlantic*. www.theatlantic.com/science/archive/2016/05/the-gas-of-emotion/482922; Jacob, K. (2018, April). A nose for feelings. *Max Planck Research*. www.mpg.de/12605031/W004_Environment_climate_062-069.pdf

also affect the organism. Think of it as a sphere of manifold beings, molecular and otherwise. Think of it as a parliament of voices and bodies that always surround and swirl around organisms. A pressing implication of the volatolome is that organisms are neither isolated nor as isolatable as modernity would have us believe they are. It seems we are always caught up in affective domains. Could we consider that depression, anxiety and other states of being that we habitually lock away in sealed selfhood have a way of escaping language, stealing into the air and constituting a territory that enlists various kinds of bodies in its mattering?

In search of answers

This strange idea that we occupy affective domains – echoed in James Hillman's insistence (Avens, 1980) that the psyche exceeds language and the mind and must be located in the between spaces in the world at large, involving more than human subjectivities – sketches an alien psychology that disrupts the unbothered continuity of therapy as a clinical alliance between two or more pre-ordinate, pre-relational subjects.

The whole idea of spillage, however, is not new. I come from the Yorùbá people, as I have said. I remember travelling for my PhD research from the rectilinear predictability of the city into the heavy creases of Yorùbá indigenous traditions driven underground by the eschatological tensions of a pristine surface. In 2012, I lived in the Christian south of Nigeria, and in that part of my world, anything that was considered indigenous was considered villainous and demonic and pathological. Not to be spoken of. Teaching at a Christian university, and quite taken by the decolonial aesthetic that spilled through the writings of Ngũgĩ wa Thiong'o, Chinua Achebe, Wole Soyinka, and others in that pantheon of Afrocentric imagination, I started to ask dangerously seditious questions about the uncritical acceptance of (Western) psychotherapeutic practices as universally appropriate ways to address wellbeing. I asked: 'What if our problems in Nigeria aren't merely an issue of a poverty of bed spaces in our neuro-psychiatric hospitals? What if the way we frame mental wellbeing, health and illness is part of the problem here? What if we have followed these moustached white men with their side-facing pictures from the 18th and 19th centuries for too long, and we've forgotten how to think about illness and wellness in ways that meet our own imperatives and local concerns?'

I decided, against the advice of colleagues and professors alike, to study with the Yorùbá shamans – what we call the *babaláwo*. They taught me strange things, some of which I cannot repeat here – but the idea that emotions were atmospheric was a prominent theme in their narratives. I remember asking one babaláwo about his nosological tools: 'How do you diagnose *this*? What is your take on, say, visual hallucinations? How do you make judgments about what ails your clients?' I was half-expecting him to pull out something like the *DSM-5* or the *ICD-11* – some indigenous version of those psychiatric diagnostic manuals – but he instead spoke about meeting these problems as if they were relational, qualitative dimensions, fiercely loose in their categoricity, and not as static or as fixed as they seemed to be in the bibles of sicknesses I was trained to sermonise.

'Sometimes, I just come out and I listen to the air. And I sniff the air, and whatever is in the air will tell me what's happening,' he said. I didn't quite believe him – it wasn't very convincing to me at the time, until I started to go deeper into these studies to understand concepts like *ayé*, a Yorùbá word that is roughly translated as 'life'. A preferred unpacking of the concept of *ayé* convenes a conspiracy (literally, 'breathing-together') that decentres agency, affective states and subjectivity from the human individual. *Ayé* suggests that 'the individual' is *spread out* – and that we're diasporic things, diasporic becomings, ecological, and *atmospheric*. Becomings, not beings, as such.

The babaláwo's air-sniffing cosmology travelled with captured Africans and sailed across the Atlantic, swirling restlessly like unused magic in slave communities and plantations that practised seditious notions of healing underneath a colonial medical enterprise. The 'fugitive sciences' of Obeah, vodou, candomblé and related systems of healing embodied resilient cultures of the body that refused presumptions of androcentricity. These were practices that were situated in the Atlantic, under the boot of the slave masters, and were about listening to 'nature', listening to the world, and treating the world as tangentially alive. The idea that health is private and that anyone could have a clean bill of health in a world that is unhealthy would have been unintelligible to the practitioners of these hidden arts.

Railway spine and the lens of trauma

In this brief genealogy of sorts lies the heart of this chapter: the effect of these concepts of spillage and atmospheric entanglements is that they pull us away from thinking that health is static, that health is fixed, that wellbeing is something that can be 'owned' as a property of the self. They invite us to lose our way. My people suggest that, to find your way, you must be willing to lose your way. And that is the invitation of these insights and what they are bringing to our attention.

Let me step into an example that might be grounded in the history of trauma as a Western concept. I believe it always makes for good reading to interrogate the modern genealogies of the concept of trauma. In the 1800s, as the Western world experienced rapid industrialisation, things began to shift around a bit. The railway was especially huge, and people were witnessing a transformed society. With this rapid industrialisation came terrible accidents, and with these accidents came many deaths and injuries.[3] But many people were damaged in a way that escaped the expertise of the medical authorities, who could not find anything that was organically amiss with them, whether they witnessed or were involved in the accidents.

The inscrutability of the tangentially biological symptoms that seemed to afflict those involved in these industrial accidents mobilised new conversations about the nature of injuries and would thus become the foundation of what we know now today as 'trauma'. 'Trauma' started out as something called 'railway spine', named by an Englishman, John Erik Erikson, and then became increasingly psychologised through the discursive matrix that involved the French neurologist and professor of anatomical

---

3. One such accident was the Staplehurst rail crash in England of 9th June 1865, which led to several deaths and many more injured persons. The famous English novelist Charles Dickens was among the survivors, reportedly tending to some of the victims as they lay dying. He was so rattled by the experience that he was said to have completely lost his voice two weeks after, and avoided train travel as much as he was able to thereafter. He died five years to the day after the accident.

pathology Jean-Martin Charcot, the English surgeon Herbert Page (who held that 'railway spine' was a 'mental condition'), and Freud, who needs no introduction (Fassin & Rechtman, 2009). Most crucial to the evolution of the concept was the incipient suspicion with which governing authorities looked upon those who demanded just compensation for the negligence of state/company actors – a suspicion that gradually gave way to growing acceptance and the crystallisation of the role of the 'victim'.

We learn in this way that the context of psychic trauma's emergence as a concept was characterised by steel engines, rapid movements, the expansionist project of the city and deeply industrial aspirations for mastery – a convergence of cosmology, the city and the citizen. To address the history of trauma as a concept, as an evolutionary concept, we must situate it within the onto-epistemological conditions of industrial growth and progress and the colonial apparatus that we now recognise today as the 'city state', or modernity, or globalisation.

The lens of trauma afforded the project of modernity a way to think about suffering without decentring the citizen-subject. In this sense, trauma constellates the city, the compensatory dynamics of the welfare state, the juridical consequences of corporate negligence, rationalised industrialisation, technology, the fragility of flesh, a politics of ascendancy, the technologies of racialisation that assign the identity of victimhood to some and not others, as well as the nature of the proper subject. Something more than a clinical reality is happening here (Fassin & Rechtman, 2009), something that is calibrated to the carcerality of modern, isolatable flesh.

These legacies burn at the heart of the Anthropocene, the geological epoch defined by *the individual*. The suffering subject (its continued productivity, its sanity, its intelligibility within audial and visual regimes of power, and its ontological separation from the wilds) is predominantly at the heart of our discussions about trauma and wellbeing. But what if the traditional liberal humanist subject is a colonial terraforming project that depends on, and is heavily subsidised by, the capitalist numbing of desire, the pathologisation of our embodied imbrications with/in multispecies ecologies, and the Procrustean delimbing of the monstrous becoming of the 'human'? What is *wholeness* and *healing* and *cure* if they render our bodies legible to technofascist arrangements of unbothered continuity? What is speaking truth to power if voice – the legibility of the subject – is power's software? If the *human* were an asylum, if African bodies were 'humanised', or located within the spectrum of the human (albeit closer to the animal end of things) (Jackson, 2020) across their transatlantic voyages to the New World, then isn't wellness an ideological commitment to and enactment of the legacies of containment?

By focusing exclusively on trauma's subject, therapy in the Anthropocene performatively reinforces the sociomateriality of the gilded subject – but by banishing the more-than-human worlds around us and in us to the instrumentality of anthropocentricity, the conditions of inflammation are reinscribed. It is like clearing the debris and seaweed off a beach, then turning around to dump the material in the ocean.[4] Or perhaps like launching a massive multi-nation epidemiological drive

---

4. It really happened – see https://bit.ly/3zUwX8J

to distribute pandemic-annihilating vaccines (using hydrofluorocarbon or HFCs – a greenhouse gas that is more than a thousand times more problematic than carbon dioxide) to safeguard the citizen-subject, while continuing to treat land and forests and other-than-human life as dispensable.

Dashing upstream

Along with rumours of migrant feelings lurking in our armpits and in the air – lending themselves to accounts of a different kind of global warming (not merely of greenhouse gases but of despair) – we are met by posthumanist, poststructuralist, eco-feminist, indigenous sciences and topographical shifts forcing us to revisit our claims about the dimensions of the self. In other words, it seems the self has travelled: where we put the self is no longer where it is, and it has become diasporic. It has left the room!

There is a sense in which we are being invited to leave the suffering subject behind and touch the conditions of suffering. There is a story about two monks out for a walk one day and they see someone drowning in the river. One monk jumps in and pulls out this body. A few feet further on, they find another man drowning, and again the monk jumps into the river and pulls him out. When a third drowning person screams for help, instead of jumping in to assist his lifesaving companion, the other monk dashes off, running upstream. His exhausted companion shouts: 'Where are you going?' And the monk says: 'I'm going to wherever they're falling in, to stop them.'

Let me give my energy and attention to focusing on the conditions, instead of the anorexic and myopic focus on the suffering, isolated subject, which is the imperative of modern conditions and which removes from our conversation the idea that the subject – existing as the matrix of geological, political, theological, gastronomical, bacterial happenings – has never been isolated.

In this analysis, trauma becomes part of how the modern names itself – an appellation purchased with the invisibilisation of intergenerational, ecological, atmospheric, ancestral, nomadic, territorial, and more-than-human matters. Trauma – now bracketed as the concatenation of capitalist ambition, urban planning, malleable steel and the Baldurian archetype[5] of the quarantined subject – hints at molecular transgressions, microbiomes, atmospheric territories, material swirls of gas, and geological events. Suffering takes on a domain-like quality, exceeding personal experience, deterritorialising the Freudian couch. Something breaks through and cracks open our isolation. We are exposed.

Intra-active psychology

It seems what is invited now is a stranger psychology – perhaps an 'intra-active psychology', christened after the term 'intra-action' formulated by Karen Barad (2007),

---

5. From the Norse myth of Baldur or Baldr, whose death is foretold in a disturbing prophecy that motivates his mother, Frigga, to travel around the world extracting from every creature a promise that they won't harm her son. Frigga omits the mistletoe from this mission, believing the plant to be harmless. Loki, the trickster, hears of this weak spot, fashions a weapon out of mistletoe, and gets Baldur killed with it. By 'Baldurian archetype', I refer to the familiar dynamic of extracting agency from the more-than-human so that the modern subject can live.

which is the idea that culture has always been nature and that there is no pre-relational distinction, or no separation, between the body and the mind. An intra-active psychology might rush upstream to where the bodies are falling in, might notice that cities are therapeutic or non-therapeutic interventions into how bodies are framed, that bodies are not static but reiterative traces of performative flows, and that furniture, texture, colour, temperature, sound, animal and climate are not just things around us but agentially vital producers and contributors to the conversations about wellbeing.

Our gaze cannot be focused extremely or exclusively on the 'subject', which is a myth, an invention of eurocentric enlightenment thinking. We urgently need speculative, decolonial, psycho-theological therapies that effect departures from the Anthropos. We must do something more than just treat ourselves, something more than just a patronising stewarding of ecologies. We must think of ourselves as always entangled with the world at large.

What does it mean to be well in unwell times? If health is what modernity is calling our present circumstances, then health itself has become toxic; this health isn't healthy. We need a different form of healthiness, or wellbeing, that addresses our indebtedness to the world we never separated from.

References

Avens, R. (1980). James Hillman: Toward a poetic psychology. *Journal of Religion and Health, 19*(3), 186–202.

Barad, K. (2007). *Meeting the universe halfway: Quantum physics and the entanglement of matter and meaning.* Duke University Press.

Fassin, D. & Rechtman, R. (2009). *The empire of trauma: An inquiry into the condition of victimhood.* (R. Gomme, Trans.). Princeton University Press.

Jackson, Z. (2020). *Becoming human: Matter and meaning in an antiblack world.* New York University Press.

Towards a sacred framework

3 | *Niki Harré*

As people, we live within two overlapping, but not quite aligned, realities. One is that we are biological creatures of planet Earth. We have a material reality that ensures we are in constant relationship with what is around us. Take breathing, for example. We breathe in about 21% oxygen, 78% nitrogen, and less than 1% carbon dioxide. We breathe out 16% oxygen, 78% nitrogen, and 4% carbon dioxide.[1] What has happened there? Well, we have given up some carbon, the building block of our body, in exchange for the oxygen we need to produce energy. Those carbon atoms re-enter the atmosphere and may be taken up by another life form – perhaps the nearby hibiscus bush. This exchange happens whether we know it or not, and whether we like it or not. We can invent vaccines to ward off viruses, cut out malignant growths and improve our diet, but in the end our bodies return to the planet that gave rise to us.

On a larger scale, as readers will know, human habits are changing the material world in ways that are both known and unknown (see Díaz et al., 2019 for a comprehensive description). Our dependence on fossil fuels is causing changes in the composition of the atmosphere and oceans with flow-on effects for many life forms. Temperatures are rising, weather patterns are changing, the oceans are becoming more acidic and many species are struggling to survive. Science and other forms of observation can describe much of this, but there are always unknowns. The myriad interactions that determine the state of the planet at any one time can only ever be partially mapped by human beings. We can never be quite sure what will happen next and when. But we can be sure that, as material beings, the state of the planet at large, and our own corner of it, matters to how our lives will unfold.

Our second reality is a personal/social reality that I call here a 'framework'. This framework is how we see the world and our default responses to it. Much of the framework we hold as individuals is socially constructed – human groups have always told stories that describe what is, how it came to be and the proper way to respond. These

---

1. These, or similar numbers, can be found on several websites that explain the chemistry of breathing.

frameworks must be informed by the material world or we will not survive, but they can never be a perfect match. As the anthropologist Eugene Anderson has written in relation to nature, human groups 'manage unevenly' (2013, p.169). We cobble together stories of the world and our place in it and use them to plan our collective lives. Each person lives within the narratives they hear and value; some of which are shared by large groups such as cultures, religions, nations and so on, and some of which reflect the particulars of their social circle, and the explanations that have resonated for them. And, to some degree or other, we also live with knowing our stories have gaps and inconsistencies – they may be good enough, but they aren't *exactly* right.

As an academic in a school of psychology, housed within the Faculty of Science at the University of Auckland, the dominant narrative I am exposed to about how the world works is one based on science. When it comes to big-picture material reality, it is a story I know and trust, although I do not consider myself a scientist. Scientists spend a lot of time on detours of various sorts (I know this from my own research!), but it still seems to me that science is by far the most accurate way we have of knowing the material world. It is remarkably transparent and self-correcting; not always and not instantly, but over time the truth does out. When there is a question science *can* answer, I can't think of an occasion when I've preferred another way of knowing. And, as far as I can tell, my preference is widely shared. Whether we are science fans, science doubters or a bit of both, we almost all use its language and many of its assumptions in our conversations with each other. Covid-19 is talked of as a virus, almost everyone takes a gravely sick child to a modern (i.e. science-based) hospital for treatment, if they have access to one, and it is taken for granted that carbon dioxide is a gas with a role to play in the temperature on Earth.

There are, however, many questions that science cannot answer. For the purposes of this chapter, it cannot tell us what we value, and it rarely provides a specific course of action for the set of circumstances we face. So, our frameworks for understanding and responding to the world must, and do, include other ways of knowing. Traditionally, these frameworks have been woven over time as people observe the place in which they are located and construct patterns of living. Currently, however, at least in large cities like Auckland, where I live (population 1.7 million, so much smaller than many, but big enough), people of different cultures and religions live together in new configurations, alongside the demand that we change our ways in response to environmental threats. We need, I think, a new framework for living together – one that respects the diversity among us and does not shy away from the material reality revealed by science and other forms of careful observation. Here, I am calling this a *sacred* framework, to signify that it is based on a leap of faith – that as human beings we can work together, and this work is worthwhile.

Two caveats

Caveat number one: please excuse the extraordinary arrogance that may appear to underlie the proposition that follows. If it helps, I am aware that what I am about to do is, in one sense, ridiculously grandiose. On the other hand, I am convinced that we must find ways to work together, and that we do not spend enough time figuring out how to do this. We wring our hands at the existence of echo chambers but become nervous when it comes to challenging the echo chambers closest to us. Even (perhaps especially) among the intellectual and politically-active left – the community I know best – there is constant pressure to label and call out 'bad' behaviour and world views: a pressure maintained by claims that they/we hold the one true interpretation of the history of human affairs. This, I think, gets in the way of inviting *everyone* into the game of living well together (see Harré, 2018a). And I think we must invite everyone in – as equals. This notion may make you bristle at the unfairness or risk of doing so – as 'they' are too powerful, self-interested, or naïve to be trusted – but I can't see what else will work. Are we serious about caring for our planet, or only prepared to do so our way? Do we really think we are going to *get* our way? When does that ever happen – and even if it does, how long will the solution last?

Caveat number two: as touched on earlier, I am located in a culturally and religiously diverse city, in a 'Western' country. The ideas I present here, then, are with Auckland in my sights. I hope they resonate with people in other Western cities and perhaps more broadly. They may not resonate for you in your context. The truth is, a lot of people I know in Auckland object strongly to my pursuit of commonality, especially given my position as a woman of European descent in a country colonised by Britain.

I speak then, not from a position of certainty, but from a position that I cannot resist returning to and sharing with others. When I enter the framework that I attempt to articulate below, I feel hopeful, generous and inspired, and I often see similar responses to it in others. As we'll get to later, it is, I suggest, a tale of joy. You can think of it as a gesture – one that is made in as good faith as I can, but designed to stretch the collective conversation rather than restrain it.

The values we share

As well as being responsive to our best understanding of the material world, a sacred framework for our time must, I suggest, have two other characteristics – it must be based on the values we share as human beings living on planet Earth, and it must be as spare as possible to allow for local interpretation and creative responses (see Figure 3.1). In this section I will discuss the values we share. I draw largely on academic research in psychology, including my own, although I hope that what I describe makes sense to people immersed in other academic disciplines and knowledge systems.

Figure 3.1: Towards a sacred framework

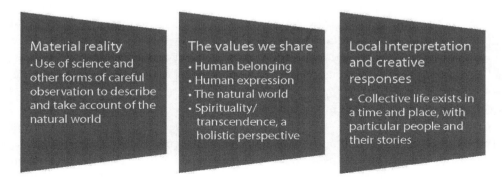

At the most basic level, people value life itself – they want to survive and they want their children to survive. All of us then, are oriented towards food, shelter and physical safety. Our biology places numerous restraints on how these needs are fulfilled, such that we can only eat certain food prepared in certain ways, human shelters look broadly similar the world over, and we are all wary of large predators, injury and disease. I won't go on: the point is that human beings – wherever we are – have rather similar problems to solve and go about solving these problems in recognisably human ways. We are also deeply social creatures, such that the need to be part of a group is likely to be a fundamental part of human nature (see Baumeister & Leary, 1995).

Over and above these basics, there have been many efforts in academic psychology to identify and describe what people consider underpins flourishing – not just the bare minimum, but the good life (e.g. Kasser, 2002; Ryan & Deci, 2002; Schwartz, 1992). As is the tendency in this field, much of this work has focused on differences in emphasis between cultures (e.g. Schwartz & Sagiv, 1995) and individuals (e.g. Schultz et al., 2005), and the implications of those differences. This can distract us from the much more basic and reliable similarities in content and emphasis. It is these similarities that I've focused on in my own research on what people value (Harré, 2018a; Harré & Madden, 2017; Harré et al., 2017). This research has been an attempt to find a language for what it is people have in common and how people respond when they feel others share their core values. I've drawn primarily from self-determination theory in psychology and its notion of intrinsic goals and motivations (Ryan & Deci, 2000), as well as the work of the philosopher and theologian James Carse, who suggested that in life there are at least two kinds of game: the infinite game, in which the aim is to keep the game in play, and finite games, in which the aim is to win (Carse, 1986). Inspired by these starting points, and with the help of colleagues and graduate students, I put together an infinite game workshop. Part of the workshop involves people generating things of 'infinite value', which can be thought of as the stuff of the infinite game we are attempting to keep in play.

Over the past decade, I've run dozens of workshops and asked thousands of people in group settings what they consider of 'infinite' value (Harré et al., 2017). Infinite values are roughly equivalent to 'intrinsic' values: that is, they are primary or core values (see Agar, 2001; Korsgaard, 1983). In workshops, they are defined as things that are sacred, precious or special; things that make the world truly alive and are of value for their own sake. I've run workshops with community activists, business networks, environmentalists, educators and students, mostly here in New Zealand but also in Europe, Australia and North America (I recognise these are all Western contexts – see my earlier caveat). Over and again, I've found that people's core values fall into four key domains. In almost all groups, the most mentioned values concern human relationships – for example, community, compassion, family and shared laughter. The other three domains are human expression – for example, learning, creativity, innovation, artistic expression, and positive emotions; the natural world – for example, mountains, the ocean and biodiversity; and spirituality/transcendence – for example, faith, the whole and love.

Other research on intrinsic values shows a similar pattern (Kasser, 2011; Ryan & Deci, 2000; Sanderson et al., 2019). Why do people gravitate towards these values?

It comes back, I think, to our shared reality as evolved, embodied creatures of planet Earth. We live in community, we die and know we will die, some of us give birth and rear children, and our lives are entwined with the natural environment in which we live. We also experience awe and mystery and tell stories about what it means to be human and why the world is as it is. This shared experience and biology – what we could call the human condition – points us toward broadly similar yearnings. Of course, the four key domains I carved out in the previous paragraph are just one way of rendering the values landscape of people living in contemporary Western societies. However, the bigger point I want to make is that the process of discovering and acknowledging that we have the same core interests provides a platform from which conversation, relationship-building and decision-making can begin.

A tale of joy or a tale of terror?

To reiterate, the importance of feeling our core values are shared is key here. Research in the UK has found both that people tend to underestimate the extent to which others hold similar 'compassionate' values to themselves, and that doing so reduces their inclination towards civic engagement (Sanderson et al., 2019). Our research here in New Zealand has also demonstrated that considering your own core values and then seeing a 'word cloud' that suggests other people also have values that align with the four domains I outlined above promotes a sense of belonging to a human community with shared values and feeling uplifted and hopeful, and safe and reassured (Harré et al., 2017). This is a 'tale of joy' in the sense described by the community psychologist Julian Rappaport (2000). First, it makes people feel positive and capable, and second, it invites them to participate in community life. Tales of joy suggest the world is a welcoming place – one in which people look out for each other and in which our talents and interests can be expressed. They encourage people to bring themselves to the community in which they live and help create a place for others.

We've also asked people to consider their core values and then shown them a 'word cloud' that indicates others hold values focused on money, status, ownership and competition (Azizi, 2018). This provokes shock and confusion, sadness and disappointment, critique of others, and a sense of disconnection. This is a 'tale of terror' in Rappaport's terms, as it suggests you are out of step and the world cannot be trusted. As one participant wrote, in response to the money/status word cloud: 'I feel slightly confused as none of my listed things were on the cloud of common things. Considered whether I'd interpreted the question wrong?' This sense of disorientation – that, at one level we know what matters most but at another level we may have got life 'wrong' – is a feeling I know well. Some readers may also recognise it. Something seems off, but I'm not quite confident enough to speak out. Maybe I've interpreted the question wrong?

The tale of terror just described is often associated with neoliberalism and colonialism (e.g. Monbiot, 2016). Indeed, I've sometimes been in business circles where the assumption that everyone is out for themself is so integral to the conversation that I've felt I was inhabiting a parallel universe (I hasten to add, that is not always the assumption in business circles). However, this tale is also a common sub-text in environmental and social justice circles: yes, you have got the question wrong – people in Western societies (or at least those of European descent) are primarily self-oriented, and money, status and ownership are what drives them. *We* are the ones who care and are up against a hostile world occupied by *others*. The intent in these latter circles may be to speak truth to power and empower those with little of it, but a side effect is to isolate people from each other. If, after all, my values are peculiar to a select group with little influence and this is a dog-eat-dog world, why would I invest in the collective? Better to build as big a fortress as I can manage and include only the few I can trust.

Furthermore, the sense that others can't be trusted creates enormous pressure to try to control every issue that shapes our life. Been diagnosed with an illness and offered treatment by a GP or hospital specialist? Better do your own research – don't, whatever you do, take the advice of the first doctor you encounter. Have some money to invest? Check out the options offered by different investment funds, consider their past returns, and remember that past returns are not a reliable indication of future returns. We become like insects, each caught in our own lonely intersection of a massive spider web. Anxiety kicks in, and our ability to care for others wanes in face of the need to protect ourselves from the carelessness we are told surrounds us.

Can we flip this? Can we dare to imagine that others, in general, can be trusted? A sacred framework, I think, encourages us to search for and discuss our common values and enables people to step into a tale of joy. Not because life becomes certain, but because life becomes shared.

Enlivening the framework

So far, I've discussed two of the three components I suggest form part of a sacred framework that can help us work together on the problems we face. The first is recognition of material reality that is underpinned by science and careful observation. The second is an emphasis on our shared values for belonging and being in community, human expression, creativity and learning, care for the natural world and a holistic perspective. The third component is the need to keep the framework spare, to allow for local interpretation and creative responses.

As someone who leads talks and workshops, I'm often presented with a difficult situation someone is facing in their workplace or community and asked for advice on what they should do. Sometimes people even ask me what my research implies for the latest war; say, Russia's invasion of Ukraine. I almost always have no response – and I've got better at saying this.

To be sacred, a framework must, I think, say as little as possible, while saying just enough to keep people interested, respectful and willing to work together. People can and must live within the interpretations, structures and poetry suited to their setting, time and preferences. This includes the myths that teach us about the land we inhabit and provide us with wisdom, comfort and direction (Campbell, 1972; Hikuroa, 2017); the institutions and rituals we enact and pass on, and the art that inspires and connects us. We get into trouble when we insist our particulars are the only way or should be directly applied to the present, even if they are designed for a world of different technologies and configurations of people. Sometimes we even worship an exotic worldview and feel it contains the wisdom we need. This is rarely true, as if it is exotic, it has not been built from the conditions we face and with the people around us.

I've put some of what I discuss into practice through intentional sustainability networks in an Auckland secondary school, Western Springs College/Ngā Puna O Waiōrea, and in my own Faculty of Science (Harré et al., 2022). These networks bring together people interested in forwarding environmental sustainability within the organisation, with just a broad concern for human and ecological thriving to guide the practical activity. Members suggest projects based on their observations and location within the organisation and are supported in instigating these. We do not attempt to agree to a single overarching goal or insist that everyone works on the same issue. Projects have included composting facilities; promoting walking and cycling; seminars on current research into biodiversity and climate change; a fashion show using materials otherwise destined for landfill or recycling, and submissions on proposed government legislation. Network members differ in their worldviews, but in this setting the work is practical, and ideological debates seldom arise. This is the case even if the project involves creating policy – for example, a waste management policy for school trips. We ask, what is feasible for our community in this situation, with these resources? Can we provide, or ask for, extra resources and assistance?

There are numerous examples of community-based projects that bring together people of different backgrounds and faiths to work within a similarly loose framework of common values (for examples, see Harré, 2018b; Hassan, 2014). Sometimes it is appropriate, and fascinating, to set out to learn the details of each other's stories, and storytelling workshops are one way to do this (Harré et al., 2006). But more often, people learn of each other's backgrounds and beliefs in fragments as they focus on the physical environment and institutions in their locality.

What we do next is never settled; every solution is temporary and is made up of real people acting in the real world. When you get your head around that and find a group of people willing to respect each other and work within the material reality they share – well that, I think, is the sacred in action.

Closing comments

As has always been the case, our livelihood and wellbeing as people is interwoven with the natural world. Any framework for working with people of different backgrounds must, and does, take account of our most objective and accurate observations of how that world works. The scientific enterprise (alongside local knowledge of place) is, in this sense, essential to our collective lives. Even if some people sincerely believe it would be better if we'd never gone down the science route – and maybe it will be our undoing in the end – it seems impossible now to turn our backs on this way of knowing. Can you really bring yourself to ignore the insights of science in your own life and choices? And if so, do you occupy a position that is widely adopted by the people you come across? For better or worse, science provides a set of assumptions and a language that is as close as we can get to an agreed knowledge system. It is by no means complete, but it is a necessary component of the framework described here. I also suggest that, to solve the problems we face, we need to keep coming back to the values we share. This is not to strip away or ignore difference, but to accept that our differences are particular solutions, which are always temporary and cannot be imposed on other people or readily transferred to other contexts.

Perhaps the reason I've dared propose a sacred framework for our time is because it is more a description of situations where I feel alive and at home, and where I sense other people feel this too, than it is a proposal *per se*. It is really an attempt to highlight *how I think we already are when we are at our best*. Like many readers, I worry about the future. My concern becomes overwhelming when I hear tales of terror and am surrounded by people who insist that the world is full of malevolence. When I see tales of joy in action – people getting on with life-enhancing solution-making alongside others, and doing so with humility and care – everything seems possible.

References

Agar, N. (2001). *Life's intrinsic value: Science, ethics, and nature.* Columbia University Press.

Anderson, E.N. (2013). Culture and the wild. In P.H. Kahn & P.H. Hasbach (Eds.), *The rediscovery of the wild* (pp.157–180). The MIT Press.

Azizi, A.A.B. (2018). *Two tales about what matters to people: How a 'Tale of Joy' and a 'Tale of Terror' influence wellbeing and values.* Honours dissertation. University of Auckland.

Baumeister, R.F. & Leary, M.R. (1995). The need to belong: Desire for interpersonal attachments as a fundamental human motivation. *Psychological Bulletin, 117*(3), 497--529.

Campbell, J. (1972). *Myths to live by.* Penguin Compass.

Carse, J. P. (1986). *Finite and infinite games.* The Free Press.

Díaz, S., Settele, J., Brondízio, E.S., Ngo, H.T., Agard, J., Arneth, A., Balvanera, A., Brauman, K.A., Butchart, S.H.M., Chan, K.M.A., Garibaldi, L.A., Ichii, K., Liu, J., Subramanian, S.M., Midgley, G.F., Miloslavich, P., Molnar, Z., Obura, D., Pfaff, A., . . . Zayas, C.N. (2019). Pervasive human-driven decline of life on Earth points to the need for transformative change. *Science, 366*(6471), eaax3100. 10.1126/science.aax3100

Harré, N. (2018a). *The infinite game: How to live well together.* Auckland University Press.

Harré, N. (2018b). *Psychology for a better world: Working with people to save the planet.* Auckland University Press.

Harré, N. & Madden, H. (2017). The infinite game: A symbol and workshop for living well together. *Ecopsychology, 9*(4), 212–224.

Harré, N., Blythe, C., McLean, L. & Khan, S. (2022). A people-focused systems approach to sustainability. *American Journal of Community Psychology, 69*(1-2), 114–133. https://doi.org/10.1002/ajcp.12550

Harré, N., Bullen, P. & Olson, B. (2006). *Storytelling: A workshop for inspiring group action.* In R.M. McNair (Ed.), *Working for peace: A handbook for practical psychology and other tools* (pp. 116–120). Impact.

Harré, N., Madden, H., Brooks, R. & Goodman, J. (2017). Sharing values as a foundation for collective hope. *Journal of Social and Political Psychology, 5*(2), 342–366. 10.5964/jspp.v5i2.742

Hassan, Z. (2014). *The social labs revolution.* Berrett-Koehler Publishers.

Hikuroa, D. (2017). Mātauranga Māori – the ūkaipō of knowledge in New Zealand. *Journal of the Royal Society of New Zealand, 47*, 5–10.

Kasser, T. (2002). Sketches for a self-determination theory of values. In E.L. Deci & R.M. Ryan (Eds.), *Handbook of self-determination research* (pp.123–140). University of Rochester Press.

Kasser, T. (2011). *Values and human wellbeing.* The Bellagio Intitiative.

Korsgaard, C. (1983). Two distinctions in goodness. *Philosophical Review, 92*(2), 169–195.

Monbiot, G. (2016). *How did we get into this mess?* Verso Books.

Rappaport, J. (2000). Community narratives: Tales of terror and joy. *American Journal of Community Psychology, 28*(1), 1–24.

Ryan, R.M., & Deci, E.L. (2000). Self-determination theory and the facilitation of intrinsic motivation, social development and well-being. *American Psychologist, 55*(1), 68–78.

Ryan, R.M., & Deci, E.L. (2002). Overview of self-determination theory: An organismic-dialetical perspective. In E.L. Deci & R.M. Ryan (Eds.), *Handbook of self-determination research* (pp.3–36). University of Rochester Press.

Sanderson, R., Prentice, M., Wolf, L., Weinstein, N., Kasser, T. & Crompton, T. (2019). Strangers in a strange land: Relations between perceptions of others' values and both civic engagement and cultural estrangement. *Frontiers in Psychology, 10*, Article 559.

Schultz, P.W., Gouveia, V.V., Cameron, L.D., Tankha, G., Schmuck, P. & Franek, M. (2005). Values and their relationship to environmental concern and conservation behavior. *Journal of Cross-Cultural Psychology, 36*, 457–475.

Schwartz, S.H. (1992). Universals in the content and structure of values: Theoretical advances and empirical tests in 20 countries. In L. Berkowitz & M.P. Zanna (Eds.), *Advances in experimental social psychology, vol. 25* (pp.1– 65). Academic Press.

Schwartz, S.H., & Sagiv, L. (1995). Identifying culture-specifics in the content and structure of values. *Journal of Cross-Cultural Psychology, 26*(92), 10.1177/0022022195261007

How green is your mind?

4 | Robin Shohet

'We have met the enemy, and he is us.'[1]

'Have you ever noticed that whenever you have a problem, you are there?'

(Source unknown)

A man walks into his GP surgery. 'Doctor, doctor' he pleads desperately, 'Do you have a vaccination to protect me from myself?'

It's a cartoon image I've had in my mind throughout writing this chapter. In this chapter, I suggest that, if we want to tackle the climate crisis, the place to start is with us, with our own thinking. The clearer our thinking, the more likely it is that our action is going to be effective.

Eckhart Tolle writes:

> The pollution of the planet is only an outward reflection of an inner psychic pollution: millions of unconscious individuals not taking responsibility for their inner space. (Tolle, 1999)

If we follow the line of inquiry that Tolle suggests, we are asked to take responsibility for our inner polluter. We no longer project on to others what is inside us. Projection offers temporary relief but creates problems further down the line. We polarise others into 'them and us', inevitably creating opposition rather than joining. If we want to wake people up to the climate crisis, I would like to suggest our starting point might be an inquiry into how our minds jump to self-justification, self-righteousness, blame and the creation of otherness (can't *they* see what is happening?) As Pogo suggests,[2] the

---

1. This phrase was coined by the American satirical cartoonist Pogo on an anti-pollution Earth Day poster in 1970 and again in a comic strip created for Earth Day 1971. https://library.osu.edu/site/40stories/2020/01/05/we-have-met-the-enemy

2. See note 1 above.

enemy might be us or, more accurately, how ready our minds are to polarise those who don't share our views.

This chapter is in three parts. Back in the 1990s, I wrote an article (Shohet, 1995) about inner pollution and how fear-based thinking prevents us acting on climate change (or, in those days, subscribing to the Green movement). The article has since been republished a few times, and I am incorporating it here, slightly updated to fit this context, as its premise is still relevant, even though the Green movement has morphed into climate activism.

Then, following Charles Eisenstein (2022), I draw a connection between the climate crisis and love. I suggest that, when our concerns and actions are fuelled by fear and separation, they add to pollution, whereas love has the power to go beyond that.

In the final section, I offer a very practical tool for reversing our negative thinking – one that has at its heart forgiveness; not the simplistic forgiveness that can lead to a moral superiority, or a repression of rage, or letting them 'get away with it', but a totally different way of thinking about injury and reparation. I am suggesting a connection between the inability to forgive and the climate crisis.

These might not appear to be related, but if we accept the possibility that pollution starts in our minds, then a failure to forgive adds to pollution. I believe we are in a better place to tackle our external environment when we have done our inner work. The inner work I am suggesting here (and of course there are dozens of techniques for doing inner work) is a particular form of forgiveness, a Hawaiian method called *ho'oponopono*. It helps us to undo some of what Eckhart Tolle (1999) would refer to as 'polluting inner beliefs' that manifest externally and, I believe, contribute to the climate crisis.

How green is your mind?

> What people are doing in planting forests and saving the whales and so on is very necessary, and more of it should be done. Nevertheless, it is still downstream. Unless something is done upstream, that is, in the process of thought, it won't really work in the long run. (Bohm & Edwards, 1992)

> Much of the time we are not very selective about the thoughts we put in our minds – nor are we aware of the toxic side effects these thoughts can have on our bodies *and the world*. (Jampolsky, 2008; emphasis added)

> There are no idle thoughts. All thinking produces form at some level. (Foundation for Inner Peace, 1996)

> There is nothing good or bad, but thinking makes it so. (Shakespeare's *Hamlet*)

Suppose you were a car and your brain/thoughts/mind were the exhaust pipe. Every time you had a negative thought, *any* negative thought, criticism or judgment – about yourself, another or God – your exhaust pipe would give off fumes. Would you be polluting the planet?

I believe that pollution begins in the mind. The *Upanishads*, an ancient Hindu text, say, 'Where there is another, there is fear.' What I understand by this is that, as long as I see myself as separate and you as 'other', I will be frightened of you and our relationship will be polarised: if I am competitive, I fear you will upstage me; if I hate you, I will fear your attack; if I love you, I fear you will abandon me. *A Course in Miracles* (Foundation for Inner Peace, 1996) talks about 'special love relationships' and 'special hate relationships' and sees both as the same: both arise out of duality or a sense of separateness, and therefore both exist in fear, not love.

Fear, I believe, is the source of all pollution. Fear lies behind the greed that fuels our exploitation of resources – fear that I must get what I can before you do, and that what I get will never be enough because my greed is fear driven and therefore irrational. Logical argument has less power over us than our emotions do. For instance, everybody knows that smoking is not good for your health, yet people persist in smoking.

I think that some of the ecological movement under-rates the self-destructive urge in each of us. According to psychoanalyst Harold Searles:

> Unconsciously we harbor the notion that since we do not immediately experience the ill effects of pollution and the like, it will not happen to us… Mankind is collectively reacting to the real and urgent danger from environmental pollution much as the psychotically depressed patient bent upon suicide by self-neglect. (Searles, 1972)

Searles connects the need for more power over nature, more industry and more technology with our desire to be in control of everything in order to compensate for infantile feelings of helplessness and powerlessness. These feelings can evoke rage, which in turn evokes fantasies of destroying everyone – mother, father, siblings, the whole world – in order to gain revenge and prove our might. Unfortunately, as is not the case with a child, we actually have the power to make such fantasies come true.

I remember in my early 20s feeling quite depressed, hating anyone who was happy, and consciously thinking that I wished there would be a world war and everyone would be as unhappy as me and/or be destroyed. As I get older, I allow myself to feel more connected to others, but my own feelings of powerlessness and helplessness still evoke in me terrible thoughts of revenge. I have moved on from being a fantasy bomb-builder but am still a gross polluter when in such states. I have learned that one way of reducing the pollution I create is not to judge myself and to overcome the shame of acknowledging my shadow by publicly speaking and writing about it, as I am doing here.

In *The Art of Hating* (1992), Gerald Schoenewolf looks at the whole business of hating, or, as I described earlier, having negative polluting thoughts. He makes a distinction between what he calls 'subjective' and 'objective' hate. When we hate subjectively, we are concerned with the immediate need to protect ourselves, to be right, to teach a lesson, to gain an advantage, to defeat an opponent or to revenge ourselves on an enemy. Objective hating, on the other hand, involves sharing our feelings of animosity in a way that aims to increase our contact and does not lose sight of the humanity of the other. It requires an understanding of others, oneself and one's motives, and a reminder not to go into subjective hate when provoked.

When we are supporting a 'worthy cause', if we find ourselves feeling judgemental or ever so slightly superior, we can be sure we are subjectively hating. One of the characteristics of subjective hate is to deny our own aggression and to project it onto those deemed to be 'unenlightened'. We become adept at provoking aggression in others in order to make our enemies look bad and ourselves look good. It is not surprising, then, that when the subjective hate of the polluter meets the subjective hate of the environmentalist, a lot of anger is generated and very little in the way of solutions.

In a chapter entitled 'Us and Them', Fran Peavey (1991) relates how she prepared for a meeting with the president of a conglomerate who owned a local napalm factory. She and her colleagues found out as much as they could about the president's personal life, relating to him in his human context, surrounded by the people who loved him and whom he loved. By the time the meeting took place, he no longer felt a stranger to them. Their aim was for him to see them as real people, not flaming radicals he could dismiss. They assumed he was carrying doubts inside himself about renewing a contract for his napalm factory and that they could voice these doubts in a non-antagonistic manner. In approaching the meeting in this way, they had moved from subjective hate to objective hate and established a real, personal contact. The president did not renew his factory's contract.

Peavey (1991) asks some pertinent questions about the truths we must face in ourselves if we are to practise non-polarisation: i.e. if we are to avoid creating 'otherness'. She realises that to work with social change without relying on the concept of enemies raises some practical difficulties. For example, what do we do with all the anger we are accustomed to unleashing against an enemy? Is it possible to hate actions and policies without hating the people who are implementing them? Does empathising with those whose actions we oppose create a dissonance that undermines our determination?

Saving our planet is as important a movement as there ever has been [*this was written in 1995*]. But unless I fully understand the mind of, say, the president of a napalm factory, I will be stuck in subjective hate and will therefore in my own way be as much of a polluter as he is.

The Indian sage Sri Ramana Maharshi once commented that we thank God for the good things that happen to us but not for the bad, and that is a mistake. I was shocked, but I think I understand. As long as we divide events into 'good' and 'bad', we are at the mercy of our minds, caught in an endless cycle of craving for what we consider to be 'good' and having an aversion to what we consider 'bad'. This means that we constantly judge everything in terms of a limiting, dualistic frame of reference.

How does all this relate to climate change?

1. The seeds of destruction are in the mind and in the emotions. Telling people about the effects of pollution is even less effective than anti-smoking campaigns. Polluting the world does not bring us instant or direct feedback, the way smoking can. Revenge can be an important component as much in those who pollute as in those who, in their campaign against pollution, are simply hiding their subjective hate behind a 'worthy cause'.

2. Campaigns against climate change will, I think, be more effective if they include some recognition of the divisive quality of human feelings and the human mind. Even as I write, I am aware of creating a new division in my own mind – between all those who have done their work on their inner polluter, versus those who just deal with the environment – a new hierarchy/duality.

3. When I look inside myself, I see how deeply polluting I am in my thoughts, regardless of my ecological credentials. Acknowledging this is a useful way of balancing any moral superiority I may try to claim. Perhaps it is true to say that anyone who is not enlightened will be polluting. Ramana Maharshi's ashram was run with great precision. Nothing was wasted. This was not because it was a movement or a conscious attempt to save resources, but a natural by-product of an undivided mind.

4. This does not mean there should not be a global movement to combat climate change. I simply want to remind myself (again) that, whenever I think I am right, I can be at my most bigoted and most unable to reach out to those who oppose me, because of the degree of my subjective hate.

I do not know if the ecology movement has adequately addressed this issue of inner pollution and it may be one of the reasons why it is not more effective. To change the mind of the president of the napalm factory, Fran Peavey (1991) had to work very hard on an inner level to release her subjective hate. I know I have not reached that state. My inner world is still full of 'goodies' and 'baddies'.

A recent minor incident in my life indicates how big an investment there is in the world for us to polarise. I received a telephone call from someone making a television programme against circumcision because I fitted all the criteria they were looking for. I am Jewish, male, articulate, have relived the trauma of my own circumcision in therapy and decided not to have my own sons circumcised. We were arranging dates for televising when I said (influenced, I think, by writing this article): 'You need to know that I can only be 95% and not 100% certain that I have made the right decision. It could be that, in later life, my sons will be angry with me for robbing them of a tradition. If I say I am 100% certain, I will, in my own way, become as rigid as those who fervently support circumcision. My wish would not be to convert or be converted, but for my five per cent of doubt to meet with a pro-circumcision person's five per cent of doubt so we can dialogue and increase both our doubts and thus create more middle ground.' At this point, the interviewer said he would have to consult his boss and would call me back. He never did. My fantasy is that my unwillingness to polarise on this issue would not make for good viewing.

I would like to end this section with an anecdote that amuses me, and with which my unloving self identifies. Many years ago, I went to listen to psychic and healer Paul Solomon. He told the story of how the CIA became interested in him because they wanted him to help them tap the secrets of the KGB. When asked if he could do it, his reply was, 'Sure. Anyone can do it. All you have to do is love the KGB more than you love yourselves.' The secrets of the KGB remain intact.

A shift to love: affirming interconnectedness

> Fear knocked at the door. Love answered and there was no one there. (Sufi maxim)

> We are victims of an energy crisis of our own fabrication. We are trapped in a crunch between eternal love and mortal fear. (Mendel, 1984)

There is in our Western culture, and perhaps in humanity as a whole, a confusion about love. I am full of love for my family, my tribe, my nation, my CIA, my football team, but not your family, your tribe, your nation, your KGB or (especially) your football team. Beneath the dominant individual consciousness there lurks a tribal consciousness that, by definition, is based on separation – on creating a 'them' in order to feel we have an 'us'. I argue that the climate movement takes us too easily and quickly into polarity, into othering others, or otherness, so even if we agree about the necessity of taking action, we are unable to work together to agree what we should do.

Charles Eisenstein (2022) has made a connection between love and climate change. He writes:

> The climate change issue is a gateway to truths about the human condition that hold whether or not you accept the dominant climate change narrative. The first of these is: *What we do to the world, we do to ourselves.* Self and other, humanity and nature are not separate. We may not die if the Amazon dies, but surely something within us dies, something precious, something sacred.
>
> My main message to the environmental movement is to shift the narrative away from our own destruction. From 'Change or we won't survive,' to 'Change or we will continue to lose what is beautiful and sacred.' It is a shift into love.

I like this framing. I think a shift to love moves us beyond separation and tribal thinking and frees us up to act together. So how to make this shift? I'd like to propose a simple, practical method of doing this.

Forgiveness

> He who is devoid of the power to forgive is devoid of the power to love. (King, 2012)

> Without forgiveness, there is no future. (Tutu, 1999)

Most of us would probably agree with the idea of taking responsibility for our thinking, although again most of us find the practice much harder, even when we know of the harm to self and other involved in not doing so. For example, when we blame or scapegoat or judge, we are, in the terms of reference above, polluting. We are hurting others and ourselves. Forgiveness in the way I am suggesting helps undo what I see as the addiction to being right. Self-righteousness reduces effectiveness of action in any worthy cause, as it usually creates opposition: being right, claiming the moral high ground, makes someone else wrong or ignorant. If we are to campaign (and introspection does not negate this – it is not a question of *either* campaigning *or* introspection, but both *and*), then, like Fran Peavey (1991), we must first start with understanding another's point of view.

So why forgiveness? What I am describing here is a particular form of forgiveness – the *hoʻoponopono* method from Hawaii. This invites us to look at the other in a totally different way: not to frame them as wrong, bad or dangerous, but to move ourselves into a position where *we take responsibility* for how we think about them. In the framework of this chapter, we become willing to contemplate not polluting them and the world with our negative thinking.

It works like this. Suppose Jack has swindled me out of my share of the money we put into a business venture. Rather than sue Jack, hate Jack or plot revenge on Jack, in the *hoʻoponopono* method, we repeat the following sentences:

> Jack, I love you. (Assumption that love is who we both are.)
>
> Jack, I am sorry. (For holding a negative picture of you that is inevitably incomplete.)
>
> Jack, please forgive me. (For not being willing to see your essence.)
>
> Jack, thank you. (For giving me this opportunity to heal the part of me you represent.)

It is counter-intuitive to think that Jack swindled me and I ask him for forgiveness. According to this philosophy, which is based on our changing our thinking, yes, Jack has swindled me, but I have been carrying around negative thoughts about him, perhaps gossiping and turning people against him. From my metaphorical exhaust pipe, I am belching out fumes. My hot, angry thoughts are contributing to global warming. I am seeing him in one dimension, letting that picture of him dominate my thinking. In that way, I am both attacking myself and him. It is as if I have made a decision to close my heart and am blaming him for it. The *hoʻoponopono* method cuts right through that.

When I teach about forgiveness, I suggest we do it for ourselves. Forgiveness has nothing to do with the other person. We say we no longer want to walk around with a closed heart. And if we are not ready to do this, that is fine. There are no 'shoulds' to doing this inner work. But it centres us, so we can be more effective in whatever form of action we choose to take. We have taken responsibility for our inner polluter.

Summarising so far:

1. Negative thoughts pollute. Not in an obvious way, but they are like radiation that is toxic but invisible.

2. We may have little control over external events, but we can take responsibility for internal ones – i.e. our thinking.

3. In doing so, we can reduce the way we pollute by such actions as blame, criticism and so on.

4. This does not negate external action, but after inquiry the action is less likely to polarise and be full of self-righteousness.

5.   The *hooponopono* method of forgiveness turns our thinking on its head and asks us to be willing to undo the polluting, 'hot' thoughts that contribute to global warming.

6.   This method can be done silently on one's own, and while not obviously related to global warming, moves us into a clearer space from which to act. We are less willing to polarise and see goodies (us) and baddies (them).

7.   None of us really knows anything for sure. Underneath what can masquerade as certainty, there are doubts. Can we meet in not knowing together? In holding this aspiration, I create more space to meet the other, whether in the consulting room or elsewhere. Rumi's words come to mind:

> Out beyond ideas of rightdoing and wrongdoing, there is a field. I will meet you there. (2004)

8.   *Hooponopono*, which suggests internally asking for forgiveness when we are ready (this mustn't be forced or made into a guilt trip), offers us a practical method of taking responsibility for our inner polluter.

I have many examples of using the *hooponopono* method with teams who have difficulties with each other, helping them to see how interconnected they are and that, in fact, we all are. In one organisation I worked with, a charity with very lofty aims, two key players did not trust each other and were locked in a power battle that threatened to disrupt the work of the whole organisation. I supervised one of them and suggested he did the forgiveness process internally before he met with the other, which he did. He reported that the meeting went far better than he could have hoped. He went in with an open mind, recognising how his negative thoughts would just keep the conflict going, and that they both ultimately wanted the same thing – the wellbeing of the organisation.

In my work with numerous charities, I have found that, behind the worthy causes, there lurks the shadow of power battles. In the words of Gerry Jampolsky (1983):

> A great deal of strife can result if people come together to pursue a purely external goal, even if the goal is very idealistic.

Forgiveness work, where we take responsibility for our thinking, gives us a practical tool to lessen strife and come together.

I would like to end with a personal story. I was having issues with my stepson. I could see no way out, and my wife felt like piggy in the middle. I did the *hooponopono* method, sometimes through gritted teeth. I was sure my negative thoughts about him and what had happened were justified. Then, one day, I heard myself say, 'It's over.' The stories of the past dropped off me. It was no longer right/wrong but a willingness to move into the present. I would not have believed this possible, but the commitment to want to see things differently kept me going. The whole family, not just he and I, are better for it. The willingness to stop making the other our enemy and take responsibility for our own negative thinking is my version of holding the hope. It is a movement from fear to love.

References

Bohm, D. & Edwards, M. (1992) *Changing consciousness*. Harper.

Eisenstein, C. (2022, March 12). *The spirituality of* _____. [Blog.] https://charleseisenstein.substack.com/p/the-spirituality-of-_____?s=r

Foundation for Inner Peace (1996). *A course in miracles*. Viking.

Jampolsky, G. (1983). *Teach only love*. Banta

Jampolsky, G. (2008). *Forgiveness the greatest healer*. Atria.

King, M.L. (2012). *A gift of love: Sermons from strength to love*. Beacon Press.

Mendel, B. (1984). *Open heart therapy*. Celestial Arts.

Peavey, F., with Levy, M. & Varon, C. (1991). Us and them. In Zweig, C. & Abrams, J. (Eds), *Meeting the shadow: The hidden power of the dark side of human nature* (pp.202–206). Tarcher.

Rumi. (2004). *Selected poems*. Penguin Classics.

Schoenewolf, G. (1992). *The art of hating*. Jason Aronson.

Searles, H. (1972). Unconscious processes in relation to the environment. *Psychoanalytic Review, 59*(3), 361–374.

Shohet, R. (1995). How green is your mind? *One Earth*, (Summer).

Tolle, E. (1999). *The power of now*. New World Library

Tutu, D. (1999). *No future without forgiveness*. Rider.

PART 2

Hope, what hope?

5 Radical hope: A dimension of the rooted soul

Hetty Einzig

The title of this chapter is taken from the book by the American philosopher Jonathan Lear, *Radical Hope: Ethics in the face of cultural devastation* (Lear, 2006). Lear uses 'radical' in its commonly held sense of far-reaching, fundamental, usually disruptive change. Here I seek to extend its usage by reminding us of the word's etymological base in the Latin *radice*, for root. The title also references comments by the Czech dissident, activist and playwright Vaclav Havel, who presided over a period of great cultural turbulence as the last president of Czechoslovakia from 1989 to its dissolution in 1992, and as the first president of the newly formed democratic Czech Republic from 1993 to 2003:

> The kind of hope that I often think about... I understand above all as a state of mind, not a state of the world. Either we have hope within us, or we don't. It is a dimension of the soul; it's not essentially dependent upon some particular observation of the world or estimate of the situation... it is not the conviction that something will turn out well, but the certainty that something makes sense, regardless of how it turns out. Hope, in this deep and powerful sense, is... an ability to work for something because it is good, not just because it stands a chance to succeed. (Havel, 1991, p.181)

These are my points of departure on my journey to explore the holding of hope as a psycho-spiritual discipline and a radical act in a time of devastation. Following Lear's enquiry into how one can maintain hope as an act of courage, I suggest we need to reanimate our imaginarium, and I offer transpersonal psychology as the practical vehicle for cultivating hopeful practice and a container for ecosystemic thinking and emergence. This can happen through truly hearing other voices and opening to other cultures. First and last, I seek to re-root hope as a dimension of the soul, which, I suggest, lives beyond the self – in nature, beauty, art, music, and in relationships.

It is in the spirit of exploration that I share my inquiry into hope and grappling after truths. I believe we can support ourselves to restore and uphold hope through dark times. Indeed, as practitioners who work with people to help them understand their challenges and fulfil their potential within shifting ecosystems, I suggest it is our responsibility to do so. That doesn't mean it is either easy or self-evident.

Regeneration – rent a cherry tree

For Christmas 2021, my children rented me a cherry tree. I was politely baffled by this gift. Why not buy me a cherry tree to plant in my garden? What did it mean to rent a tree? Where's the joy in this second-hand relationship with an arbitrary tree? Plenty, as it turns out.

At the end of January, I received my first newsletter from the Rent a Cherry Tree farm in Kent. As I read about 'bud break' and 'blossom walks', of the 1200 hours of chilling that the tree buds need every winter to 'break endodormancy', the mycorrhizal fertiliser to encourage a strong orchard-wide root system, and the jaunty names of the varieties – Merchant, Vanda, Kordia, Penny, Colney, Korvik, Sweetheart and Regina – my cherry tree took root in my imagination. An urbanite with unrequited longings to grow sweet peas and vegetables, I had become a foster parent – albeit from afar – for a tree of the Penny variety, number 63b in row 11.

In Japan, cherry blossom is the literal and symbolic flower of the spring, a time of renewal, and a reminder of the fleeting nature of life. After their beauty peaks at around two weeks, the blossoms start to fall. I had fallen in love a little, alive to the poignancy of the short span of our romance: *mono no aware*[1] encapsulated.

I had become a stakeholder, is one way of putting it – another, which I prefer, is that I had entered a world of growing hope…

Reanimating our relationship with landscape

Animism, the belief that all things – animals, plants, rocks, rivers, weather systems, human handiwork and, perhaps, even words – are animated and alive was relegated to the margins or actively repressed by the European Enlightenment of the 17th and 18th centuries. Seen as superstition, backward and the preserve of 'primitive' cultures – all blockers to the ideal of reason, logic and scientific progress – animism is still today regarded in Western cultures with a certain embarrassment (Eldridge, 1996).

James Lovelock and Lyn Margulis introduced Gaia theory – Earth as a self-regulating, complex system – in the 1970s. But, while this has educated our understanding, it has not sufficiently changed our behaviour (Lovelock, 2000).

However, the belief that objects, places and creatures all possess a distinct spiritual essence is the foundation of Japan's main religion, Shinto, still (alongside Buddhism) vital in a country that is also a global leader in electronics and technology and whose people enjoy one of the longest life expectancies in the world. Animism could be on the verge of a modest comeback in our self-consciously 'enlightened' societies as 'a

---

1. *Mono no aware* is an acute sensitivity to the transience of lovely things; a melancholy awareness that everything beautiful will fade, combined with a rich enjoyment of this short-lived beauty.

language in which to think of the world' (Burley, 2018). David Attenborough's television series have done more than any scientific or academic research to awaken us to both the wonders and the familiarities of the lives of plants and animals.

Scientist and founder/director of the Center for Native Peoples and the Environment, Robin Wall Kimmerer has written eloquently on how the English language depersonalises and thereby disrespects the natural world:

> we make that maple an object; we put a barrier between us, absolving ourselves of moral responsibility… if a maple is an *it*, we can take up the chain saw. If a maple is a her, we think twice. (Kimmerer, 2013, p.57)

Landscape – trees, water, fields and the built environment – is not something out there. It is the often unconscious but very real container for our individual and cultural lives. In psychological terms, a 'container' is that which contains and mediates our raw feelings and, like the crucible, transforms these into meaning through relationship, as in the primary parent-infant dyad. In the same way, landscape contains us, and through relationship lives within us in an entangled interchange of inner and outer. Landscape links us to Earth and also to time – a felt sense of continuity from past into the future (see also Sheldrake, 2020). 'Our work,' says Kimmerer, 'is to learn to speak the grammar of animacy, so that we might truly be at home' (2013, p.58).

Like the parental, coaching or therapeutic space, landscape holds us so we can develop our individual lives, and our individual lives are infused with the world around us, including our relationships – just as we permeate them. Enrique Salmon (2000), an academic from the Raràmuri people in the Sierra Madre, Mexico, terms this 'kincentric ecology'.[2] He describes the Raràmuri worldview thus:

> Indigenous people view both themselves and nature as part of an extended ecological family that shares ancestry and origins… an awareness that life… is viable only when humans view the life surrounding them as kin. (Salmon, 2000, p.1327)

In the tundra of northern Norway, the Sámi people today hold the same concept. Artist Máret Anne Sara says:

> For us the reindeer is a very close relative. Humans, nature and animals are interdependent and equal. What's happening to the reindeer is our story as well. (Higgins, 2022)

This same idea of kinship moved the American hunter-forester turned ardent environmentalist Aldo Leopold to propose in 1949 the concept of the land ethic, which expands community to include the natural environment:

---

2. I am grateful to Charmaine Roche for introducing me to this term and to Enrique Salmon's paper that he presented at a webinar on 'Decoloniality as narrative resistance to climate change', on 8 March 2022, as part of the Climate Coaching Alliance festival.

In short, a land ethic changes the role of Homo sapiens from conqueror of the land-community to plain member and citizen of it. (Leopold, 1949, p.113–114)

Salmon introduces us to the word *iwigara* – a concept useful for expanding our Western idea of soul. *Iwigara* includes origins, history and spiritual guidance, and an embodied richness where language, identity, spirit and actions are enmeshed in a continuous co-creative flow.

As Sara says of her world, 'destroying any part of this is like suicide from our perspective'.

The imaginarium – under threat

One way we can approach *iwigara* in terms of Western-European heuristics is through the concept of the imaginarium. The imaginarium is a cultural repository of visual references that stimulate feelings and imagination. As well as a rich flow of personal images (think of Proust's iconic madeleine – now a go-to referent for how taste, smell and sound bend time and space), our surroundings, especially our natural landscapes, supply our imaginarium with universally recognisable symbols – sun, moon, birds, trees, water. My cherry tree has entered my imaginarium.

Today our imaginarium is being profoundly shaken. The images of climate change that come to me – of rooftops straining above floodwater, of wildfires ripping through forests, of strip-mining and mountains of plastic, of the terror of refugees crossing the seas in leaky dinghies – coalesce into a fist-size stone that sits somewhere around my solar plexus.[3]

In mid-January 2022, after weeks of leaden-grey cloud and rain, the sky in London shone a spectacular cold, metallic blue – I felt it a blessing. And yet. News reports warned that pollution levels in the city that day were at their highest since 2018. And those disconcertingly high temperatures over the New Year? England experienced its warmest on record.

A bright blue sky and warm days are no longer guaranteed indicators of hopefulness or sources of joy; instead, they are sinister signs of seismic shifts in our landscapes. As weather patterns shift and our landscapes are increasingly damaged, our containers start to feel unstable, unsafe, even threatening. When places and people meant to keep us safe threaten or hurt us, our imaginarium is turned painfully upside down. This can be traumatic (Davenport, 2017[4]).

Anxious questions occupy me: how can we hold hope in the face of despair? Can hope co-exist with guilt? With shame? How can we nurture hope in these times of

---

3. See also Sally Weintrobe's (2021) reflections on the personal emotional taxation of holding the crisis in mind: '… when this author comes close to the climate crisis, she can find in her hands a melting iceberg, a small migratory bird caught in a hurricane, a climate refugee: moments of piercing sadness. Recently she finds shame: individual shame and species shame. Her species caused this crisis. In the space of just fifty years (in large measure) humans have squandered, polluted and damaged support systems that life depends on. Feelings about this require considerable working through.'

4. See pp.70–80 in Davenport's book for an acute account of one person's trauma reaction and the responses of clinicians and community.

chronic anxiety – and, increasingly, acute fear? What might it mean to hold hope in the face of the lure of despair or cynicism or fury?

We are at a watershed moment (Hawken, 2021). As we emerge from the 40-year 'cold war' of denial and cover-up by the fossil fuel industries (McKibben, 2019; Milman, 2023), terms like the Great Turning, the Great Transformation and the Great Transition, and an emphasis on regeneration, rather than growth, are entering the discourse to describe our era and our potential. If we are to articulate new narratives for a future where we can find ourselves and our agency, we need to replenish our imaginarium with objects that re-energise concepts of care and relationships, of repair and restoration, of goodness, beauty and soul. We need this refreshed language to revitalise our imaginarium with hope. This fuels our courage and leads to engagement and action.

At the moment the future is looking shaky and goodness seems an academic concept. To feel hope, we must have a sense of home as a safe place and of continuity into the future.

A sense of the future

In *Radical Hope*, Jonathan Lear (2006) explores the holding of hope when a whole culture is destroyed. In what is, in part, a parable for our times, Lear reviews contemporary accounts of the decimation in the late 19th century of the indigenous North American Crow Nation, and enquires into questions of ethics, courage and virtue as constituents of hope in the face of cultural devastation. He quotes from an interview with Chief Plenty Coups:

> when the buffalo went away the hearts of my people fell to the ground, and they could not lift them up again. After this nothing happened... (Lear, 2006, p.2)

Records show that this renowned chief went on to do many things, including successfully securing his people's tribal lands as the largest of the North American reservations. Lear takes the Chief's words to mean that, without the context of life as they knew it, symbolised by the buffalo (a key icon in the Crow imaginarium), it was not possible to conceptualise a good future.

For Lear, this is a question for moral psychology – where ethics, psychology, philosophy and theories of mind intersect. This moral dimension is not part of mainstream coaching and psychology. But the inquiry into whether 'the formations and transformations of the psyche help us to lead a good life with others' (Lear, 2006, p.104) is ever more urgent.

For the most part, visions for the future are based on the past. A key element of the current turbulence is that our narratives of the past are being overturned – not just by historians and academics but by large-scale movements like #MeToo and #BlackLivesMatter, by environmental activists and writers, by scientists, artists and campaigners. So, if the past is not what we were led to believe, if the stories that framed our collective identities are shown up to be disingenuous at best and fraudulent at worst, what does that mean for our sense of self and our capacity to shape new futures?

Futures philosopher Bill Sharpe (2013) developed his Three Horizons model to help us envision the future – the 'patterning of hope', he calls it – by exploring three vectors. The first horizon is the current dominant pattern or culture; the third horizon is the future pattern – 'working creatively with the unknown, the partially known and the uncertain' (Sharpe, 2013, p.22). The second horizon is that of 'ambiguous innovation', of experimentation. It stops us getting trapped in the 'incremental improvement that holds us back from the third horizon' (Sharpe, 2013, p.25). This second zone of working focuses our eyes and ears on noticing the seeds of the future emerging today.

The global north is at this inflection point now. Do we retreat into glossy fantasy worlds – an endless supply of Netflix movies, cookery programmes and game shows; or can we face current realities and conceive of a good future that we could build together in active hope (Macy & Johnstone, 2022)?

Contested narratives

The scale of emotional recoil at Russia's invasion of Ukraine in February 2022 points at a sensitive spot beyond our natural horror of war. I sense it relates directly to the widespread re-examination of the European Enlightenment and the imperialism it spawned. Enlightenment ideals of science, logic and progress – to bring the light of reason to superstition – are being widely contested, and the dark side of these lofty ideals – colonialism, the violent suppression of other lives, other voices and other world views – is increasingly exposed.

For example, I grew up in the UK with a story that followed Caesar's 2000-year-old boast, 'Veni, vidi, vici.' Enabled by the heroic alliance of science and Christianity, Britain 'civilised' the rest of the world. It constitutes a cosmic shock now to allow ourselves to see the invalidity and hear the facts that expose the British Empire – the largest in human history, which at its peak in 1920 covered almost a quarter of the globe – as effectively a programme to suppress, exterminate and dominate peoples and environments in the biggest land grab ever.

There is an unravelling going on. The Establishment – the institutions of government, health services, law and order, religion, education – is increasingly fractured. Deep beliefs about justice, truth and democracy are being re-examined. This is part of the fabric of culture. We may not articulate our current unease as a prolonged divorce from the narrative of Empire, but its impact on us is as profound. A foundation story bestows on its people a sense of belonging and collective self-esteem. When it cracks, we feel the pain.

As Western ontologies lose cogency and vitality, our sense of being in the world, our contributions, work and efforts at leading a 'good life' become deflated of meaning. It's not just the 'bullshit jobs' (Graeber, 2018) that cause psychological and societal harm. These are acute symptoms of a chronic loss of meaning as cultural norms creak with the strain in a world in deep trouble. My clients work in a range of sectors that are considered worthwhile – but they too sometimes feel their work to be 'not enough' or to lack meaning. Many of them yearn for something different, for greater integrity. This yearning is a key factor, I believe, in what is referred to as the Great Resignation: people in mid-career leaving their jobs in large numbers (Cook, 2021; Morgan, 2021).

Environmental sustainability is not separate from social justice and psycho-spiritual wellbeing (Williams, 2021). The destruction of the natural world – that which holds our lives within a bigger frame – is a significant contributor to the anomie and disaffection felt by increasing numbers of people. Facing up to climate change and the loss of our landscapes and creatures is an existential crisis that is bound up with the dissolution of Western foundation stories. Since our sense of identity is in large part founded on our commitments to a certain life and narrative, this can be experienced as 'a rip in the fabric of one's self' (Lear, 2006, p.65).

Entropy and emergence

Entropy is a term from thermodynamics, physics, weather and economics. But its definition – 'lack of order or predictability; gradual decline into disorder' – would fit many people's lived experience. One way to look at the wars, environmental destruction, pandemics, biodiversity and cultural loss is as symptoms and signs of entropy: the winding down of the artefacts of a particular life form called homo sapiens. All life forms obey the laws of entropy: disorder leads to breakdown and dissolution.

This is not the first time that humans have believed the end is nigh. 'Things fall apart; the centre cannot hold,' Yeats famously wrote in 1919 (2009). But it is the first time we have the science to show what and how we are destroying the complex fabric of life on Earth. It is of a different order to contemplate the destruction of landscapes we are embedded in – the planet we call home – and, further, to know that it's in large part what is referred to as the WEIRD world (Western, educated, industrialised, rich, democratic) that has caused – is causing – this destruction.

Planetary devastation can feel too terrifying to contemplate – eco-anxiety is now a recognised and pervasive condition (Rao & Powell, 2021). However, two years of Covid-19 brought us face to face with the fragility of life. I like to believe that the enforced retreat of several lockdowns gave us time to reflect. Can this direct experience of vulnerability enable us to extrapolate to a wider plane – to the whole of life?

To write about hope in this context felt almost impossible – depression or denial seemed preferable. Almost. For the counterpart to entropy is the principle of emergence: new growth will always push through the cracks. Finding a lens and a language so we can notice these small shoots and nurture them became an imperative. I looked for different stories.

Thoughts about our global predicament and our human responsibility are demanding ever more loudly to enter the arena of our thinking. In a tone of hopeful revision, historians, anthropologists and environmentalists are turning to non-Western cultures and to indigenous ethical codes for alternatives to the bankrupt systems of the global north that have for so long taught us separation from the places and people we are interconnected with (Graeber & Wengrow, 2021; Akala, 2018; Mishra, 2013). Offering props and frameworks to help us engage, storytellers, activists, filmmakers and artists are emerging into the global spotlight to re-animate the imaginarium of the post-industrialised world with new images of hope (Hawken, 2021). From stories of pain and oppression emerge narratives of courage, resilience, kindness, beauty and humour (Adom, 2022).

Our current enmeshed environmental, psycho-social and spiritual crisis is now mainstream. As normalisation gathers pace, more of us are sensing that this complexity *can* be thought about, that it involves us all and that tangible actions, however small, can be taken.

Soul – breath and root

The word 'soul' comes from the old English *sawol*:[5] the spiritual and emotional part of a person; that which animates existence. Seen as the core of life, in ancient German it is connected with the sea (*saiwaz*), as the resting place of the soul before birth and after death. Soul links with spirit as breath and energy.

As a disease of the lungs, Covid-19 brought breath centre-stage in our imaginariums during the pandemic, and we learned only too vividly how our breath co-mingles with that of others. We rediscovered parks, woods and trees to breathe in, with renewed appreciation, the oxygen they offer so freely. 'Forest bathing' became popular as welcome balm for body and soul.

When Vaclav Havel talks of hope as a dimension of the soul, rather than locate this imaginatively within our body or vested in a panoply of religious artefacts – as Havel, a Catholic, might have done – we can return to its roots as that which animates existence, and conceptually reconfigure both soul and hope in ways that serve us to better engage with our current crises.

Breakthroughs in neuroscience, like the identification of mirror neurons (Rizzolatti & Craighero, 2004), polyvagal theory (Porges, 2017) and the understanding of brain as body-wide (Feldman Barrett, 2017), tell us we are, like all mammals, co-regulating creatures, our sense of self, our emotions and our health formed through interaction with others. Network theory (Christakis & Fowler, 2008; Christakis, 2010) shows how we influence each other even at distance, and mycorrhizal understanding (Sheldrake, 2020) tells us trees do all this too. As the science is increasingly validating Jung's concept of the collective unconscious, it is also challenging theories of individual consciousness. Can we now take the small but significant step of understanding soul (perhaps consciousness itself) as existing beyond the body, rooted in and interacting with our environments?

In psychosynthesis, the most prominent model of transpersonal psychology in the West, the core assumption is that, while the human being *has* a personality (multiple, changeable, complex), it *is* a soul (essential, enduring and oriented towards good). Conceptualised for a secular society as our Higher Self, this is situated in the model of the psyche on the borders of the individual and the collective: part of me and also part of 'out there'; part of the sea of life. We live as part of the world, as a cell of the whole, and the health of the world is dependent on our individual awareness, choices and right action. The transpersonal psyche emphasises porosity, fluidity, multiple levels of awareness and a continuity of past, present and future – a flow of time.

The ecosystemic nature of the transpersonal is in the name: the prefix 'trans' emphasises going beyond, across and through the personal. Developed by the Italian

5. www.etymonline.com/word/Soul

psychiatrist Roberto Assagioli (1888–1974) under the long, dark shadow of two world wars, psychosynthesis is an ontology – a way of looking at life and being in the world – that highlights interdependence and spirituality as an inherent part of being human (Einzig, 2013, 2020).

Steeped in wisdom traditions of both East and West and fluent in several languages, Assagioli was an early proponent of Freud's revolutionary ideas. But he came to see the limits of psychoanalysis, its scant attention to beauty, love, courage, hope and altruism. Like Carl Jung, Assagioli broke from Freud's model on the crux of spirituality. Psychosynthesis 'is not against psychoanalysis… but it insists that the needs for meaning, for higher values, for a spiritual life, are as real as biological or social needs' (Assagioli, n.d.) This is nothing to do with faith, dogma or organised religion, but, as Salmon aptly puts it, 'the awareness that one's breath is shared by all surrounding life' (Salmon, 2000, p.1331). Assagioli's aim was to create a practical psychology with the express purpose of helping those 'who refuse to submit passively to the play of psychological forces which are going on within them' (Assagioli, n.d., cited in Einzig, 2020).

Radical hope reminds us of the Latin *radicalis,* 'of or having roots'. This points us to both an uprooting and a re-rooting. For hope to take on fresh relevance for our times, we must, I believe, both examine the roots of our assumptions and re-root hope within the natural world. What if, for example, we reversed our Eurocentric romantic relationship with nature as an awe-inspiring spectacle and saw instead that: 'The natural world… is not one of wonder, but of familiarity. The human niche is only one of a myriad of united niches that work together to continue the process of *iwigara'* (Salmon, 2000; p.1328)? When I think of my cherry tree, it is her ordinariness and the way she blossoms in my imaginarium that I celebrate.

Crucible moments: Crisis, pain and failure as creative grist

At the start of a recent series of group supervisions for hospital staff, we (the facilitators) asked what the participants' hopes were for the sessions. A doctor took a deep breath and said quietly but firmly, 'I want a space to talk about failure. As a doctor you are expected to have an answer to everything – in a society that doesn't brook failure. I want for us to be able to show fear rather than hiding it.'

Failure and crises are a normal part of life, rather than due to personal lack or limitation. We know this. Yet we react as if we didn't. Pain is inevitable, but shame, depression and anxiety need not be. Learning how to face the failures and crises of everyday life with courage and compassion, rather than shame and suppression, is a key skill we could all usefully develop – it would serve us well in facing the greater pain and greater shame of our failure to care for our Earth. The transpersonal works very deliberately with failure and crisis as opportunities for creative breakthrough. Our imaginarium is examined and enriched. Imagery, evoked through drawing and guided visualisations, helps us, when we are ready, to take the necessary distance from the fear and pain of crisis so we can stay awake to the possibilities of emergence. Perspective enables us to come to terms with those aspects of ourselves we find shameful and meet our grief and rage with compassion.

During World War II, as a Jew, Assagioli was forced to hide in the mountains with his family, his home was torched and he was incarcerated by the fascist military, not knowing if he would be put to death. He later lost his only son to tuberculosis. Rather than raging against fate, Assagioli talked of 'collaborating with the inevitable'. Keeping in mind the natural law of emergence, even the deepest losses can acquire meaning. With all care and sensitivity to the pain, attending also to what is seeking to emerge through situations of great difficulty, rather than solve, pity or excise them, allows for the discovery not just of new dimensions of strength in ourselves but also of what could be born through us (Einzig & Whitmore, 2021).

This reframing attunes our capacity to embrace unknowing, uncertainty and paradox. As every difficult situation provides creative possibilities for personal courage and transformation, crisis becomes a portal to hope: to the opportunity to see, hear, think and do something different.

Courage and creativity – reconsidered

It takes courage to hold hope in the face of devastation.

I am a child of the Holocaust. My mother escaped from Nazi Germany in her early teens on one of the last *kindertransport* trains to leave Berlin. This was in April 1939, just months before the outbreak of World War II. I absorbed the experience of the refugee. From my earliest years, I learned about fear, uprootedness, instability and the longing for *heimat* that translates into the primary need for roots.

I also learned about courage and hope. My mother had an apparently unwavering faith in the redemption of art, in the energy and idealism of the young, and in the fundamental goodness of ordinary people, given the supportive circumstances of justice, care and integrity (see Smail, 1987). Despite a proclivity to gloom, she sought and found joy; despite a fiercely activist stance as a political citizen, she sought and found spiritual nourishment. In the aftermath of devastation, when all hope for humanity seemed lost, she chose to have children. As she recounted later, 'after so much death, I knew I had to create life'.

Aristotle is our point of return when we consider courage (Aristotle, 2000). Situated in tolerating danger, facing fear, enduring pain and loss and in the exercise of good judgement, courage aims at what is beautiful, fine or wise. Traditionally associated with the soldier in battle, courage was translated to the boardroom, the sports field and the coaching arena as a constituent of the fight to win. But if it is the cultural context that lends our individual acts their significance, when this fractures, as it does today, these strivings for success can seem meaningless. Are we polishing our skills, aiming for high performance and striving for excellence in a vacuum?

Are we being called upon to reformulate courage, not just personally but as a species? Following Aristotle, instead of emphasising bravery, we can see courage in our capacity to face and endure the pain of multiple losses, and hold hope, nonetheless. Paul Tillich called this the 'courage to be' (1952/2000). Endurance is not a gritting of the teeth. Better conceived as a 'being with', it is a call for fortitude, patience and grace. The etymology of courage reminds us also of love: rage of the heart (*coeur* in French). We stand for what we love.

The Symposium is a workshop created by the Pachamama Alliance (2006) that groups of us delivered for some years across the globe. We were coaches, facilitators, artists, activists and citizens, young and old, from many different countries, committed to working for a fundamental shift in our human presence on the Earth. In the Symposium, we talked about a key element of the work being to 'hospice the old': that is, to assist with respectful care ways of being in the world that have lost legitimacy or meaning, that are dying out, so they may pass with dignity. The other half of this work is to 'midwife the new' – to be alert to the seedlings, to aid new forms into life.

Just as courage is not self-confidence, creativity is not the simple realisation of eureka moments (Einzig, 2017). In his research into how innovation leaders tackle overwhelming challenges, Brett Macfarlane discovered that only those who could sustain a hopeful outlook 'were concerned with doing the work of regeneration'; only hope held them in the 'productivity zone' (Macfarlane, 2022). These leaders demonstrated a hopeful mindset through tolerance, empowerment and composure, and, significantly, with ambivalence and humility.

In contrast to conventional heuristics of innovative courage manifested in bold action, these are important findings. Macfarlane relates these qualities to Melanie Klein's (1997) concept of the depressive position – when the developing child confronts the reality of paradox and imperfection in themselves and their parents. Klein thought this phase was a prerequisite for creativity, for engaging with real work. Far from being a weakness, ambivalence is an important element of a relational approach – a recognition of interdependence and the realities of holding multiple, often competing priorities in mind. Maturity, then, is to be creative despite the limitations of the real world and one's own doubts; to move forward together with courage inflected with humility, care and the willingness to engage with the uncertain work of birthing the new (Einzig, 2017).

> Reversing the climate crisis is an outcome. Regenerating human health, security and well-being, the living world and justice is the purpose. (Hawken, 2021, p.11)

Paul Hawken's clarion call articulates the agenda. These questions thence follow: Can we find the courage to sublimate our individual goals and desires to the good of the whole, of the wider planetary project? Can we move from destructive modes of being to regenerative ones? These surely are key to what is being asked of us now. If, like the Raràmuri, we believe 'that all life shares the same breath' and that 'we are all related to, and play a role in, the complexity of life' (Salmon, 2000, p.1328), we might engage with the work hopefully.

Radical hope – the holding of goodness beyond self

The pivotal moment for Chief Plenty Coups in choosing how he should lead his people to survive the destruction of their way of life came in the form of a dream. A new character enters his imaginarium to guide him forward: the chickadee bird (similar to the UK blue tit). A symbol of honest guidance, the chickadee indicates the path to be taken. The Chief recognises that things will change in ways he cannot now imagine, so the future cannot be faced in the way the Crow have faced challenges before.

We must do what we can to open our imaginations up to a radically different set
of future possibilities. (Lear, 2006, p.93)

As he grapples with what a hopeful vision might mean, the Chief commits to the
idea that 'something good will emerge even if it outstrips my present limited capacity
for understanding what that good is' (Lear, 2006, p.94). This commitment to both
emergence and to goodness beyond the self, like Havel's (1991) holding of hope without
knowing if something will turn out well, defines radical hope.

To hope for mere survival is not enough: to continue living, an honourable way
forward must be found. The key issue is to find ways to carry forward ethical principles
of courageous goodness across the limbo of transition into new ways of being. Ancient
sagas of spiritual awakening, such as Dante's *Divine Comedy* (1939/1971), are metaphors
of this journey. In this epic of fear, confusion and trials of courage, Dante is tested in the
fire of inferno and the bleak wastes of limbo as essential stages to access 'paradise': the
goodness that lies beyond the self. The individual's task is to manifest it (Dante, 2004).

Transpersonal psychology offers practices to enable us to build goodness through
being and doing. Following Aristotle, Assagioli lists the will as a spiritual dimension:
our capacity for good judgement, choice, discipline and action in the world. Practical
action is emphasised. When we draw on collective energies beyond the personal, our
Higher Self (or soul) infuses our will with courage, love, responsibility and solidarity,
fortifying our capacity for personal sacrifice in service to others and the greater whole
(Assagioli, 1988/2007).

Radical hope is indeed radical (in the disruptive sense) as it requires us to
move from the burden of individualism – with its narrow purview – to the flow of
collaboration, based in the understanding of Self or soul – indeed consciousness itself
– as both inside us and without. As practitioners, we can commit to steadfastly hold the
space for new and innovative expressions of goodness to emerge through, not despite,
our challenges and pain.

Envisioning – putting soul into the future

Radical hope is manifested not in bold actions but in the courage to dream when all seems
lost. To hold such hope cannot be explained by logic or science. It is a dimension of the
soul. To bring our hearts to the table, to the land itself, and to entertain, beyond reason
and against current evidence, a vision of a better world is to choose to live in radical hope.

It is often said that humans are not good at thinking long term and not good
at acting selflessly (Kahneman, 2011). But when we contemplate the ancient stone
monuments and burial chambers, the temples and cathedrals that took centuries to
build, the olive orchards that would not yield for decades and the planting of forests
that would mature only for future generations, we know this to be false. These masons,
architects and farmers knew they would not see the fruits of their labour. These future-
builders worked in service of a vision – the inspiration of the cathedral, the beauty of
the mature orchard. Their visions lent them purpose. And at a certain point, when that
vision no longer held relevance because of changing circumstances – contingent on
climate, disease, wars, change – that culture died.

It is the law of entropy.

The issue is deeper than one of competing narratives. As a culture dies, we lose the embedded concepts with which we can construct a narrative. I think this is true of humankind today. If those who hold power shape the narrative, then we need a 'middle ground' to envision the new (Lear, 2006, pp.29–30). A space, ritualised perhaps, structured certainly, where we can lay down past certainties or fierce allegiances, fixities of right and wrong, and move into the space of possibility is vital for ethical inquiry – and today it is clearly an imperative. This is where, as Lear notes, the current narrative can be contested, where several narratives can be put forward and, from disagreement, new narratives can grow.

The middle ground is a place where warring nations can put down their weapons and explore shared hopes. We find 'middle grounds' in the social dreaming of analytic practice, the group and team facilitations of coaching, in the peace and reconciliation processes of nations, in citizens' assemblies and in the many dialogue and decision-making circles held by communities the world over.

We need more spaces where we can dream together in radical hope, governed by an alliance of heart and mind and fuelled by courage. Could this also be the work of the psychological and coaching professions: to create many more secular-sacred spaces in which to dream together?

Hope rooted

A stronger picture of radical hope as a dimension of soul has emerged for me through this enquiry. Concerned with relationship and interdependence, it is nourished by a courage that is enduring as well as bold.

Radical hope is rooted, grounded in the soil, trees, forests and rivers, the landscapes we love, that we nurture and that contain us, and that are present in the breathing we share – *iwigara*. A transpersonal ontology gives us a framework and a language to cultivate that hope and thread it into new stories for the future. Rooted, this is a hope that can contain shame, despair and fear, along with joy, collective visioning and active engagement.

As I read about my cherry tree and the work that goes into ensuring her fruitfulness, I shifted, through imagination, from being a puzzled recipient of an odd gift to pleasure at my new responsibility as 'Penny's godmother'. I will take a keen interest in her health, read every update, and trust in the expertise and goodwill of Michael, her farmer.

That I was to hold this privilege for only a year struck me with Havel's (1991) 'certainty that something makes sense'. We do not, cannot, own a tree. She is her own self, her roots carefully entwined with those of her orchard sisters in the mycorrhizal networks under soil and grass – and with mine through my imaginarium. My responsibility for my cherry tree has limits and a term – as do our lives here on Earth. Such are the ethics of land (Leopold, 1949) and of care (Gilligan, 1982), and the natural laws of the transpersonal: our inherent interdependence.

We hold the baton of the journey for a while – with a radical hope and a fierce compassion as we share in life's breathing. And then we hand it on...

References

Adom, K. (Producer). (2022). *Unearthed narratives*. DBK Studios/Sky Studios.

Akala. (2018). *Natives: Race and class in the ruins of empire*. Two Roads.

Aristotle. (2000). *The Nicomachean ethics* (T. Irwin, Trans.). Hackett Publishing Co.

Assagioli, R, (1988/2007). *Transpersonal development: The dimension beyond psychosynthesis*. Inner Way Productions.

Assagioli, R. (n.d.). Cited on https://psychosynthesistrust.org.uk/about-the-psychosynthesis-trust/about-psychosynthesis/

Burley, M. (2018, October 29). 'A language in which to think of the world' : Animism, indigenous traditions, and the deprovincialization of philosophy of religion, part 1. *Religious Theory: E-supplement to the Journal for Cultural and Religious Theory*. https://jcrt.org/religioustheory/2018/10/29/a-language-in-which-to-think-of-the-world-animism-indigenous-traditions-and-the-deprovincialization-of-philosophy-of-religion-part-1-mikel-burley

Christakis, N. (2010). *The hidden influence of social networks*. [Video]. TED2010. www.ted.com/talks/nicholas_christakis_the_hidden_influence_of_social_networks?language=en

Christakis, N. & Fowler, J. (2008). Dynamic spread of happiness in a large social network: Longitudinal analysis over 20 years in the Framingham Heart Study. *BMJ*, 337, a2338. www.bmj.com/content/337/bmj.a2338

Cook, I. (2021, September 15). Who is driving the Great Resignation? *Harvard Business Review*. https://hbr.org/2021/09/who-is-driving-the-great-resignation

Dante Alighieri. (1939/1971). *The divine comedy* (J.D. Sinclair, Trans.). Oxford University Press.

Dante Alighieri. (2004). *The inferno of Dante Alighieri* (C. Carson, Trans.). Granta.

Davenport, L. (2017). *Emotional resiliency in the era of climate change: A clinician's guide*. Jessica Kingsley Publishers.

Einzig, H. (2013). *Psychosynthesis: A practical psychology for our times*. https://hettyeinzig.co.uk/wp-content/uploads/2019/10/Psychosynthesis-A-Practical-Psychology-For-Our-Times.pdf

Einzig, H. (2017). *The future of coaching: Vision, leadership and responsibility in a transforming world*. Routledge.

Einzig, H. (2020). *Transpersonal coaching*. https://hettyeinzig.co.uk/wp-content/uploads/2021/01/TRANSPERSONAL-_COACHING-_Hetty_Einzig.pdf

Einzig, H. & Whitmore, J. (2021). Transpersonal coaching. In Passmore, J. (Ed.), *Excellence in coaching: Theory, tools and techniques to achieve outstanding coaching performance* (4th ed.) (pp.158–181). Kogan Page.

Eldridge, R. (1996). Is animism alive and well? In D.Z. Phillips (Ed.), *Can religion be explained away?* (pp.3–5). Palgrave Macmillan.

Feldman Barrett, L. (2017). *How emotions are made: The secret life of the brain*. Picador.

Gilligan, C. (1982). *In a different voice*. Harvard.

Graeber, D. (2018). *Bullshit jobs: A theory*. Penguin.

Graeber, D. & Wengrow, D. (2021). *The dawn of everything: A new history of humanity*. Penguin.

Havel, V. (1991). *Disturbing the peace*. Vintage Books.

Hawken, P. (2021). *Regeneration: Ending the climate crisis in one generation*. Penguin.

Higgins, C. (2022, March 31). 'Our traditions have been criminalised' – the Arctic artists bringing protest to the Venice Biennale. *The Guardian*. www.theguardian.com/artanddesign/2022/mar/31/

criminalised-sami-artists-arctic-venice-biennale-loggers-miners-global-heating-culling-protest

Kahneman, D. (2011). *Thinking, fast and slow*. Penguin.

Kimmerer, R.W. (2013). *Braiding sweetgrass: Indigenous wisdom, scientific knowledge and the teachings of plants*. Penguin.

Klein, M. (1997). *Envy and gratitude and other works 1946–1963*. Vintage Classics.

Lear, J. (2006). *Radical hope: Ethics in the face of cultural devastation*. Harvard University Press.

Leopold, A. (1949). A Sand County almanac. Cited in T. Heberlein (2012), *Navigating environmental attitudes* (pp.113–114). Oxford University Press.

Lovelock, J. (2000). *Gaia: A new look at life on Earth*. Oxford University Press.

Macfarlane, B. (2022). *Tackling overwhelming challenges: How innovation leaders work with anxiety, authority and frustration*. Presentation at OPUS annual conference, Examining the Organisational, Social and Cultural Challenges of the Anthropocene. [Online.] 11–13 February.

Macy, J. & Johnstone, C. (2022). *Active Hope: How to face the mess we're in with unexpected resilience and creative power* (Revised ed.). New World Library.

McKibben, B. (2019, June 19). What oil companies knew: The great climate cover-up. *The Guardian*. www.theguardian.com/environment/audio/2019/jun/19/what-oil-companies-knew-the-great-climate-cover-up-podcast

Milman, O. (2023, January 12). Revealed: Exxon made 'breathtakingly' accurate climate predictions in 1970s and 80s. *The Guardian*. www.theguardian.com/business/2023/jan/12/exxon-climate-change-global-warming-research

Mishra, P. (2013). *From the ruins of empire: The revolt against the west and the remaking of Asia*. Penguin.

Morgan, K. (2021, July 1). The Great Resignation: How employers drove workers to quit. *BBC Worklife*. www.bbc.com/worklife/article/20210629-the-great-resignation-how-employers-drove-workers-to-quit

The Pachamama Alliance. (2006). *The Symposium: Awakening the dreamer, changing the dream*. Pachamama Alliance.

Porges, S.W. (2017). *The pocket guide to the polyvagal theory: The transformative power of feeling safe*. W.W. Norton & Co.

Rao, M. & Powell, R.A. (2021, October 6). The climate crisis and the rise of eco-anxiety. [Blog.] *BMJ Opinion*. https://blogs.bmj.com/bmj/2021/10/06/the-climate-crisis-and-the-rise-of-eco-anxiety/

Rizzolatti, G. & Craighero, L. (2004). The mirror-neuron system. *Annual Review of Neuroscience, 27*, 169–192. https://doi.org/10.1146/annurev.neuro.27.070203.144230

Salmon, E. (2000). Kincentric ecology: Indigenous perceptions of the human-nature relationship. *Ecological Applications, 10*(5), 1327–1332.

Sharpe, B. (2013). *Three horizons: The patterning of hope*. Triarchy Press.

Sheldrake, M. (2020). *Entangled life: How fungi make our worlds, change our minds and shape our futures*. Vintage.

Smail, D. (1987). *Taking care: An alternative to therapy*. J.M. Dent & Sons.

Tillich, P. (1952/2000). *The courage to be*. Yale University Press.

Weintrobe, S. (2021). *Psychological roots of the climate crisis: Neoliberal exceptionalism and the culture of uncare*. Bloomsbury Academic.

Williams, J. (2021). *Climate change is racist: Race, privilege and the struggle for climate justice*. Icon Books.

Yeats, W.B. (1919/2009). 'The Second Coming'. In *Collected Poems*. Vintage.

6 Rewilding hope

Nick Totton

I very much agree with the perception on which this book is based – that therapists have an important role to play in the global environmental catastrophe we are now experiencing. However, I will be arguing that this role is emphatically *not* about flying the flag of hope but about supporting clients in facing and moving through despair, along with the accompanying fear, grief and anger; only then may it be possible to revisit hope and reconnect with it in a more grounded way.

Of course, therapists cannot facilitate this work in our clients unless we have at least begun (because there is no end in sight) to process our own despair, fear, grief and anger, and perhaps what I say here will encourage and support such a beginning. We need to start not by *abandoning* hope, but by *releasing* it, out of our control and into the wild, to make its own way.

After all, what exactly are we being exhorted to hope *for*? Some *deus ex machina* techno-fix that allows us to carry on consuming the world without actually rendering ourselves extinct? Or the neat and convenient excision of the human species in a sort of Rapture event, leaving behind an eco-paradise? Or an equally miraculous way of squaring capitalism's reliance on permanent growth with the necessity of a steady-state (at best) economy? I suggest that, given the interlocked catastrophes that face us, we must accept the impossibility of tracing any path from the doomed present to the desired future. This is not to say that such a path will not come into existence – but rather that, under the pitch-dark sky of our times, only a wild and grievous hope can offer us any star to navigate by.

Unthinkable

The environmental philosopher Timothy Morton has suggested that the scale of environmental catastrophe identifies it as a 'hyperobject': something we are irretrievably and continuously affected by, yet truly cannot conceive. 'Hyperobjects,' he writes, 'are real whether or not someone is thinking of them. Indeed... hyperobjects end the possibility of transcendental leaps 'outside' physical reality (Morton, 2013, p.2).

The effect of this, he argues, is that:

> the normal certainties are inverted, or even dissolved. No longer are my intimate impressions 'personal' in the sense that they are 'merely mine' or 'subjective only': they are footprints of hyperobjects. (Morton, 2013, p.6)

Morton argues, paradoxically, that 'the world has already ended' with the dawn of the Anthropocene and the advent of the environmental hyperobject. Recognising this fact, rather than incapacitating us, actually makes effective action possible, he proposes, waking us from the dissociative freeze created by the message 'that the world is about to end "unless we act now"'. In other words, to abandon hope is to create a basis for it.

Activists, artists, psychologists and intellectuals have struggled to find an adequate response to the hyperobject of environmental collapse. In his famous paper 'Deep Adaptation', Jem Bendell (2020) has suggested that we accept the imminent collapse of civilisation as a done deal and start thinking about how to respond to it in ways that may 'reduce harm, save what we can, and create possibilities for the future while experiencing meaning and joy in the process' (p.1). His paper doesn't mention any species except the human, which seems to me part of the problem he wants to address: so much of what is written and spoken focuses exclusively on the human consequences of environmental catastrophe, ignoring the other-than-human world for whose destruction we are responsible and whose destruction is a major contributing factor to our own.

Covid-19 should bring this relationship home to us: it is probably just one of the increasingly frequent pandemics that will spring from human encroachment on wild ecosystems (see Tollefson, 2020). This not only threatens many species with extinction but also puts us in contact with robust 'weed species' – rats, bats and others – carrying diseases that can jump across into humans. The trade in wildlife as pets or food exacerbates the situation.

In contrast to Bendell's concentration on humanity, *Uncivilisation: The Dark Mountain manifesto* (Kingsnorth & Hine, 2009) agrees with his prognosis but suggests that, since we are all 'poised trembling on the edge of a change so massive that we have no way of gauging it… it is time to look down' and see what has put us there (p.9). It concludes with 'Eight Principles of Uncivilisation' (p.20), one of them being that 'humans are not the point and purpose of the planet', and another that:

> the end of the world as we know it is not the end of the world full stop. Together we will find the hope beyond hope, the path that leads to the unknown world ahead of us.

Like Morton, both of these initiatives suggest that the desperate struggle not *actually* to avert future catastrophe but rather to insist that it is possible to do so may have become an enormous and unhelpful burden: a burden that we need to find a way of releasing. This brings to my mind the image of the face of actor Leonardo DiCaprio, in the film *Titanic*, sinking into the depths of the ocean as he releases his grip on the improvised raft so it can float and Rose can survive. So too must we release hope to find its own way, to become an unknown and unknowable future, about which we know only that it does not have a starring role for the human race.

Having mentioned *Titanic*, which I last saw some years ago, I thought I had better take another look. This was just as well, since I had misremembered: my image was of Jack (DiCaprio) deliberately letting go of the raft. In effect, Jack does enable Rose's survival of course, by staying in the freezing water, but it strengthens my analogy to notice that it is actually Rose who prises Jack's stiff, dead hands loose so that he will sink and she will float.

Unbearable

Psychotherapeutic theory suggests that there are two basic ways to deflect from the fear and grief of ecological catastrophe: on the one hand, avoidance/denial, and on the other hand, over-activity. These can both be understood as variations of what Klein (1935) and Winnicott (1935) call the 'manic defence': a concept that was initially used in relation to unbearable internal reality, but that I suggest applies equally well to unbearable external reality. In both cases, emotional pain is drowned out by compulsive *activity*, mental and/or physical.

The manic defence is widespread in our culture, and it can be a factor in the kind of endless activism that leads to burnout. I am most certainly not criticising activism – more of it, sooner, might conceivably have changed what we now face, and this catastrophe is so extreme that there is no obvious limit to action; nothing that is 'enough', no easy way to pace oneself. I think, though, that this objective situation sometimes interlocks with a need to keep *doing* so as to suppress *feeling* – something that Winnicott compares to living with the radio permanently on to drown out depression (1935, p.131).

The sort of manic defence that I particularly want to discuss here is the empty invocation of *hope*. We hear this constantly (I don't want to name and shame any individuals; it is a collective phenomenon): 'I stand for hope'; 'We must never give up hope'; 'Without hope we are lost'. Or, at slightly greater length: 'I have to believe that human ingenuity will find a solution.' I *have* to believe – because in truth I don't, but I cannot bear the truth.

Winnicott refers to this attitude as 'ascensive', a project of continually *rising up* as a defence against sinking down into:

> an aspect of depression which is implied in such terms as 'heaviness of heart',
> 'depth of despair', 'that sinking feeling', etc. (1935, pp.134–135)

'Clinically,' Winnicott says, 'we see not so much the denial as the elation that is related to the denial, or a sense of unreality about external reality, or unconcern about serious things' (1935, p.133). At its worse, this becomes what he calls a 'manic, internal omnipotence' that stops 'everything (the good included)' (p.140). In a different account he sums up:

The central fact denied in manic defence is death in the inner world, or a deadness over all; and the accent… is on life, liveliness, denial of death as an ultimate fact of life. (Winnicott, 1988, p.87)

There are different versions of manic defence seen in environmental activists, in climate-change deniers, and in those not actively involved with the issue. For activists, it is expressed in hectic campaigning and compulsively positive thinking – often an explicit belief that thinking 'negatively' will make bad things more likely to happen, so that we have to control our thoughts and feelings. For deniers, obviously, there is the attitude that none of this is worth paying attention to because it cannot be absolutely proved.

For those who ignore the whole issue, the constantly switched-on radio referred to above is social media and the single-minded pursuit of pleasure and consumption.

It is just when we are manic-defensive, that we are *least likely to feel* as if we are defending against depression. At such times we are more likely to feel elated, happy, busy, excited, humorous, omniscient, 'full of life', and at the same time we are less interested than usual in serious things and in the awfulness of hate, destruction, and killing. (Winnicott, 1935, p.132, original italics)

According to Melanie Klein (1935), manic defences are typified by three feelings: control, triumph and contempt. In the last case, one tries to believe that the loved object is of no importance and their condition doesn't matter. I relate this to two phenomena in particular: one is the treatment of other-than-human life as insignificant and ours to mistreat as we will – an attitude that has caused the current catastrophe, in reaction to which some parts of society are doubling down on the control, triumph and contempt, for example by proposing 'solutions' that protect only humans.

But on the other side of our currently polarised culture, there is the masochistic fantasy of the human race dying out and other life forms breathing a sort of sigh of relief – often expressed as 'the world is better off without us', because we are so messed up. However, this isn't going to happen. Millions or billions of humans may die, but as a species we're not going anywhere in a hurry. On current form, we will throw virtually every other species – together with many powerless humans – out of the sledge rather than change our ways, ending up with us, the cockroaches and other so-called weed species, and the microbes.

Releasing hope into the wild seems to me quite a precise analogy to the practices of rewilding that are becoming so widespread. The essence of rewilding, what distinguishes it from traditional conservationism, is *letting go*: letting go of control (and the implicit triumph and contempt – 'I know best' – that accompany control); trusting the keystone species – and what could be more of a keystone than hope? – to find its own way and enrich the ecosystem by means we may not have anticipated. Trusting hope to find its own way, I suggest, means letting go of control over *what we hope for*: letting hope be bigger and freer than our limited and self-centred perspective.

Unstoppable

All the above is, in a sense, a preamble, preparing the way to directly address the role of therapy and counselling in relation to environmental catastrophe. I have already heavily implied some of what I am now going to say directly. Whether we are dealing with environmental catastrophe or personal unhappiness, it is not our job to offer *hope*. Surely most of us know that working with depressed or anguished people is not a matter of trying to cheer them up? Very often, we are doing something that might seem like the direct opposite: helping people to face – facing *with* them – just how much pain they are actually in, rather than trying to evade it. A lot of what we call depression is about avoiding feelings that seem even more unbearable – usually feelings of grief or rage. If hope is involved, it is the hope that our feelings will not actually be unbearable after all.

Joanna Macy has written:

> We do not and cannot know whether we are here to serve as deathbed
> attendants for our world or as midwives to a new chapter of life on earth.
> (Quoted in Rust, 2011)

We do not and cannot know, and we perhaps need to pay equal attention to both possibilities – to hold them in balance, one in each hand. But my sense is that many of us are not doing this – partly to avoid scaring people at large, but perhaps partly also to avoid scaring ourselves.

Let's test this out. I'm going to offer a brief statement of what seems to me, and to many who have explored the situation, the probable outlook for the future. I'm going for a middle-of-the-road scenario here: things could conceivably be much less bad than this, and they could conceivably be far worse, but those scenarios are outliers. I invite you to read what I have written below slowly, perhaps speak it out loud, and scan what happens in you, notice your responses on every level – thoughts, feelings, sensations, impulses. It's not about trying to have the 'right' response, it's about noticing and accepting how you actually *do* respond, including any resistance or avoidance. Whatever it is, it's okay, and useful to bring into awareness.

> Within a human lifetime from now, this planet will suffer irreversible,
> catastrophic environmental wounding. Large areas of the earth will become
> uninhabitable by humans and by other species that currently live there. Our
> current global civilisation will be hugely damaged, and possibly destroyed
> altogether. Many millions of humans, and many billions of other-than-human
> beings, will die prematurely; huge numbers of species will become extinct.

Now read it again, preferably out loud, and try to stay in touch with the meaning of the words as you say them. Then put this book down and take time to process. Think about your reactions – how much were they essentially defensive, how much were you able to let in?

If we are able to quieten ourselves and relax our defences enough to take into our bodyminds the likelihood – in my view, the strong likelihood – of catastrophic environmental collapse over the next 50 years, then what are our options, as therapists and as human beings? How can we survive this knowledge? What is there left to do, practically and emotionally? If catastrophe is coming, is there any point in trying to do anything?

Well, catastrophe is always coming, and always has been coming, for every living being: we are all going to die. Impermanence is built into existence, and many people at some point in their lives feel that this fact makes life meaningless. Most of us eventually decide that the only source of real meaning is in present satisfaction, productive activity, what Wilhelm Reich called 'love, work and knowledge' (Reich, 1975).

And something will almost certainly survive. We are facing the end of *our* world, not of *the* world; and whatever the world becomes, there will be humans in it, probably in great need of succour. But I would hope – wildly – that, either with or without catastrophe, a change comes about in human culture that recognises our need for kinship with the other-than-human and enables us to let go of our claim to specialness. There will be a future; but a future in which human beings no longer claim centre stage. One way or another, the world of human exceptionalism is coming to an end.

The philosopher Donna Haraway has thought more deeply about this than most of us, especially in her book *Staying with the Trouble* (2016):

> In urgent times many of us are tempted to address trouble in terms of making an imagined future safe, in terms of stopping something from happening that looms in the future, of clearing away the present and the past in order to make futures for coming generations. Staying with the trouble does not require such a relationship to times called the future. In fact, staying with the trouble requires learning to be truly present, not as a vanishing pivot between awful or edenic pasts and apocalyptic or salvific futures, but as mortal critters entwined in myriad unfinished configurations of places, times, matters, meanings. (Haraway, 2016, p.1)

When I first read this passage, I thought 'This is what wild therapy is about.' Wild therapy is an approach to ecopsychology that I started to develop in about 2009. It became a book (Totton, 2011, 2021), then a training course, which I eventually passed on to other trainers, and finally, a community of practitioners. Its motto is 'Bringing therapy into the wild, and wildness into therapy'; one of its key principles is that humans are neither more nor less than animals (Totton, 2021, pp.85–87).

In what Haraway calls 'the thick present' that opens up when we release past and future to stay with the trouble, we are faced with a vast project of *cherishing* – a simultaneous celebration and mourning of all life forms, together with a transformation in our perception of multispecies relationships.

I believe that there is a point of inner balance from which we can fight hard to stop something happening while at the same time accepting that, if it *does* happen, it will be as part of a bigger picture, and the overall richness of the cosmos will not be lessened. But to reach this point of balance is a big step; we can't do it all in one go. Some of us may not even want to go there, preferring to stay with the battle, and if we are thinking ecosystemically, we can accept that every reaction, every position has a function. In thinking this way, we are identifying with the system itself, rather than simply taking a role within it. But a crucial condition for even approaching that inner balance is that we first need to grieve.

We need to grieve. It's an organismic need, like the need to shake in order to release shock from the system. Just as a person needs to grieve the loss of a loved one, we need to grieve the loss of our world. I think we cannot actually say the impact of a lost world is *greater* than the loss of a partner or a child; in fact, every such loss *is* the loss of a world. In both situations, the catastrophe is absolute, and the chances of collapse into fragmentation and despair are high. For many people, thinking about their grandchildren is what allows or forces them to connect with environmental catastrophe.

Ecologically aware psychotherapists and counsellors need to prepare to be among those who act as therapists to the human race, as it increasingly wrestles with its grief, fear, anger and guilt. This process, I think, is already under way, though largely subliminal and unrecognised: many, especially young people, are operating in a nihilistic haze where the underlying, usually inexplicit slogan is 'We're fucked, so who gives a fuck.'

At the heart of Winnicott's description of the manic defence is the principle that 'essential to healthy development is a certain seriousness' (Winnicott, 1988, p.86). If we reach to the largest perspective that we are momentarily capable of, then the situation is neither 'good' nor 'bad' – these concepts just don't encompass such a hyperobject – but it is deeply, profoundly serious, and it demands from us a correspondingly serious response. Our heads can't stretch far enough; our language can't stretch far enough; our survival-centred organismic selves can't, on their own, stretch far enough. But our hearts, once open, can stretch a very long way indeed. And what opens our hearts is letting ourselves grieve.

Larry Eddy, a Chemehuevi Paiute Salt Singer, says this:

> The great Creator told us, I'm going to teach you these songs, but before I teach you these songs I'm going to break your heart. (Quoted in Hebner & Plyler, 2010, p.17)

The songs are too big and too serious for our heart to contain without it first being broken open and rebuilt on a larger scale. This project of breaking and rebuilding is, I suggest, where therapy needs to be focused in the future.

References

Bendell, J. (2020). *Deep adaptation: A map for navigating climate tragedy* (2nd ed.). IFLAS occasional paper 2. https://lifeworth.com/deepadaptation.pdf

Haraway, D.J. (2016). *Staying with the trouble: Making kin in the Chthulucene.* Duke University Press.

Hebner, L. & Plyler, M.L. (2010). *Southern Paiute: A portrait*. Utah State University Press. http://issuu.com/usupress/docs/southern_paiute

Kingsnorth, P. & Hine, D. (2009). *Uncivilisation: The Dark Mountain manifesto*. Dark Mountain Project. https://dark-mountain.net/about/manifesto

Klein, M. (1935). A contribution to the psychogenesis of manic-depressive states. *International Journal of Psycho-Analysis, 16*, 145–174.

Morton, T. (2013), *Hyperobjects: Philosophy and ecology after the end of the world*. University of Minnesota Press.

Reich, W. (1975). *Listen, little man!* Epigraph. Penguin.

Rust, M.-J. (2011). *Double vision: The gestalt of our environmental crisis*. Marianne Fry Lecture, Bristol. https://archives.mariannefrylectures.uk/2011/M-J-Rust-text.pdf

Tollefson, J. (2020). Why deforestation and extinctions make pandemics more likely. *Nature, 584*, 175–176.

Totton, N. (2011). *Wild therapy: Undomesticating inner and outer worlds*. PCCS Books.

Totton, N. (2021). *Wild therapy: Rewilding our inner and outer worlds* (2nd ed.). PCCS Books.

Winnicott D.W. (1935). The manic defence. In *Collected papers: Through paediatrics to psychoanalysis* (pp. 129–44). Hogarth Press/Institute of Psycho-Analysis.

Winnicott, D.W. (1988). *Human nature*. Routledge.

7 | Coming home to a posthuman body: Finding hopefulness in those who care

Caroline Frizell

Entrance

This chapter is a small part of the unfolding of a posthuman[1] call for alternative corporealities, as we find our way through the environmental crisis. Here, I explore the potential of finding hope in the corridors of grief that are opened when we face the reality of what is happening environmentally, and I argue for the ways in which posthuman discourses in embodied practice can foster ethical cultures of care. The environmental crisis has been fuelled, in part, by a lack of care, in systems that privilege particular voices over others, creating a hierarchy of matters that matter. The creation of cultures of care can generate hope in the context of the socio-political, economic and environmental injustices that accompany advanced capitalism. In this exploration of the posthuman body as compassionate and empathic force, my eco-feminist, posthuman voice, as a dance movement psychotherapist (DMP), researcher, educator, mother and carer, resists patriarchal power structures and the oppression of dominant discourses and turns towards new and different ways of inhabiting the world.

I invite you to join me in my wonderings and wanderings through this writing, as I draw on, oscillate between and bring together different kinds of knowledges, including (in no particular order) imaginings and dreams, movement practices, critical theories, personal lived experience and professional practice. At the same time, I will shift gear between writing genres, moving back and forth from the academic to the prosaic to the poetic, and sometimes take you into the first-hand expression of the dance itself. This intentional disruption of the illusion that specific knowledges can be privileged over others reflects the mellifluous process of gathering the assemblage that has become this chapter.

---

1. Posthumanism provides a thinking apparatus for animating ideas about being human that move away from the rational, thinking 'man' towards an eco-feminist, embodied experience that is embedded as just one small part of an intra-dependent ecological community.

Before entering the entanglements and contradictions about posthuman bodily home-(be)comings, and the search for hopefulness in those who care, I will begin with a note on the posthuman body as a basis for the convergence, divergence and multiple possibilities that emerge in this chapter.

A note on the posthuman body

The notion of posthuman bodies invites a process of defamiliarisation with anthropocentrism and a disidentification with the dominant cultural values that infuse our subjectivity. Posthumanism problematises ideas about the human body as it becomes inscribed with characteristics that purport to be universal yet uphold only partial definitions of humanhood and considers the multiple and diverse ways of inhabiting humanness (Braidotti, 2022). The term 'human' has come to define a homogenous group, the members of which are identified with characteristics that privilege particular attributes over others. If I try to define these characteristics, I invariably stumble and find myself falling into a hierarchical exceptionalism, along with other 'isms', such as racism, sexism and ableism.

Posthuman eco-feminism, with new materialist feminism as its precursor, is embedded, embodied and grounded in multiplicities and differences that refuse (as far as is possible) binary thinking (Braidotti, 2022): that is, the kind of thinking that positions mutually exclusive opposites against one another. The posthuman convergence operates at interfaces between, first, social structures that foster inequalities; second, environmental phenomena, including destruction and degradation, and third, technological and digital interconnections (Braidotti, 2022). Coming home to a posthuman body means entering a complex entanglement of material-discursive phenomena that is infused with a hopefulness that enables us to care and a carefulness that enables us to hope. Despair whispers from the blurry edges of that home-coming, asking for an audience.

The dance of despair

Some years ago, I shared a car ride to an ecopsychology gathering with a (then) stranger. We discussed our thoughts about the forthcoming gathering and my fellow traveller enquired about my hopes for the event. I hesitated before hearing myself say that I was 'hoping to gain further insight into being with diversity'. Arriving at the conference, I pitched my tent due west. A speckled butterfly rested on the grass next to me, lingered for a moment, then flew off.

As I erected my tent, I wondered what I had meant by 'hoping for further insight into diversity'. The thought followed the butterfly's flight path and my mind turned to a workshop I was due to run at the conference, entitled 'The Dance of Despair' (Frizell, 2014), which had been largely inspired by a difficult experience on the organising committee. The shadow side of the hopeful solidarity of like-minded folk was powerful and not without its casualties. As eco-devotees, we were surprised by unexpected whisperings of inevitable power struggles lurking in the shadows. Some ugly dynamics were screaming to be heard; when they were largely ignored, their destructive potency began to swell. The tent now pitched, I took this confusion into the thinking, moving body and found a dance of despair surfacing from the murky waters. Letting my weight sink into the earth through my feet, I stepped forwards onto my right foot, arms outstretched and mouth opening wide, as if to scream, but no sound emerged, just a deafening silence. The intensity of my despair erupted through an almost imperceptible flick of my wrist, a shift in the angle of my head, an impulse in my elbow and a small twist of my spine. Dropping to the ground, the fingers on one hand reached tentatively and awkwardly backwards, feeling their way into an eternal night. In my mind's eye, a butterfly alighted, unseen and unheard in that darkness, and the bewitching humming of a lullaby erupted from the silence to soothe the belly of the world. Slowly, I sank further down to roll upon my back and lie, staring up at the passing clouds, feeling the breeze brush softly against my skin. Around me I sensed displaced figures struggling to exist in a wasteland, standing inert, disconnected and alone. A buzzard circled overhead and, swooping down, carved bold arcs in the air, her haunting cry lingering in the blueness of the sky. I smiled to myself as hope and despair collided in my mind, '… cutting together-apart…' (Barad, 2014, p.168) in many directions. However well-intentioned we are, in that coming together, it seems that hopeless despair sits on the edge of diversity as competing elements vie for position in an atmosphere of scarcity.

Advanced capitalism rolls on.

Sinking into hopelessness

The relentless pursuit of progress and development at the expense of the delicate balance of life itself has characterised advanced capitalism in this post-industrial world. Blatant inequalities are evident in the privileges enjoyed by the super-rich, while others have to choose between eating or heating. Rising house prices and second-home ownership drive local inhabitants out of their communities. What do we do in the face of the eco-psychotic, profit-driven desecration of our homeland? Brutal contractions of services in health, social and community care provision have deprived many of basic amenities. At the same time, a culture of managerialism has fostered dehumanising, risk-averse, soul-less systems of uncare (Weintrobe, 2021), as crude, number-crunching outcome measures determine the way services are run and define the support that is provided in the name of care.

As a senior lecturer in higher education, I am aware of the damage that can be caused by cultures of uncare, in which the marketisation of education reduces members of a working community – for example, lecturers, administrative staff, cleaners and technicians – to dispensable commodities in the face of economic efficiency. I can find myself sitting at a meeting, urged to focus on 'blue-sky thinking', being asked where the organisation wants to be in five or 10 years hence. At that moment, I find that an ethical duty of care brings my focus back to the colleague with a casualised contract sitting next to me, who is in imminent danger of losing her job in the name of efficiency. I refuse blue-sky thinking until the present community is protected.

Along with the many oppressions within our species that operate at the intersections – for example, of race, ethnicity, gender, sexual orientation, disability, poverty and many others – the oppressions of anthropocentrism operate in tandem to the detriment of our ecology. Climate chaos and ecological disruption, including extreme biodiversity loss, is out there. It is around us. It is between us. It is infused into our subjectivity as the extinction of species rumbles on. As I glance out of the kitchen window, I notice the blueberry plants flowering unusually early after a warm winter, but there are no insects around to pollinate them. When the insects arrive, the pollen will be gone. Our balance of life is seriously out of kilter. We are inhaling the poison that we have pumped into the air. We have a food system that includes the abhorrent treatment of animals. We find the landscapes we have loved decimated as building regulations are reduced, making it easier for entrepreneurs to develop land for profit.

Signs of an ecology out of balance are everywhere. I work in both London and South Devon, and some years back my commute was disrupted when the railway track at Dawlish fell into the sea in the winter storms. The not-so-terrible and relatively small inconvenience to me of a slower replacement bus service from Newton Abbot to Exeter served as a reminder of a far more terrible and far greater existential precarity posed by climate chaos. As the climate changes, there are small signs all around us of an ecology shifting out of kilter. In a tattered *Guardian* newspaper cutting (now serving as a bookmark), Mark Cocker (2007) describes sidestepping a tortoiseshell butterfly lying lifeless on his doorstep one February morning. The butterfly had misjudged its emergence out of hibernation after an unusually warm winter and was now dying. He notes how this 'filigree of death' on his doorstep holds a powerful symbol of the catastrophic impact of global warming. In the 15 years since that was written, the climate has become increasingly unpredictable, yet the drive to maintain business as usual is pervasive, despite constant reminders that business-as-usual-as-we-know-it is unsustainable.

It can be tempting to pull the duvet over my head, park my body in a suspended state of denial, consume comfort food and drift into an ecstatic dreamland of TV dramas, or scroll social media as an escape. An alternative, perhaps, is to run at the challenge head on, engaging in frenetic firefighting activity, from which I will undoubtedly burn out. Anything to avoid being with the suffering and risk sinking into the hopelessness. It's easier not to care too much. We have created the monster that is advanced capitalism and we are simultaneously created by it, and in that state of hopelessness, we can find our capacity to think has collapsed. Like adolescents struggling to free ourselves from the sticky web of dependency, we have succumbed to an antisocial, anti-environmental tendency, trashing the family home (aka Earth) with a hedonistic house party of economic progress and productivity.

Moments of hope

In his paper presented to the British Psycho-Analytical Society in 1956, titled 'The Antisocial Tendency', Winnicott (2015) suggests that an individual's acting out behaviour represents an expression of hope: a hope, that is, for a responsive environment. Less consciously, the young person is yearning for parental love and care. Winnicott gives an example of a young person who, in the face of emotional deprivation, steals as a symbolic acting out of their entitlement to something precious. According to

Winnicott, this behaviour is a less conscious drive that compels the attention of another. In therapy, this cry for help can be met with a capacity to think, to sense and to stay with the difficult feelings. The irony, then, is that the antisocial behaviour itself implies hope, in a displaced scramble to fulfil a yearning for connection, love and belonging. As we (you and I, that is) glance back through our post-industrial, late capitalist lens at the wider antisocial and anti-environmental tendencies of our species, this dynamic mirrors the way in which the anti-environmental consumption and exploitation of the Earth's resources might be seen as a displaced yearning for connection, love and belonging that brings us close to our intra-connected, intra-affective, intra-dependent, entangled place of becoming.[2]

The optimist in me fumbles in this place of hopeless despair, with an unfounded certainty that, somehow, I can find meaning that can help me think constructively towards a better future. Winnicott's idea that our destructive acting out behaviour is, in fact, a moment of hope, brings me some solace. The posthuman eco-feminist in me rises from the embers of that hopeless despair towards creating a new agenda that refuses the patriarchal oppression of progress and productivity at all costs. I step into my later years with a growing confidence that things can be different. As a woman in my 60s, I look back on my life with gratitude for the opportunities I have had, and I hope that, in some small way, I can harvest my learning and offer it back to the world. Poynor (2023) highlights the importance for the elders of the profession to share the messy truths of their experience, in which the boundaries between the personal and professional are porous. In a co-authored chapter with my colleague Helen Poynor, we articulate our work together in a way that takes the reader into the experiential dimensions of this process (Frizell & Poynor, 2023). The personal and professional converge in a heartfelt ethics of care, for each other and for the world around us.

Like many women (and not so many men), I have spent many years navigating the responsibility of organising and securing care for family members with additional needs. This has been as sister to a brother with schizophrenia, as daughter to a dying mother disabled by a stroke, as daughter to a father growing gracefully towards 100 years and as mother to three now grown-up daughters, one with complex needs. Like many women (and what sometimes felt like against all odds), somehow alongside those familial responsibilities, I managed to pursue a career as a dancer, a dance artist in the community, a dance movement psychotherapist (DMP) and an academic. For the past 15 years I have managed to work full time. Yet, just recently, I had a stark wake-up call reminding me of that tightrope that many women navigate in balancing careers with family responsibilities. It was also a reminder of the fragility of support systems in which individuals are vulnerable to wider operational oppressions. My daughter's care home was going through a crisis. The combination of Covid and Brexit impacted on

---

2. As a posthuman practitioner working with(in) diverse moving bodies (homo sapiens or not), I engage in a continuous process of *becoming*, within dynamic relations of difference, in which material bodies serve as dynamic agents of affective experience, always on the edge of creating new worlds (Frizell, 2023). Throughout this text (and beyond), I tend to use the word *becoming* (rather than being) to represent (for language can *only* be a representation, rather than the thing itself) the immersive, fluid potential of experience that is infused into any mo(ve)ment.

staff recruitment, with reduced availability of care and reliance on inexperienced and often disinvested agency staff. Furthermore, overseas volunteers were finding their visa applications refused. In addition, the disruption of coming in and out of lockdowns, coupled with a change in management that introduced an uncaring managerialism into the mix (priding themselves on making 'difficult decisions' at the expense of residents), caused the placement to break down and the funding authority to withdraw its support. Overnight, my daughter lost her home of 15 years and returned to live with us full time.

The shock included a realisation of the brutal, systemic failures of care in which the efficient use of resources took precedence over the lives of individuals. It was almost too much to bear. The process lacked compassion, as well as an ethical duty of care, and was emblematic of an advanced capitalist system. My personal story is one of many that illustrate wider divisions and inequalities that have been accelerated and amplified by the pandemic. Frameworks of uncare (Weintrobe, 2021) that adversely impact individuals and their families are symptomatic of a wider system that serves the individual interests of the privileged at the expense of subordinated others and the wider ecology. Weintrobe identifies how a neoliberal agenda has colonised the individual and collective mind with a deregulation of care that serves the interests of exceptionalism and notions of 'superior entitlement' (2021, p.86).

It can all feel hopeless.

Chains of solidarity

Yet, I find glimmers of hopefulness hovering in a conviction that we are intra-connected and that we can affect and be affected by the world. There is hopefulness in the principles of a posthuman eco-feminism that does not take subjectivities for granted. Braidotti (2022) describes this kind of transversal thinking as creating a chain of solidarity while remaining open and available to differently lived realities. That chain of solidarity is embedded in the diversity of post- (not just) human bodies.

Hopefulness is a place of potential transformation and might be said to begin in the imagination (Solnit, 2005). Solnit urges faith in the power of individuals to make change and cites an example of a small group of women standing in protest outside the White House in Washington DC, as part of the Women Strike for Peace (WSP) movement. One woman said that, although their conviction was strong, it seemed futile to be standing with this small group of women in the rain. Yet she heard later that another high-profile activist had spotted them from afar and had been inspired to take further action by the strength of their conviction.

I remember a child with whom I worked in a school. I'll call her Kemi. The work often seemed hopeless as she persisted with her repetitive expression. Every week, it seemed, was the same. She entered the room and ran in circles around the periphery, before calling me to support her in lining up the toy animals in order of size. She then said 'snails', looked at me knowingly, and paused a moment, before lifting both hands above her head and bringing them both slowly down in a zig-zag pattern with the palms facing each other. This movement became our mo(ve)ment of connection, and whenever Kemi saw me around school between sessions, she and I would greet each other by lifting both hands above our heads and bringing them both slowly down in a zig-zag pattern. For me, it represented a moment of hope in which we were acknowledging each other and becoming present to each other. The meaning was in the doing and the embodied connection.

Daring to hope

The intra-active entanglement of alternative corporealities is the material connection that brings us into alignment with the substance of life. Macy (Macy & Young Brown, 1998) suggests that we must first meet with our despair as we face the reality of the destructive forces of the human species. In honouring our pain for the world, we can re-invigorate our connection. Haraway (2016) reminds us that:

> (g)rief is a path to understanding entangled shared living and dying; human beings must grieve with, because we are in and of this fabric of undoing. (p.39)

The hopelessness in the face of unbearable loss is the grief that we need to feel, rather than defend against. The following vignette illustrates how, as a practitioner, I can provide a space in which hopelessness and despair can find a space for expression.

> I listen to the client disclosing how he leads his life as a competent, successful professional. He is likeable, confident and socially well-equipped. Yet he finds himself waking alone in the night, staring terrified into the darkness, as existential anxiety courses through his nervous system. As we explore his experience together in the sometimes-silent relational space between us, he finds that his less conscious wisdom pulls him to the wooden floor. There, he curls into a foetal position, sensing a great grief for the world. In that moment, all I can do is connect with that despair in solidarity; his, mine and the world's.

Whether I am working outside or indoors, that despair hovers. In that moment, I resist the temptation to find a rational understanding and try instead to 'come to some kind of knowing through a holding and a wonderment' (Bernstein, 2005, p.73). Bernstein, a Jungian analyst, notices this 'Great Grief' (2005, p.71) that is held by clients who have a heightened sensitivity to the destructiveness of the Western psyche in relation to the wider ecology of life and whose 'psyches are connected to and respond to nature as living essence – not in an *as if* context of symbolic meaning only, but as ongoing feeling *connection*' (p.78; original italics).

In some moments, the only solace is in our solidarity. We 'are not one and the same, though we are in *this* posthuman predicament together' (Braidotti, 2022, p.13), and glimmers of hope shimmer from that shared predicament: the 'us' that includes the client in his foetal curl, me as therapist and fellow traveller, the wooden floor, the oak beams, the spider in the corner of the room, the woodlouse by the door, the birdsong that breaks the silence and the shaft of sunlight that stretches through the window. As a dancer from birth, I have some faith that the spontaneous dance deep inside and between each of us will support our resilience and strengthen our resolve in the face of adversity. Embodied expression offers us a language to articulate that vulnerable, violated place and to delve into our creativity as a forum for discovery. The extemporising moving body is powerful in its fragility, creative in its unpredictable shape-shifting and convincing in its wayward wandering.

Some of my work takes place outside on moorland in the south west of England. As I step out onto the moor to prepare for sessions, I immediately experience an aliveness and responsiveness in my body as I respond to changing temperatures, wind direction and rain, and I breathe in the changing terrain. Rust (2020), an ecopsychotherapist, notes a natural tendency to sink into the body as she enters areas such as forests, beaches, moors and cliffs. I need to arrive with respect, open to the possibilities of posthuman ethical porous relations of care, solidarity and dialogue. This is the place of eco-feminism, in which I question my capacity to listen and filter through the power relations that determine how I listen, what I privilege when I listen and what I identify with when I listen. I take my work outside with caution and humility, however, careful that I am relating to the landscape in dialogue and as a partner, rather than a resource.

There have been occasions when my intuition has made it clear that my intention to work outside, for whatever reason, needs to shift. I was once due to run an outdoor workshop at an eco-psychotherapy gathering and all my plans had centred around facilitating the workshop on a secluded grassy verge. In my final preparations, I was unable to settle, despite the warm, balmy weather. My intuition was taking me into the large, musty, damp, main tent, rather than remaining outdoors. It seemed that, on this occasion, I needed to go inside. I found an available tented indoor space and was grateful to the good-natured team of volunteers for shifting bales of straw to create a space conducive to a movement session. I was touched by their enthusiasm and fresh-faced generosity. Within minutes, their long, strong, youthful limbs had moved the cuboid bales of golden straw to the sides of the tent. I alerted the organisers and, at the allotted time, the participants arrived, young and not so young, bringing eager enthusiasm, along with sceptical caution; some with expectations and some without. I was moved by the expression of commitment embedded in the act of simply turning up, itself an act of hopefulness. As we began, sitting in a circle on the carpeted floor of the tent, the pungent smell of canvas and damp earth hung in the air. One participant, a child, held something in the palm of their hand and shared with the group a small orange and black striped caterpillar that they had found on the grassy verge.

When I wandered outside after the workshop, I noticed a similar caterpillar clinging to the stem of a wildflower on the grassy verge. I knelt down, adjusting my focus to the intricacies of that small patch of land, to find an abundance of similarly striped caterpillars nestling inconspicuously in the grass. Some were still and some moving, with that gentle undulation of the body unmistakably exclusive to caterpillars. I realised that, had I pursued the idea of working outside on that particular spot, I would have inadvertently disturbed that creature community. I took heed to tread with care.

Coming to a close

I continue to take heed to tread carefully as I gather the inconclusive threads of this assemblage of thoughts. As when tented gatherings come to an end, on the final morning I might open my eyes to the sun shining through the canvas and smell the pungent air following a night of rain. As the blackbird's playful tune fills the tent with sound, I might deliberate about leaving my tent up so that it dries, notwithstanding the risk of further rain. I might hold an unrealistic hope that the rain will stay away just long enough, and find myself surprised by the inevitable downpour. I might then dismantle the tent and put the sodden package into a wheelbarrow. I might feel a surge of gratitude to the space for hosting my small tent, along with sadness as I gaze back at the trace of my stay that manifests as a rectangular patch of yellowing, flattened grass. I might stand quietly for a moment, acknowledging the muddy space, before trudging up the hill towards the car with my wheelbarrow.

And, as this chapter comes to a close, I look back at the trace that has been left by the process of this writing, like a footprint in the sand: that intensity of thinking that any writer knows; the discarded phrases; the paragraphs that took a turn just too far away from the path to be useful; the iterations that sit in the folder labelled 'recycling'; the pile of books by the writing desk that have become my imaginary friends; the wisteria visible from the window that looks out from my writing desk, now in full bloom as I finish this chapter. I reflect on how this writing has provided me with an opportunity to consider those psychological, emotional, material and spiritual responses and practices that allow me to find a hopefulness in the face of the climate emergency.

As I reflect here, across this process over time and the assemblage of thoughts that have gathered, I linger on that spontaneous response to the stranger in the car on my way to a tented conference when I expressed my hope of gaining further insight into be(com)ing with diversity. I realise that perhaps I was leaning into the idea of kinship. To find kinship is to find connection and to inhabit an empathic responsibility (care) for others, while remaining cautious of the process of other-ing (uncare). Haraway (2016, p.1) notes how kinship is made up of 'the florid machinic, organic, and textural entities with which we share the earth and our flesh', and that making kinship is an imperative in the face of irreversible destruction of the planet that confronts us. She also cautions us against a simplistic, generalised and/or appropriated leap too quickly into a 'common humanity' and 'multispecies collective' (p.207) and the like, without addressing specific historical and contemporary oppressions and injustices. To make kinship and to evolve cultures of care potentially turns each of us towards our own shadows and the familial, socio-cultural and political inscriptions that bring us to think the way we think, because '(i)t matters what thoughts think thoughts. It matters what knowledges know knowledges…' (p.35).

Creating different ways of thinking, of knowing and of becoming together can interrupt existing norms and create new agendas of ethical solidarity and care. In order to play a part, I need to develop a capacity for holding the multiplicities of sameness and difference and all the contradictions in between. As a practitioner, I can then become part of the unfolding of a posthuman call for alternative corporealities, not in anything particular that I do, but by developing alternative ways of thinking about, seeing, listening, sensing and *becoming with* the world. The small part that I play can sometimes seem futile in the face of the enormity of the climate crisis. However, I trust that the less conscious moments of hope can be unearthed as a reaching out for love, care and belonging and that my hopelessness and despair can become part of a wider current within turbulent waters. One way to move with this tide is to trust the spontaneous, improvised dance of intra-connection that always hovers on the edge of becoming something new. In that material-discursive dance, I discover a language through which I can move into a place of solidarity with fellow travellers, face the vulnerability of hopelessness and discover a renewed energy through the wisdom of compassion and ethical care.

References

Barad, K. (2014). Diffracting diffraction: Cutting together-apart. *Parallax, 20*(3), 168–187.

Bernstein, J. (2005). *Living in the borderland: the evolution of consciousness and the challenge of healing trauma.* Routledge.

Braidotti, R. (2022). *Posthuman feminism.* Polity Press.

Cocker, M. (2007, 12 February). Country diary: Claxton. *The Guardian.*

Frizell, C. (2014). Reflections on the dance of despair. *Transformations,* Winter, 9–11.

Frizell, C. (2023). The cat, the foal and other meetings that make a difference: Posthuman research that re-animates our responsiveness to knowing and becoming. In C. Frizell & M. Rova (Eds.), *Creative bodies in therapy, performance and community: Research and practice that brings us home* (pp. 50–61). Routledge.

Frizell, C. & Poynor, H. (2023). The matriarch and the mollusc and all things in between. In C. Frizell & M. Rova (Eds.), *Creative bodies in therapy, performance and community: research and practice that brings us home* (pp.180–190). London: Routledge.

Haraway, D. (2016). *Staying with the trouble.* Duke University Press.

Macy, J. & Young Brown, M. (1998). *Coming back to life: practices to reconnect our lives: our world.* New Society Publishers.

Poynor, H. (2023). 'Is that yoga or are you just making it up?' In C. Frizell & M. Rova (Eds.), *Creative bodies in therapy, performance and community: Research and practice that brings us home* (pp.101–108). Routledge.

Rust, M.-J. (2020). *Towards an ecopsychotherapy.* Confer Books.

Solnit, R. (2005). *Hope in the dark: The untold history of people power.* Canongate Books.

Weintrobe, S. (2021). *Psychological roots of the climate crisis.* Bloomsbury Press.

Winnicott, D.W. (2015). *Deprivation and delinquency.* Routledge.

8 | Holding hope, letting go
Emma Palmer

Active Hope is a practice. Like tai chi or gardening, it is something we *do* rather than *have*. (Macy & Johnstone, 2012, p.4)

Hope is found where risk is faced. Hope involves risk… we can't just hope for reform. We have to take risks. The word risk is very interesting; the Latin etymology involves the words 'running towards danger'. Running – not walking, not shuffling, not ambling, but running towards danger. (Samuels, 2021)

Imposter

I've avoided writing this for months – avoiding dwelling with the pain of climate emergency as fires rage; wrangling with the inner Imposter. Talking with Imposter is a good enough starting point. It's congruent and welcomes what's here, in keeping with the spirit of wild therapy, embodied-relational therapy, meditation practice, and pre- and perinatal somatic psychology – things I love.

Imposter syndrome, with its throttling self-doubt and sense of fraudulence, is helpful/painful to notice. If you too recognise Imposter, take time to pause, breathe, and see how it agitates as well as silences and stops us acting. Let's pause, noticing how Imposter limits us in response to the climate emergency ('It won't make any difference anyway'). How it limits who we are and what we do therapeutically, in our families, neighbourhoods, workplaces or spiritual groups of which we are a significant part.

Systemically, let's notice how Imposter mutes the voices of so many everyday wise folk. How Imposter actively silences those already structurally marginalised because of racism – I would say colour, but white's obviously a colour too, going unquestioned, as the colour of majority rule – plus class, gender, education, sexuality, age, other-than-human nature, many other intersecting identities.

In the face of climate emergency, who *isn't* an Imposter? Attempting to say something timely and useful is stretching, especially with climate denialism embedded in and shaping consensus reality. The great news is that we can be united in being out of our collective depth.

It's only recently that I have seen how much consent I have given Imposter – understandably, in terms of adaptive childhood behaviours and character structure (see Kamalamani, 2012a). It's more complex than that, too, isn't it? Consent has only recently become much more explored. As therapists, we know that we are conditioned and, in turn, each of our actions shape conditions, from our first breath – or our earlier decision to become incarnate. Born into a complex web of human conditioning: family, friends, state, economy, religion, culture. Let's pay loving attention here to the dance/tension between our individuality and our part in a collective body of beings in ever-changing phenomena.

We

The 'us' of community and social cohesion has been further eroded in the past few decades by the constant underlining of the individual and success, wealth and status, at the cost of investing time in relationship and community. It is described by Weintrobe as 'neoliberal exceptionalism and the culture of uncare' (2021). Here, I mean genuine community cohesion, rather than the propaganda and promotion of so called 'British values' in the past few, politically divided years (Cowden & Singh, 2016).

In my childhood and 1980s teenage-hood, the rise of individualism was an essential and celebrated part of the neoliberal project. That, and the bombardment of what we 'need' in order to look richer, more beautiful and more successful, playing on our status anxiety (de Botton, 2004). We have been branded from the outside as consumers rather than breathing beings; our runaway consumption provides the necessary fuel for the (now failing) neoliberal project. Closer to home, is the mushrooming in the vast number of therapy training courses perhaps another manifestation of this?

In the neoliberal project we are positioned as competitors against one another, rather than remembering our commonality, our cooperation (see Bregman, 2020) and the reality of our interdependence. Consensus reality systematically persuades us to identify with 'I' rather than 'we', with the ensuing loss of 'we-ness', including forgetting our deep knowing that we are part of 'nature'; other-than-human and more-than-human life and our beautiful complexity. We've lost muscle in coming together, acting with the whole community of life in mind. A timely reminder in the Covid-19 pandemic was the strengthening of neighbourly connection – fetching groceries, collecting medicine for one another.

I pause here, take a breath and notice how I relate to 'I'. Then I change tack and notice how I relate to 'we'. I listen to what is happening in my body: 'I' constellates around my core, drawing me in and upwards; a few more breaths, and 'we' encourages my shoulders open, awareness drawn to the expansiveness of my energy field, with subtle heart opening. Loved ones come to mind. What happens for you? Who's part of your 'we'?

'I-ness' can be our therapy 'normal'. It can be a lonely trade; I can find my 'I-ness' is reinforced, limiting the energy for 'we'. Thank goodness for therapy that draws on systems thinking and includes intergenerational influences in our work, hopefully countering how parts of our trade are inevitably following the trends of the neoliberal project.

In the face of climate emergency (and other interrelated crises), individual action isn't enough, is it? It's a fabulous starting point to recycle, to insulate our home – if we're lucky enough to have one – to switch to renewables, to drive less, to stop flying, to eat less meat and fish or go vegan, to go through the process of choosing not to have children or have one if we were planning two (Kamalamani, 2016).

The CEOs of the oil corporations, investing millions of dollars in concealing the extent of climate emergency, would love us to keep believing we can change the world through recycling alone. We need to keep challenging that current *status quo* together. We need to follow in the footsteps of Polly Higgins' (2010) legacy of 'Earth Protectors' and the commitment to protect the Earth in whatever form that takes: in the climate-change policies of our therapy organisations, how we collaborate with clients, and how we take collective action.

The size of the cloth

> There is no such thing as a single-issue struggle because we do not live single-issue lives. (Lorde, 1982).

When I hear the words 'climate emergency', or read the latest UN report, or hear of species going extinct in this sixth extinction catastrophe, or see needless habitat destruction in pursuit of commercial greed and political expediency, or other slow-burning disasters, part of me freezes, immobilised. Part of me breathes out, re-engaging with whatever I'm doing that feels most useful. Part of me wants to distract myself. On a good day, I feel the pulse-like drum beat of my love for the Earth.

I've been aware of 'global warming', as it was then known, since the mid-1980s, yet my body still has this range of responses. How could it be otherwise? Let's notice our responses. Let's include the responses we are less happy to admit: denial, dissociation, overwhelm, and the desire to distract – noticing our personal go-tos. Let's remember, too, to notice the love and care for the Earth and one another.

It's sobering to acknowledge how human actions, particularly those of the wealthiest of us in the global north, have impacted the climate, caused the raising of Earth's temperature by burning fossil fuels, deforestation, large-scale livestock farming, large-scale military infrastructure, adding greenhouse gases to those that naturally occur atmospherically. Maybe the split, the forgetting that we're part of 'nature', is inevitable – even necessary – to avoid feeling the agony of the destruction we have so far inflicted, witnessing the institutionally sanctioned oppression upon which late-stage capitalism depends, with marginalised humans and other-than-human and more-than-human life consistently disregarded. It can literally feel maddening to be complicit in a system with harm at its heart.

Eruptions

As we dwell with climate emergency, waking up to its size and scale, let's keep breathing. Let's notice that movement is happening too, from the cellular level and beyond. In recent years, there's been a gathering pace of collective 'eruptions' and increasing public stands against oppression, embodied, for example, in #BlackLivesMatter, following

George Floyd's murder in 2020, and the 2019 international emergence of Extinction Rebellion activists, urging leaders to 'tell the truth' about the 'emergency on planet Earth'.

Earlier still, the 2017 #MeToo movement gained popularity in the wake of the Weinstein allegations: '#MeToo' was a phrase originally coined by New York-based civil rights activist Tarana Burke in 2006, emerging from her work with young women of colour who had experienced sexual abuse. This is a subject close to my heart, too, as Deborah A. Lee and I co-edited a book for therapists in its wake (Lee & Palmer, 2020).

Let's pay attention to the small eruptions: for example, the increasing awareness of some friends and family, some of whom haven't considered themselves as 'political' to date. Or the eruption of younger therapy colleagues, imploring colleagues to be more in touch with the way the world is *now*. How is erupting energy for you? Notice the excitement. Notice the fear? Notice the parts of us that have been erupting, perhaps marching, campaigning, persuading, protesting, building. Notice the parts that keep deadly quiet, resisting movement – apart, perhaps, from running away.

Power

One oppression is an echo of all oppressions, with misuse of power at its core. When I am talking about climate emergency, I am talking about all of the above. The subject of power in the therapy room – its use and misuse – has direct parallels for me with our respect, or lack of it, for other-than-human and more-than-human life. How we bring in anti-racist practice and recognise white supremacy, attending to our internalised racism and patriarchy, are related to how likely it is that we will, as a species, divert some elements of climate disaster.

It's why we need to talk about race, or gender, or sexuality, or class, or disability, and many other things, alongside talking about climate emergency and the interrelated crises. It's why I have been critiquing the neoliberal project. Climate emergency isn't an 'environmental' problem, just as racism isn't a 'social' problem; they are both current and historic misuses of power – power that is personal and systemic. Let's remember, in parallel, the potency of our desire to create an equitable world.

Balance

The more we engage, perhaps the more we start to remember we are part of multi-dimensional, beautifully complex ecosystems, in which one species was never meant to be without predators. How do we regain balance? In our therapy work, and beyond, recognising the significance of intersecting identities is a starting place. In helping to explain the oppression of African-American women, civil rights activist and legal scholar Kimberlé Crenshaw (1989) coined the term 'intersectionality', highlighting how traditional feminist ideas and anti-racist policies exclude women of colour because they face an overlapping of many discriminations that are unique to them.

Intersectionality explores the importance of recognising that sexuality, gender, race, class, disability, whatever the nature of the embedded, structural oppression – are interconnected forces supporting an intersectional perspective, and giving that experience a name. When we recognise this, we realise we all have an intersectional experience. Take a moment to absorb those words, to sink into what your intersectional experience might be. Or perhaps notice the privileges of the constellation of your class, colour, level of wealth and education and so on. Maybe notice, in your heart of hearts, what or who seems to you 'other' (see Turner, 2021). Take time to notice any clarity and confusion with love.

Other-than-human and more-than-human life is another marginalised 'community' – a vast one. Given that we humans are part of, rather than separate from 'nature', we oppress parts of ourselves when we oppress and cause harm to so-called nature.

Having glanced at the size of the cloth, I'm now drawn to noticing the play between 'out there' and 'in here' – what brings us balance, a still point, while staying engaged? There can sometimes be an over-emphasis on what's 'out there'. Conversely, as therapists, perhaps our tendency is our focus on 'in here'. Let's see how fluid we can become in dancing between the two – even if the duality is ultimately rather a false one.

Let's offer the pacing, timing, space and compassion that we would offer our clients, particularly those taking in fully the interrelated crises for the first time. Let's offer that to ourselves, too. We know crisis can touch the parts of us that love life, as well as the parts that want to give up, when the grief and terror are too much - love and grief both being completely understandable and healthy responses to the size of the cloth.

Out there/in here

I hit overwhelm this morning, crying into my Earl Grey tea and wishing it would all go away. To engage with climate emergency, I need to let reality in more, while seeking creative and collective forms of expression and engagement. How do we find ways of turning towards, opening our hearts? How do we turn towards climate emergency and actively engage, so it does not become 'other' – something happening on a different continent, with all the potential for disavowal discussed by Weintrobe (2012)? How do we notice the impact 'in here', digesting, talking with friends and colleagues, finding still points – a process that in turn offers still points for others whose lives we touch?

So, I'm taking a breath. Perhaps feel your connection with your seat, your feet on the earth. Notice with kindly attention how you are. Notice the busyness or quietness of your mind. Notice your feelings, even the trickier or more hidden ones. Pay kind attention to your breath; whether it's high or low in the body, whether your breaths are shallow or deep. Follow its rhythm with curiosity.

Perhaps bring to mind a favourite seascape, woodland, or a corner of your backyard or local park. Or perhaps another being comes to mind, or physically enters the room where you are sitting. What do your senses tell you? What's happening in your heart?

Let your mind wander into the changes you've noticed in your lifetime. What's changed in the place you grew up, or in places you love? If you are a gardener, recall how the season's patterns are changing beyond their regular variability. Notice parts of you that are changed by awareness of climate change, and how you know and recognise these changes. How is it to notice? What happens in your body? What stays the same? If attention wanders off, where does it go?

Pay kind attention to your breath. Notice your contact with the earth, as well as the invisible energetic thread winding through the core of your body, stretching skywards.

How is it to let in the pain of witnessing human destruction – breathing and seeing which parts are fully present, which parts might have switched off and gone numb or are doing whatever they are doing; bearing witness, paying attention?

Maybe notice how you have silenced and how you have been silenced in engaging with climate emergency and other crises. These might be subtle or everyday occurrences. How do you experience oppressive behaviour and how is it to notice our own oppressive behaviours – even micro-tones of voice? How do we meet the climate-denying parts within? Sitting here, see what peace and kindness we can offer these parts.

Notice, listening carefully, how you have been placed, from the outside in, in the hierarchies we 'Western' humans seem to love to reinforce, in the therapy trade, in our families, within local communities, friendship groups, workplaces, training organisations, professional bodies, through to our place in the human pecking order. How has that 'placing' helped and hindered? How have we tried to find a place? And, breathing out, where do we feel we naturally belong?

Come back to the rise and fall of your breath, your feet on the solidity of the earth. Maybe bring to mind a treasured friend, sensing energetically how you often feel in their company. Recollect the life in their eyes, their laugh, maybe the lilt of their voice. Breathe some more.

The guest house

> Moving on, as a concept, is for stupid people, because any sensible person knows grief is a long-term project. (Porter, 2016, p.99)

Therapeutically, we are likely well-versed in supporting clients with the range of emotions that arise in response to climate emergency, as well as in supporting the practice of hope, referring back to the Macy and Johnstone (2012) quote with which I opened this chapter. Perhaps we are even better placed, having spent the recent past living with the uncertainty of the Covid-19 pandemic.

Let's give ourselves time and space to meet and digest our responses, perhaps cultivating a practice of active hope. I'm reminded of George Monbiot's declaration (2019): 'Despair is a sin.' I guess he meant how despair in response to the climate emergency can be as immobilising as climate denial, albeit from different origins. Yet surely despair is just despair? The more we let it, the more open we are about it, the more it is free to come and go. Sometimes it may stay for longer than at other times, but hey, no need to add self-or-other pathologising, or a layer of post-Christian guilt-tripping into the mix.

Despair is despair, love is love, hope is hope, terror is terror. Can we let them be fully here? I am reminded of Rumi's poem 'The Guest House' (Rumi, 2005). Do look it up if you don't know it, because its spirit conveys way more clearly what I am stumbling to say here.

How can we let all of our beautiful human mess be here – as rich as the finest compost? How can we support one another to do this? It sounds obvious – maybe it's too obvious – but the 'we' – having conversations in kindly-held spaces within us, between us, in large groups, in and beyond therapy – is supportive in staying engaged in the face of climate emergency. What seems common as we fully face the inter-related emergencies is the emergence of grief. Participating in collective grief work – as well as the practice of hope – through the powerful 'Work That Reconnects' developed by Joanna Macy (Macy & Brown, 2014) can be deeply supportive and transformative.

In our work, many of us are likely to be well-versed in supporting bereaved clients. Facing the grief of climate emergency or the sixth extinction catastrophe feels similar and different. The range of feelings is the same, the scale and context are different. In grieving for what we have collectively done to the planet, and continue to do, the possibility for overwhelm is vastly increased, making it entirely understandable that it is harder to stay engaged.

Perhaps it is hard to stay engaged, too, because this is collective trauma. Facing the consequences of an ever-hotter planet, the changes themselves are scary, as is the woeful lack of action by the world's most powerful governments. Knowing that I am here and breathing, that I am part of the web of 'mutual causality' that has given rise to these interrelated crises (borrowing the term from Macy (1991), who in turn, adapted it from Buddhism), can also be trauma inducing. It's vital to come into relationship with our part in this, especially those of us living privileged lives in the global north: to see the consequences of our actions as well as realise that we are as valuable and as unique a part of life as anything and anyone else. That might mean facing deeper grief, and also the emergence of greater aliveness as we see with clearer eyes. We need one another to do this – including other-than and more-than human friends and community.

Holding hope as a body of therapists

Hope, for me, is about the balance of action and reflection. I am reminded of Green Tara, a well-loved Buddha from the Tibetan Buddhist tradition. Tara has one leg tucked up in meditation posture, and the other stepping into the world (see Kamalamani, 2012b). I'm not sure, thinking of Samuels' quote above (2021), how many of us are willing or able to run towards danger in the pursuit of hope. Yet the spirit of that rings true, given the size of the climate emergency and the interrelated crises and how much is at stake. Perhaps Green Tara can remind us of this balance, and how, perhaps paradoxically, the more active we are, the stiller we might need to become. It doesn't have to be 'being' versus 'doing' or 'in here' versus 'out there'.

Here we are, reading this, with a vast range of skills between us, and, I'd imagine, an astonishing amount of love and curiosity in our hearts. I'm deliberately starting with 'us' as a collective body, given the default focus is so often on the individual. Maybe a holding hope starting point is acknowledging that of which we are already a part: human as well as other-than and more-than-human communities; perhaps membership organisations, peer support groups, teachers you know or have known and loved. Take a moment to note down all those you know who also hold hope. Our networks can be thoughts, ideas, a training you did years ago that somehow woke up your love of other-than-human life. Ideally, this is an exercise to take to a peer group or discuss with a friend – how we are linked with one another in the web of interconnected life.

As we see ourselves in a 'family tree' or lineage of people, beings, associations, we realise we are in good company, that the practice of hope can be regenerative as we inspire others in and through how we live. We might want to join established organisations already acting and holding hope – the Climate Psychology Alliance,[1] or Psychotherapists and Counsellors for Social Responsibility,[2] for example. Or offer our skills in national or local organisations that aren't specifically therapy focused, or faith communities of which we are a part.

Reflecting on my earlier observation that 'one oppression is an echo of all oppressions' in respect of climate emergency, the work of networks like the Black African and Asian Therapy Network[3] come to mind, with its primary aim of addressing the inequality of appropriate psychological services for Black, African, South Asian and Caribbean people. Or Pink Therapy,[4] the UK's largest independent therapy organisation working with gender and sexual diversity. Other organisations have emerged to support clients and therapists from unrepresented backgrounds, bringing about much-needed awareness and change. Perhaps our calling is towards anti-oppressive work, or anti-racist work, or understanding whiteness. Or perhaps making therapy or therapy training more accessible for all; an exciting prospect – therapy without borders.

Continuing with oppression and liberation in mind, much of the conventional therapy we have been taught has its roots in the same beliefs, assumptions and norms of the global north. Some of you reading this will be therapy tutors and lecturers. What needs to change to challenge this orthodoxy, in terms of content and process? How can we in the wider therapy body support this? How can we become aware of how our privilege upholds the status quo? If we have privileges, how do we choose to use our voice and potency in being an ally or accomplice? Perhaps as therapists we might experience a political coming of age, in terms of recognising the extent to which climate change isn't being addressed governmentally and working out how to cope with that, given that it can feel akin to gaslighting.

Has therapy become too tame? Or our membership bodies? As a 'wild' therapist, practising this form of ecopsychology (Totton, 2021), I guess I would raise that question, given that I have witnessed repeatedly what can be learned when we not only practise and train in wilder places but also invite the wilder parts of ourselves and others into our everyday experience. If therapy is partly a reflection of consensus reality, how ready is it – are we – as a body of people, to do what we can in the face of the climate emergency?

Maybe we also need to take the time to find out what our particular role is in the broader therapy body. Are we here to tell stories or create plays that offer alternatives to dystopia and apocalypse? To offer spaces to re-imagine, to envision, to dream? Are we here to support climate activists at the frontline, or are we off to the frontline ourselves? As we stay rooted – the roots of the word 'radical' – what are our bodies moved to do?

---

1. www.climatepsychologyalliance.org

2. www.pcsr.org.uk

3. www.baatn.org.uk/about

4. https://pinktherapy.com

What does the precious planet and all her inhabitants need us to do? Are we listening carefully?

And let's pause and celebrate what we are already doing.

Holding hope with clients and for ourselves

What do I do when a client shares their fears about climate emergency? With the increasing awareness of what's become known as 'eco-anxiety', and given phenomena like Brexit and Covid-19, the world is talking politics more openly. The climate emergency is now a more commonplace theme in therapy. As with any theme, I hope to be as aware as possible of my own response to it so I can be as receptive as possible when a client brings it into the therapeutic space.

If we agree, as discussed earlier, that facing climate emergency, let alone living with the consequences of the emergency, is part of a collective trauma, what do we need to do to support clients to name this, perhaps even to provisionally normalise it without that becoming passive acceptance? How do we resource ourselves to stay with this?

1. Slowing down. When I first started meditating, I came across an aphorism that went something like this: 'Sit as if you have a thousand years, and never waste a moment.' It comes to mind when I'm losing the balance between being and doing. How do we sense spaciousness in ourselves and hold its possibility with clients, while also taking seriously the urgency, the immediacy of the longing to engage? What a gift it is to be alongside someone – ourselves, a client, or trainee – supporting them in the art of this balancing act.

2. Body like a mountain. Another Buddhist aphorism comes to mind: 'Body like a mountain, heart like the ocean, mind like the sky.' How do we stay grounded in facing climate emergency and other interrelated crises? As well as learning what helps us stay grounded, how do we also remember to look at the sky? To daydream? How do we know well enough our own patterns of incarnation? Learning about post-Reichian character structure has been immensely helpful here for me (Kamalamani, 2012a). How do we pay attention to the edges, to what's emerging – newer, liminal parts, as well as the parts we already know? How do we help hold that liminal space for clients?

3. Dreaming. Dare we listen to, and act upon, our wildest dreams? How do we encourage that in clients, too, rather than staying problem focused? I'm reminded of the compassionate challenge of the late Polly Higgins' book title: *Dare to Be Great: Unlock your power to create a better world* (Higgins, 2020). Wild dreaming is a fabulous counterbalance to climate emergency. I'm struck every time I participate in 'social dreaming' (Lawrence, 2005) on retreats I'm leading, or at ecopsychology events, tuning into the collective dreaming of all other beings.

4. Earth stories. As well as finding a regular outdoor spot to sit and listen to what the non-human world has to say, it can be a rich exercise to tell our 'Earth stories' (see Kamalamani, 2017) in exploring our relationship with Earth and other-than-human and more-than-human life – perhaps key moments and significant relationships told from many perspectives. We might also become better acquainted with our particular locality and its flora and fauna – a useful ecopsychological practice we can do anywhere: discovering the type of earth on which we live or the secret waterways running beneath the bus lanes; the rich history of place and the relishing of life everywhere.

5. Family trees. Simple genealogical charts can be invaluable here. Potentially knowing where we're from – and facing the not knowing – can provide useful continuity and information in how present-day ruptures often echo ancestral ruptures. Extending the notion of family trees further still, where do we feel we are from in terms of people, places, theories and action to which we are drawn? Lineages can be made of inspirational people or other species or cultures with which we feel aligned. This can offer rich healing for us from the ancestors, and from us to them, and can literally be rooting, resourcing, 'knitting us up' with wider webs of life and the temporal perspective of 'deep time' or 'kairos time'.

6. Power and potency. How do we work with the implicit power imbalance in our therapy rooms? How do we notice the nuances of when and how therapy 'rules' serve us, rather than our clients? Can we apologise when we make a mistake? (Do we notice our mistakes?) Do we notice how our privilege, compared with that of a particular client, makes our experiences notably different? Or do we tend to focus on our commonality, glossing over uncomfortable differences? Is there a way of making the therapy sessions we offer more accessible and affordable?

7. Liberation. How do we work in the therapy room knowing that we, too, will have absorbed prejudices and are likely to act sometimes in oppressive ways? This could range from our embedded assumptions about class and colour through to thoughts about the superiority of our particular therapy modality. What are we doing to ensure we're not maintaining the oppressive status quo? What do we need to learn or who do we need to talk to if this is new news?

8. Bridging. As therapists, we are well-placed to support clients in what can be difficult conversations, as they seek to talk to family and friends about how they're living differently in response to climate emergency. Trickier still, perhaps, is how we communicate with those who deny climate change. What we know about communication is also invaluable in our inner dialogues and self-talk, especially if thinking we're not enough or not doing enough are familiar scripts.

9. Living. Are we living as fully as we are able? Facing climate emergency is tough. Can we keep on living, enjoying the bits of life we enjoy, in the face of this? Do we, can we, encourage this in clients, too?

'Holding to nothing whatever'

I love these words from a well-loved Buddhist teaching called the Heart Sutra (Sangharakshita, 1989, p.25). They resonate with me more than holding hope. I've got an inkling of how to practise it – but it is only an inkling, sensed in moments of spaciousness and beauty, the wind in my hair. I'll keep on engaging with climate emergency and the interrelated crises, taking my place when I can in the erupting movements – and sitting still, too. What's the alternative? I'm here and alive. Unless we are billionaires, with the money and desire to move to Mars, there is nowhere else to go. I have no idea whether we are in 'end times' or in the birth of a new era – most likely both/and. I am not sure whether speculating is time well spent. I am fascinated by the notion and practice of 'meaningfreeness' (Loy, 2000, p.xvi), introduced to me by my friend and mentor David Loy. In accepting meaninglessness, in yielding to what can seem like a dreaded nothingness of life – nothing fixed, everything always changing – we might start to realise the playful state of meaningfreeness. Can we act freely and fully without being attached to, identified with, the outcomes of our actions? Can we play? In a similar vein, I appreciate Nick Totton's 'boundlessness' (Totton, 2010). Both 'meaningfreeness' and 'boundlessness' seem to echo particular facets of 'holding to nothing whatever'. Or the mythical words of the Buddhist figure Padmasambhava: 'I do not have, I do not understand, I do not know'. In these times, I find this a radical counterbalance to having to have and having to know. I'm getting better at showing up and not knowing.

References

Bregman, R. (2020). *Humankind: A hopeful history*. Bloomsbury Publishing.

Cowden, S. & Singh, G. (2016). Community cohesion, communitarianism and neoliberalism. *Critical Social Policy, 37*(2). https://doi.org/10.1177/0261018316670252

Crenshaw, K. (1989). Demarginalizing the intersection of race and sex: A black feminist critique of antidiscrimination doctrine, feminist theory and antiracist politics. *University of Chicago Legal Forum, 1*, Article 8. http://chicagounbound.uchicago.edu/uclf/vol1989/iss1/8

de Botton, A. (2004). *Status anxiety*. Hamish Hamilton.

Higgins, P. (2010). *Eradicating ecocide*. Shepheard-Walwyn Publishers.

Higgins, P. (2020). *Dare to be great: Unlock your power to create a better world*. The History Press.

Kamalamani. (2012a). *Meditating with character*. Mantra Books.[5]

Kamalamani. (2012b). Green Tara. *Somatic Psychotherapy Today*, Fall, 42–44.[5] https://tinyurl.com/ya6cty2k

Kamalamani. (2016). *Other than mother: Choosing childlessness with life in mind*. Earth Books.[5]

Kamalamani. (2017). Calling the Earth to witness: Telling our Earth stories. *Thresholds*, Spring.[5]

Lawrence, W.G. (2005). *Introduction to social dreaming – transforming thinking*. Routledge.

Lee, D.A. & Palmer, E. (2020). *#MeToo: Counsellors and psychotherapists speak about sexual violence and abuse*. PCCS Books.

Lorde, A. (1982, February). *Learning from the 60s*. Malcolm X celebration weekend, Harvard University. www.blackpast.org/african-american-history/1982-audre-lorde-learning-60s

---

5. Until 2018, I was known as 'Kamalamani', which is why my books and articles are published under this name in these references.

Loy D. (2000). *Lack and transcendence: The problem of death and life in psychotherapy, existentialism, and Buddhism*. Humanity Books.

Macy, J. (1991). *Mutual causality in Buddhism and general systems theory: The dharma of natural systems*. State University of New York.

Macy, J. & Brown, M. (2014). *Coming back to life: The updated guide to the work that reconnects*. New Society Publishers.

Macy, J. & Johnstone, C. (2012). *Active hope: How to face the mess we're in without going crazy*. New World Library.

Monbiot, G. (2019, April 20). No more excuses. *The Guardian*. www.monbiot.com/2019/04/20/no-more-excuses

Porter, M. (2016). *Grief is the thing with feathers*. Faber & Faber.

Rumi. (2005). The guest house. In C. Barks (Ed. & Trans.), *Rumi: The book of love – poems of ecstasy and longing* (p.179). Harper Collins.

Samuels, A. (2021, September 9). *Covid and climate: Apocalypse and alternatives*. [Video.] www.andrewsamuels.com/andrew-samuels-ranting-during-the-pandemic

Sangharakshita, B. (1989). *The FWBO Puja book: A book of Buddhist devotional texts* (5th ed.). Windhorse Publications.

Totton, N. (2010). Boundaries and boundlessness. *Therapy Today, 21*, 8.

Totton, N. (2021). *Wild therapy: Rewilding our inner and outer worlds* (2nd ed.). PCCS Books.

Turner, D. (2021). *Intersections of privilege and otherness in counselling and psychotherapy*. Routledge.

Weintrobe, S. (2012). *Engaging with climate change: Psychoanalytic and interdisciplinary perspectives*. Routledge.

Weintrobe, S. (2021). *Psychological roots of the climate crisis: Neoliberal exceptionalism and the culture of uncare*. Bloomsbury Academic.

PART 3

From theory to practice

9 | Building change-making capacity: Active Hope Training

Chris Johnstone

Our world situation is often experienced as scary and depressing, leaving people feeling overwhelmed, anxious, defeated or in despair. Psychologically orientated practitioners have a special role to play here because they're used to helping people face difficult issues, explore their reactions and engage in a constructive response. This chapter introduces a structured transformative process designed to help people grow their capacity to face disturbing world crises such as climate change and play their part in responding. Called Active Hope Training, it is based on the Work That Reconnects framework described in *Active Hope,* the book I wrote with US author and activist Joanna Macy (Macy & Johnstone, 2022). The approach can be applied as a personal practice, in one-to-one conversations, and in groups. In an outcome survey of 165 people completing an online version of Active Hope Training (November 2022), more than 92% of participants reported that the course had significantly strengthened their motivation to act for positive change and their belief that they could make a difference, leaving them feeling less overwhelmed by their concerns for the world and personally nourished by their experience of taking part.

The blocked response

In a 2022 course-joining online survey, I asked people how serious they thought the problems of our world were. On a scale of 0–10, where 0 represents no problem at all and 10 is catastrophic, the average response from more than 1800 participants was 8.8. I then asked how well developed, on a 0–10 scale, they thought our collective response was. With 0 as no response and 10 as a widespread, engaged and inspiring response, the average rating was 3.4. This mismatch between the size of our world problems and the size of our collective response is itself one of our biggest issues. As Joanna Macy observes:

> Of all the dangers we face, from climate chaos to nuclear warfare, none is so great as the deadening of our response. (Macy, 2021, p.37)

How do we cultivate the opposite of a blocked or deadened response? Perhaps first we need to understand what gets in the way. Some of the barriers to engagement are linked to structural factors in our society that require a collective, political response. There are also obstacles more related to the way we think and feel, to our view of reality and our patterns of conversation. These might be more amenable to a psychologically informed approach.

Active Hope Training addresses four such areas, where the hurdles blocking engagement and helping factors that might promote it are related to:

- our view of hope
- our responses to pain for the world
- the way we view our power to make a difference
- our experience of connectedness with the world.

Let's look at each of these in turn, and at ways psychologically informed understanding and practices, especially those used in Active Hope Training, can enliven and energise empowered responses to world issues.

Our view of hope

Hope is often thought of as a feeling that things are going to work out well. A striking finding of recent surveys is how common it is for people not to have this when thinking about our collective future. For example, in a survey of 10,000 young people in 2020, **more than half (56%) saw humanity as doomed (Hickman et al., 2021). This widespread** collapse of hope has a profound impact on our collective psyche. It is one of the factors blocking an engaged response, as illustrated by the example of Jane, someone I interviewed when writing *Active Hope*. Like many of the young people in the survey mentioned above, Jane saw humanity as stuck on a downhill path of self-destruction. 'What's the point of doing anything,' she asked, 'if it won't change what we're heading for?' It isn't just lack of hope that's an obstacle here; it is also the belief that something isn't worth doing unless you're reasonably hopeful you will succeed.

The questions 'Are you hopeful?' and 'What do you hope for?' are based on different understandings of what we mean by hope. The first views it as a positive assessment of probability, the second as much more about desire. In reply to the first question, Jane shook her head. With the second question, her energy shifted as she described what she'd love to see happen in our world.

I learned about active hope from working in the addictions recovery field. I'd often see clients who had failed so many times in their attempts to stop drinking that they'd lost all hope that their life could improve. Feeling stuck on a slope of decline, they'd tell me, 'Sure, I'd love to make things different, but I can't see that happening, so what's the point of even trying?'

Yet there were also times when I saw a shift happen, such as when someone who'd previously told me 'I've given up giving up, because it never works' showed up sober and with deepened engagement in recovery. I witnessed in clients like this a different relationship with hope, where it became not so much something they had but something they did. This version of hope is quite different to hopefulness; it is a living energy of engagement expressed by taking steps in a hoped-for direction.

When facing our concerns for the world, we can apply this active form of hope in a three-step process. First, we start from where we are by taking in a clear view of reality, acknowledging what we face and how we feel. Second, we identify what we hope for, in terms of the direction we'd like things to move in or the values we'd like to see expressed. And third, we take steps to move ourselves and/or our situation in that direction.

This recasting of hope involves a shift in emphasis from outcome to process. Instead of asking ourselves 'Will it happen?' or 'Am I hopeful?', we can focus on the sequence of events and actions that helps something happen or become more likely. For example, a central narrative thread of Active Hope Training is that crisis can become a turning point, and that we can each play a role in a larger story of change we call the Great Turning. This is the multi-levelled shift from an industrial society committed to economic growth to a sustainable society committed to supporting the flourishing of life. Whatever your level of hopefulness about whether this Great Turning will happen, the active hope approach involves asking, 'Do you hope it will? And if so, how can you be active in supporting your hope, in moving in its direction or making it more likely?'

When shifting emphasis from outcome to process with the Great Turning, an evocative question to explore is 'What would this larger story of change look like if it were happening through you today?' It is through our actions and choices that larger stories can happen through us. Three types of turning are easily within our reach: turning up with an intention to play our part; turning away from ways of doing, being and thinking that cause harm, and turning towards those that support the flourishing of life.

Just as mindfulness or tai chi are practices we can engage in each day, active hope is a practice for collective wellbeing that can be integrated into our daily lives. The three-part process of facing what we face as we take in world events, identifying what we hope for and engaging in action to support our hopes is something we can come back to again and again. It is also something we can get better at.

Courses in mindfulness and tai chi are taught all around the world. In a similar way, Active Hope Training is increasingly being offered in courses designed to help participants become more skilful and familiar with the practice of active hope, while also experiencing support and solidarity from fellow practitioners. This type of training aims to help people grow their capacity, motivation and intention to act for positive change by introducing tools, insights and practices that support these. More recently, a free, video-based online form of Active Hope Training has been developed. The journey this offers is mapped out in the infographic in Figure 9.1.

Our responses to pain for the world

What does a picture of happiness look like? What does a picture of mental health look like?

Some years ago, I felt so very far from either of these. Worries that we were heading towards a societal collapse kept me awake at night, and I was so distracted by feelings of alarm, guilt and despondency that, for several weeks, I found it hard to function

Figure 9.1: A set of seven practices taught in the Active Hope Foundations Training course (with thanks to Carlotta Cataldi for the infographic)

normally. As I sank into my dip, a friend tried to comfort me by saying, 'There's no point worrying about things you can't change.'

What I was experiencing was pain for the world – an umbrella term for the range of uncomfortable feelings brought up by distressing world events. The way we respond to these feelings is shaped by the beliefs we have about them. If we'd like our lives to be a picture of happiness, pain for the world might be viewed as an unwelcome disturbance to be pushed away. In the picture model of mental health, where wellbeing is judged by how things appear in a snapshot assessment, I had enough symptoms of depression to receive that diagnosis. My friend thought he was helping me protect my mental health by encouraging me to look in a different direction. But how can we even begin to address the problems of our world if we find them too depressing to look at?

By contrast, a process model of mental health involves considering the role distress might play in a larger sequence of events. There is a shift here from focusing on the picture of how things are at a particular point in time to instead viewing reality more as a series of frames in an unfolding process, like in a film. For example, have you ever felt grateful for your anger, anxiety, guilt or sadness? When such feelings activate us to address issues that bother us, they can be thought of as 'inspirational dissatisfaction'.

It was in the late 1970s that Joanna Macy discovered the powerful transformative impact of helping people hear and share their inner responses to concerns for the world. At an international conference dominated by presentations of disturbing facts and figures, she facilitated a group session where she invited participants to share their experience of how it felt to live in a time of planetary crisis. The workshop was deeply touching for those who came, leaving them feeling energised and nourished by a deepened sense of solidarity. Building on this experience, she developed a methodology for 'despair and empowerment' workshops, which became the Work That Reconnects. Over the past 40 years, this approach has spread internationally and reached hundreds of thousands of people. Its aim is to help people connect more strongly with their own inner voice, with a sense of supportive community, and with the world we belong to.

The Work That Reconnects guides participants on a transformative and strengthening journey that moves round a spiral of four stages (see Figure 9.2). If we're going to face disturbing information, it helps first to begin by resourcing ourselves, so that we can face difficulty from a stronger starting point. The first part of the spiral invites participants to connect with gratitude – a social emotion that points our attention beyond ourselves to the network of support we receive from.

Figure 9.2: The spiral of The Work That Reconnects

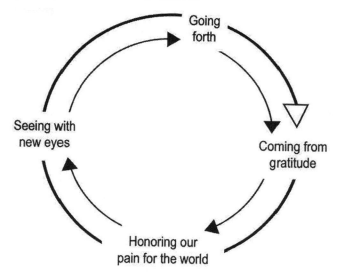

The second part of the spiral is called 'Honouring our pain for the world'. When we honour something, we give it our respectful attention and recognise its value. There's a different meaning being given here to pain for the world. Rather than being viewed as a threat to wellbeing or symptom of disease, it is regarded as an essential alarm call, alerting us to our planetary emergency. Fire alarms aren't pleasant to listen to, but they do mobilise life-saving responses. In a similar way, expressing our concerns can be an important step in engaging our responses to them.

Research in health psychology has shown that, when people are given an opportunity to voice their concerns and make their own argument for change, they're more likely to take action (Amrhein et al., 2003). The approach of motivational interviewing is based on recognising this; it seeks to draw out 'change talk' that supports the case for taking steps in a particular direction. A simple way of applying motivational interviewing to yourself is simply to ask yourself what issues concern you so much that you're motivated to do something about them. An alternative is to use a sentence starter rather than a question: take the opening phrases of a sentence as a starting point, speak these out aloud (or write them down) and see what words naturally follow. I invite you to try these examples:

- Some world issues I'm troubled by include…
- When I look at the future we're heading into, I'm concerned that…
- What particularly alarms me is…

When our conversations give us room to express our pain for the world, they can play an important role in helping mobilise our response. However, what happens when people describe a problem but can't see how to address it? Significant here is the way we view our power to make a difference. That's what we turn to next.

The way we view our power to make a difference

In a survey commissioned by the UK charity the Mental Health Foundation in 2007, more than 2000 people were asked how they felt about global issues. The most common response, identified by more than half the participants, was powerless.[1] Yet how do we know where the boundary is that divides issues that we feel are within our power to influence from those that seem beyond it? It is common for people to feel defeated when they take on a difficult challenge. Thinking that 'there's no point worrying about things you can't change' is a blocking factor in the process of working out what to do about an issue. Turning away from worries about the world may stop people giving the attention needed to find a way forward. Helpful here is the psychology of a growth mindset and the powerful three-letter word, 'yet'.

Psychologist Carol Dweck, in a much-watched 10-minute TEDx talk (2014), describes how a school in Chicago gave a grade of 'not yet' rather than 'fail' when students didn't pass a course. 'If you get the grade "not yet", you understand you're on a learning curve,' she said. 'It gives you a path to the future.' The growth mindset is based on recognising that, when we feel defeated by a challenge that seems beyond our power, it doesn't mean it will always be like that. Adding the word 'yet' after 'I can't do anything about this' places the experience of defeat in a context of larger possibility.

In workshops, I often ask participants if they can think of a time when they were convinced they couldn't do something, yet later found a way to do it. Whether it is giving up smoking, learning a new language, changing a career or starting to run marathons in later life, it isn't unusual for people to move through a phase of not believing something is possible before they discover they can do it.

---

1. Reported at http://news.bbc.co.uk/1/hi/uk/7033102.stm

Cognitive reappraisal has been described as one of the most effective strategies for emotional regulation (Webb et al., 2012). It involves taking a different view of something in a way that changes its meaning and emotional impact. The third stage of The Work That Reconnects spiral is called 'Seeing with new eyes', and it invites people to do this. If we're feeling overwhelmed by the scale of the crises we face, this third stage involves seeking out perspectives that nourish our sense of possibility. By doing this, we're applying the growth mindset to our capacity to make a difference in the world, drawing on insights and practices that strengthen our resolve to find and play our part.

One form of cognitive reappraisal used in Active Hope Training is drawing on the narrative framework of adventure stories. It is common for such epic tales to begin with a community facing an overwhelming threat. The central characters often feel underpowered, but that doesn't stop them. Instead, they begin a quest of seeking out skills, tools, training and allies that might help them find a way forward. Mythologist Joseph Campbell (2008) described obstacles faced along the way as 'threshold guardians' – features of the story that test the ingenuity and commitment of the protagonists. My friend Sarah told me this perspective had transformed her experience of facing the daunting task of a setting up a new project. When struggling, she'd say to herself, 'This is my adventure, these are my threshold guardians.' Rather than giving up, she knew her next step needed to be to seek out allies or new skills, or take a pause to recharge.

At the heart of the 'seeing with new eyes' phase of Active Hope Training is a shift in the way we view and experience our power to make a difference. What if power, like hope, were not so much something we had and more something we did? A question that supports this shift is 'What happens through you?' For example, in Figure 9.3, the circle happens through the squares. If a single square wanted to make a circle happen, it might well see the task as beyond its power. Yet each square plays a role in helping the circle happen – in making it more likely. This is a different way of thinking about cause and effect. The question 'Which square causes the circle?' might seem a nonsense, but asking 'Which square plays a role in causing the circle?' suggests a collaborative view of power. It is through the squares acting together that the circle emerges. In a similar way, it is through our actions and choices that our power to make a difference happens through us.

This shift in how we view power opens up a sense of agency. Many of the big changes we might hope for aren't things we, as individuals, can make happen. Yet turning up with an intention to play our part is a doable thing and is how the Great Turning happens through us.

Our experience of connectedness with the world

When I trained in family therapy in the early 1990s, I felt a sense of revelation at the idea that families feel and act through the people in them. Rather than making sense of behaviour in purely personal terms, when you consider the family as a living system that is more than the sum of its parts, another layer of understanding emerges.

When people are anxious about a relative who is unwell, it is as though the family feels through its members, this shared feeling mobilising their response.

Figure 9.3: Which square causes the circle?

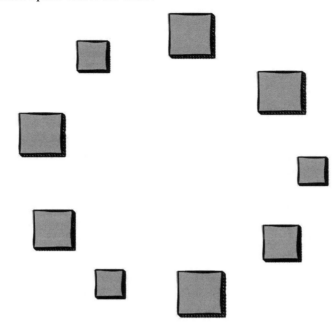

Systems thinking views our world in layers, with entities at each level that are more than the sum of their parts. A person is more than just a collection of organs, a family more than just separate people, a community more than just a collection of households. Gaia theory takes this principle up some more levels to regard the planet, with all its forms of life, as a self-regulating living system. If we were to consider ourselves to be a part of, rather than apart from, our living Earth, could we then think of eco-anxiety as our world feeling through us? Could our love of life and care for life also be ways our world feels through us?

Active Hope Training follows a sequence that begins with appreciation and gratitude, then holds a space to honour our pain for the world. Seeing with new eyes helps us recognise our connections to a larger network of resources and develop a more encouraging view of our power to make a difference. Building on these, the fourth stage of the spiral, called 'Going forth', brings a focus to finding and playing our part in responding to our planetary emergency. We're more likely to feel part of a team if we play a meaningful role within it. When we actively support our hopes for our collective future, it is as though we are finding our place within the larger team of life.

Outcome survey

The Active Hope Foundations Training was launched as a free online course in March 2021. It involves nine hours of video spread over seven weekly sections. Participants are also invited to try out a key practice each week, lasting perhaps 30 minutes. People can start the course at any time and work through it at their own pace. However, as it requires a time commitment of more than 12 hours, it needs some dedication to complete it. Nearly 5000 people dipped into at least some of the course in its first 20 months, more than 40,000 pages/videos were viewed and more than 2500 comments were added to the discussion forum. However, only 165 people completed both the course and a post-course survey in this time. Some of them said they'd found the course life-changing. The post-course survey asked them to rate a series of potential outcomes on a five-point scale ranging from 'not at all' to 'very much'. Table 9.1. shows the results.

Table 9.1: Post-course survey findings

Participants' ratings of the following outcome statements:	Not at all	Slightly	Moderately	Quite a lot	Very much
1. It has strengthened my belief that I can make a difference in the world	1.8%	3.6%	19.4%	41.8%	33.4%
2. It has helped me feel less overwhelmed or defeated when facing my concerns about the world	2.4%	3.6%	12.7%	47.3%	34.0%
3. It has increased my motivation to act for positive change	3.0%	2.4%	13.4%	39.4%	41.8%
4. It has helped me develop a deepened sense of connection with life and with the living Earth	3.0%	4.3%	12.7%	36.4%	43.6%
5. It has been personally healing and nourishing for me	2.0%	3.0%	12.2%	34%	48.8%

More than 92% of responses were either 'Moderately', 'Quite a lot' or 'Very much' for each of these statements, suggesting the course had a significant impact.

Circles of active hope

The Work That Reconnects was developed as an approach to groupwork mainly delivered in workshops. When writing *Active Hope*, Joanna Macy and I aimed to guide readers on a similar transformative journey, reaching a wider audience than just those who might come to a workshop. As the book offers processes that work well as solo practices, partnered conversations or in small groups, it can be used to support shared journeys round the spiral, as well as personal ones. The free online course provides another way of engaging with this material.

Circles of Active Hope are small groups that come together to engage in Active Hope Training, whether guided by the book, the online course, one or more small group facilitators or a combination of these. Many aspiring facilitators have found the prospect of bringing a few people together to explore the book or online course a less daunting challenge than running a workshop. The book or online course acts as a co-facilitator that provides a framework and a structured process to follow. What seems to work particularly well is having a combination of three elements: first, a group that agrees to meet to follow either the book or online course together, which could be just two people, a few friends or a larger group. The second element is the book or online course, with people agreeing to read or watch a particular section before each meeting. A third element that has deepened people's experience and satisfaction, particularly when meeting online, has been to have a partnered practice session between each group meeting.

We've recently developed a Circles of Active Hope facilitator training to help prepare and support people to form such groups. Could this catch on? And what might happen if it did?

Holding the hope by growing our capacity to activate it

Does hope spring from action or action spring from hope? If we see that as a 'chicken-and-egg' question, where each element is needed for the other, it gets pretty bleak in places where hope disappears. By viewing hope more as something we *do* than *have*, and applying a growth mindset to our capacity to engage in this active form of hope, it becomes possible to rekindle the spark where it goes out. There are skills, insights, practices and good company that help us do this. We can hold the hope by growing our capacity to activate it, so that it happens through us, through our choices and actions in each day. That's what Active Hope Training aims to support.

References

Amrhein P., Miller, W.R., Yahne, C. & Palmer, M. (2003). Client commitment language during motivational interviewing predicts drug use outcomes. *Journal of Consulting and Clinical Psychology,* 71(5), 862–878.

Campbell, J. (2008). *The hero with a thousand faces* (3rd ed.). New World Library.

Dweck, C. (2014, December 17). *The power of believing that you can improve.* [Video.] TEDx Talk. www.ted.com/talks/carol_dweck_the_power_of_believing_that_you_can_improve?language=env

Hickman, C., Marks, L., Pihkala, P., Clayton, S., Lewandowski, E., Mayall, E., Wray, B., Mellor, C. & Susteren, L. (2021). Climate anxiety in children and young people and their beliefs about government responses to climate change: a global survey. *Lancet Planetary Health, 5,* e863–73. www.thelancet.com/action/showPdf?pii=S2542-5196%2821%2900278-3

Macy, J. (2021). *World as lover, world as self* (30th anniversary ed.). Parallax Press.

Macy, J. & Johnstone, C. (2022). *Active hope: How to face the mess we're in with unexpected resilience and creative power* (revised ed.). New World Library.

Webb, T.L., Miles, E. & Sheeran, P. (2012). Dealing with feeling: A meta-analysis of the effectiveness of strategies derived from the process model of emotion regulation. *Psychological Bulletin, 138*(4), 775–808.

10 Imaginative engagement with the climate crisis: The role of climate and ecology fiction

Maggie Turp

> Protest that endures, I think, is moved by a hope far more modest than that of public success: namely, the hope of preserving qualities in one's own heart and spirit that would be destroyed by acquiescence. (Wendell Berry, 1990)

The opening quotation refers to 'the hope of preserving the qualities in one's own heart and spirit that would be destroyed by acquiescence'. This chapter considers how climate fiction – cli-fi – might help in the realisation of that hope, and also what light psychoanalysis can cast on the difficulties involved. I begin by asking what the hope of 'non-acquiescence' might involve. Three interlinked tasks come to mind: 1) striving to remain emotionally and thoughtfully engaged and able to bear witness; 2) making space to mourn and help others mourn all that has been precious and familiar and is now spoiled or gone, and 3) holding on to our capacity for compassion, joy and fulfilment in life.

Global heating and existential threat

Between the arrival of the invitation to write this chapter and its submission date, the IPCC published its *Sixth Assessment Report* (2022), headlined 'Code Red for Humanity'.[1] The news is bad, the forecast bleak. The planet is heating faster than we previously thought. To have even a 50% chance of staving off dangerous world-wide warming, emissions need to peak by 2025 before falling by 43% by 2030. (By way of comparison, emissions rose in 2021 by a record 5.5%.) Here in the UK, the by now familiar absence of an appropriate government response confirms what many of us have for some time felt to be inevitable: the juggernaut of growth-dependent capitalism will continue to roll, wreaking further havoc on the environment and discharging more CO_2 into the already overloaded atmosphere. There are some welcome exceptions to

---

1. https://news.un.org/en/story/2021/08/1097362#:~:text='Code%20red%20for%20humanity'&text=We%20are%20at%20imminent%20risk,%2C%20to%20keep%201.5%20alive.%22

the overall gloomy picture – an area of Helsinki, Finland's capital city, pushing ahead with measures to become carbon neutral by 2040; a process in development to enable steel to be produced without the use of fossil fuels. Such initiatives are pinpoints of light in an overwhelmingly dark sky.

The physical effects of climate breakdown – unprecedented floods, storms, droughts, heatwaves, food shortages and displacements of people – are a very present reality for people in the global south, while remaining still a future threat – for the most part at least – for those of us in more temperate areas. By contrast, the emotional effects are already upon us all. A letter in a recent edition of *New Scientist* bears the title: 'Global catastrophes also threaten to destroy hope' (2022, p.32). The author outlines the psychological consequences of the encroaching climate crisis for people in Western, industrialised countries, most of whom are still relatively unaffected by extreme weather events:

> The assumptions that we could undertake years of study to achieve a qualification, confidently commit to decades of paying a mortgage to buy a house and raise a child in a stable environment have been severely shaken. A different mindset is developing and it is one beset by pessimism. (Watkins, 2022, p.32)

Cli-fi and psychoanalysis

> The central concern of psychoanalysis has been with the question of how to live – or, more precisely, how to live without excessive mental pain or catastrophe to the self or others. (Rustin & Rustin, 2002, p.5)

Facts and figures are undeniably important. But scientific papers, however well written, cannot engender the same sense of emotional connection as a good story. Psychoanalysis, the original 'talking cure', reaches for words with which to weave a skin around experiences people bring to therapy, moving what was previously 'unthinkable' – exiled from consciousness by stringent defences – to something 'thinkable', something storied into a narrative and available to be thought through (Plotnitsky, 2014).

Cli-fi – a term coined in 2007 by journalist and literary theorist, Dan Bloom (Liggett, 2018) – offers a parallel opportunity in the world outside the consulting room, providing possible models of '*how to live without excessive mental pain or catastrophe to the self or others*' (Rustin & Rustin, 2002) while staying present to the changes and challenges associated with the climate and ecological crises. By a process of imaginative identification, we have the opportunity to experience the circumstances in which characters in a novel or film find themselves. We share their fears, dilemmas, triumphs and setbacks. We are offered a 'practice run' of events that, if encountered in reality and without preparation, would almost certainly precipitate us into a traumatised 'fight, flight or freeze' state of mind. Marie Cardinal (1984) wrote a book about her experiences in psychoanalysis and chose as the title, *The Words to Say It*. In fiction too, we are offered the words to say it, words to articulate what we are thinking and feeling, to come to know more clearly who we are, what we believe and where we stand.

Cli-fi is a fast-expanding genre. Over the last ten years, there has been a proliferation of cli-fi novels and films. (For readers unfamiliar with the genre, a list published in *The Guardian* (Armitstead, 2021) offers a good starting point.) Contributions range from post-apocalyptic writing, portraying a future where civilisation has collapsed, to stories set in a relatively familiar landscape, either in the present or in an altered but readily-imaginable near future. Novels set in the global south, often in the present day, have recently grown in strength and number, adding important narratives of the differentiated impact of climate change from across the globe.

Research suggests that the more books of fiction people read, the more sophisticated is the reader's theory of mind and, consequently, their ability to remain present to and empathise with the experiences of others (Oatley, 2016). Novels prompt us to put ourselves in the position of others and consider certain questions: Why does this character behave in the way they do? How would I feel in their situation? What would I do? What obstacles would stand in my way? How might I overcome them? In the case of those cli-fi novels set in the present or near future, these questions come to the fore in the context of imminent climate and ecological collapse. The hope is that, in a situation where many of us find ourselves struggling with despair or immobilised by uncertainty and anxiety, we may nevertheless find a way to remain engaged.

Denial and disavowal

In the Climate Psychology Alliance,[2] a group with which I am actively involved, we have noted a qualitative shift in defences against the reality of encroaching climate catastrophe. Where once the primary defence on display was denial – nothing different is happening; there have always been climate fluctuations – the most prevalent defence now is disavowal – climate change is real but it's not a crisis, science is scaremongering, we still have time, technological solutions will be found. An aggressive edge comes to light when these defences are challenged, whether by other people or by the climate itself. For example, during the 2022 UK heatwave, at a time when the Meteorological Office was advising people to stay inside, MP John Hayes, a member of the UK Conservative party, branded those taking precautions as 'heatwave snowflakes', 'cowards' and 'everything that is wrong with modern Britain' (Stone, 2022).

Psychoanalysis has from the start concerned itself with the question of defences, their function and the price tag attached when they take over and run the show. In her book *Sent Before My Time*, psychoanalyst and moral philosopher Margaret Cohen (2003) offers an eloquent account of disavowal as she reflects on her work as a psychotherapist in a neonatal intensive care unit. The context is, of course, very different to that of the climate crisis but the two are linked by experiences of pain, fear, guilt and loss. In both situations, survival itself is at risk. Cohen pays close attention to the defences that are activated, reflecting on her own responses and those of others. She describes her efforts to observe a very premature baby, 'Ewan', who develops meningitis and starts fitting:

2. www.climatepsychologyalliance.org

> I observed for a few more minutes, then could not bear it any more. I looked
> around the unit, taking time off. (p.13)

Ewan's parents are told he will probably be blind and at this point his mother says that she 'cannot bear to look at him'. As everyone succumbs to the overwhelming urge to look away, Ewan is left to struggle alone in his pain and helplessness.

Cohen discusses how the effort *not* to look away, to try and imagine and articulate Ewan's experience, militates against our natural desire to protect ourselves from mental pain. It is easier by far to become busy and distract oneself with some other activity. And yet to look away, to cease to bear witness, is to lose integrity, to move into a 'rubbery, indifferent or cruel state of mind where these things do not matter – they simply have no meaning' (Cohen, 2003, p.63).

Psychoanalyst Sally Weintrobe (2021) takes the discussion into the political arena, arguing convincingly that 'cultures of uncare' are actively encouraged by the current neoliberal political system – a system that shamelessly models disregard for and exploitation of others. On the other side, there are resilient 'cultures of care', such as the culture of the UK National Health Service. Psychoanalyst Melanie Klein (1952) placed the conflict between creative and destructive parts of the self at the centre of her work. There is, of course, ample evidence of destructiveness, but this is far from the whole story. Graham Music (2014) cites evidence showing that the desire to help others and the pleasure we take in doing so are part of our make-up from the earliest years of life. The cultures of care that have survived and thrived in the unpromising context of neoliberalism are evidence of the resilience of this lively and life-oriented part of the self.

To return to the question of resisting the pull towards indifference and disaffection, making common cause with others is widely recognised as a source of strength and support. In what follows, I hope to show that climate and ecological fiction can also serve as a resource. I have chosen two climate fiction novels for detailed analysis: *Weather* by Jenny Offill (2020), set in the present day, and *The High House* by Jessie Greengrass (2021), set in the near future.

Weather by Jenny Offill

Weather is a first-person narrative in a series of anecdotal passages by 'Lizzie', whose character is established by way of her interactions with customers at the university library, where she works, and with her husband Ben, her son Eli, and her troubled brother, Henry. The 'weather' in question is not for the most part the literal kind – sunshine, wind and rain – but the weather of everyday life, of work and relationships. Lizzie emerges as tolerant, patient and compassionate. We get to know her as she lends an ear to the troubled and sometimes bizarre stories told by library users and responds with advice, often accompanied by a joke. We follow her as she lets people off library fines, pretending that there are none to be paid; as she rescues a trapped wasp; as she helps her small son negotiate the scary terrain of the school playground, and as she supports her neurotic, barely coping – and later not coping at all – brother.

The story develops as Lizzie begins to work for Sylvia, a climate and environmental campaigner who was previously her doctorate tutor. Sylvia produces a podcast, 'Hell and High Water', and is much in demand as a conference speaker. The climate crisis becomes the book's dominant theme, explored by way of comments and questions emerging at conferences, Lizzie's silent reflections, and her conversations with Sylvia:

> [Lizzie] I try to reach Sylvia as I wait for the bell.
> 'I have to call you back,' she says. 'I'm about to send off this article, but I have to come up with the obligatory note of hope.' (Offill, 2020, p.67)

This passage calls to mind a time when I ran a support group for climate scientists at a leading London research institute. The group members spoke of the burden not only of knowing how bad things really were but also of having to inject an upbeat note into their communications, whether in conversations with non-scientist friends or in media interviews. This enforced double-speak left them feeling isolated and in bad faith. Behind the strictures imposed upon these scientists – and, indeed, upon us all – is the view that hope – the kind of hope that relates to putting things right in the external world – is always positive. According to this narrative, anxiety and dread push in on us and force us into retreat. Hope, on the other hand, is associated with courage and positive action. This widely shared perspective can keep us from seeing the shadow side of a certain kind of hope – the tyranny of the message to remain upbeat at all costs and the toll it takes on our fragile hearts.

Psychoanalysis offers an alternative perspective, one that acknowledges the need to remain present to and grieve our losses. In *Mourning and Melancholia* (1915), Freud argued that failure to mourn sets the scene for 'melancholia' – or, as we would say today, 'depression'. We are in sore need of spaces and places to grieve our losses – the animals and insects struggling to survive or already extinct, the chemicals polluting our rivers and poisoning our fish, the plastic clogging our seas, and not least, the loss of a future where we could reasonably imagine that things will get better rather than worse. Climate fiction opens up a much-needed psychic space for sadness, regret and mourning.

One of the most powerful passages in *Weather* calls to mind Maggie Cohen's (2003) writing on the loss of integrity involved in 'looking away' from baby Ewan's damage and distress. It articulates the hope that we will, at times of crisis, find the courage to bear witness to suffering; that we will retain our humanity by resisting the urge to look away. It is addressed by Sylvia to a conference audience:

> 'What it means to be a good person, a moral person, is calculated differently in times of crisis than in ordinary circumstances,' she says. She pulls up a slide of people having a picnic by a lake... 'Suppose you go with some friends to the park to have a picnic. This act is, of course, morally neutral, but if you witness a group of children drowning in a lake and you continue to eat and chat, you have become monstrous.' (Offill, 2020, p.21)

Many of us who take to the streets to demonstrate with Extinction Rebellion do so in the spirit of not becoming 'monstrous', of not standing quietly by while further damage is inflicted and children are already drowning.

Humour is often in short supply in climate fiction, not surprisingly in light of the subject matter. *Weather* is a welcome exception. We are presented with a character, Lizzie, who is able to maintain an ironic sense of humour, not only at home and in her work at the library but also as she accompanies Sylvia to conferences:

> One thing I'll say about it: lots of people who are not Native Americans are talking about Native Americans. (p.51)

> One thing that's becoming clear on our travels: people are really sick of being lectured to about the glaciers. 'Listen, I've heard all about that,' says this red-faced man. 'But what's going to happen to the American weather?' (pp.72–73)

The election of Donald Trump halfway through *Weather* significantly darkens the mood:

> 'It's going to be too much,' Sylvia said. 'People who do this kind of work will break down, people will get sick and die…' (p.115)

Lizzie begins to fantasise about escaping from the ominous threats on the horizon. She talks to Ben about getting a gun, buying land somewhere cooler (with money they don't have) and developing survival skills. As Lizzie succumbs to disavowal, Sylvia responds with a stringent reality check (Freud, 1911):

> 'Do you really think you can protect them? In 2047?' Sylvia asks. I look at her. Because until this moment I did, I did somehow think this. She orders another drink. 'Then become rich, very, very rich,' she says in a tight voice. (Offill, 2020, p.127)

Disillusioned and yet unable to fully take Sylvia's words on board, Lizzie becomes unsure of how to be or what to do: 'I distract myself by staying up late, Googling prepper things' (p.147). She takes a break from inner turmoil by watching mindless TV – including a so-called reality show, *Extreme Couponing*. It is her self-deprecating brand of humour that signals a return to actual reality:

> Then one day I have to run to catch a bus. I am so out of breath when I get there that I know in a flash all my preparations for the apocalypse are doomed. I will die early and ignobly. (p.187)

Over time, Lizzie's brother's mental health worsens, and his partner throws him out. He moves in with Lizzie and Ben, sleeping on their couch. Lizzie's tolerance of her brother's frailties, her refusal to judge, her loyalty and lightness of touch are among the elements of the book that express the beauty and poetry present in everyday life. Holding onto the thread of living, regardless of what the future holds, is shown to be inherently meaningful, a stance of hope of a particular kind.

As the book draws to an end, there is a sense of growing disarray. The narrative becomes more fragmented. The talk of prepping fizzles out. Lizzie and Ben focus on getting dental work done and their moles checked as the only kind of preparation that comes to mind. Circling back to Lizzie's relationship to Sylvia and her tireless campaigning, the book concludes with a coda from a website, Obligatory Note of Hope,[3] referring to the value of making common cause with others, not so much in the hope of turning things round as in the spirit of doing what is right for its own sake and finding sustenance in the resolve of others:

> Slowly, I began to see collective action as the antidote to my dithering and despair. There's a way in for everyone. Aren't you tired of all this fear and dread?

The High House by Jessie Greengrass

Whereas *Weather* is a novel of present-day observations and reflections, *The High House* has a narrative extending over two generations. Published in 2021, the novel has been well received and was shortlisted for a major literary award. It is an example of a 'back to nature', 'survival' story, depicting how the 'prepper' situation – characterised in *Weather* as nothing more than a comforting fantasy – might look in reality. In a book rich in reflections, many of the themes that emerge overlap with those central to psychoanalytic enquiry. These include the nature of attachment, questions of need and dependency, and the meaning of individual survival in the absence of community.

The story plays out in England, in a watery coastal location reminiscent of the East Anglian coast. It is narrated in alternating sections by Sally, Caro and Pauly. The story begins with Caro, her father – an academic – and her stepmother, Francesca – a climate scientist – living together close to the coast. (We are given no information about Caro's absent birth mother.)

> [Caro] This was when it was still the beginning of things, when we were still uncertain, and it was possible to believe that nothing whatever was wrong, bar an unusual run of hot Julys and January storms. (Greengrass, 2021, p.11)

Francesca, who understands only too well the difficulties that lie ahead, is often irascible and seemingly unable to empathise with those who have not yet fully faced the reality:

> How can they stand to enjoy it, this weather … They act as though it's a myth to frighten them, instead of the imminently coming end of our fucking planet. (p.11)

In an interesting comment on disavowal, Caro reflects that Francesca:

> … didn't have the habit the rest of us were learning of having our minds in two places at once, of seeing two futures. (p.11)

In climate psychology discussions, we sometimes reflect on the ways in which we

---

3. www.obligatorynoteofhope.com

likewise manage the situation by 'being in two places at once', moving by turns from facing and thinking about the frightening reality to setting those thoughts and feelings aside and losing ourselves in other activities and concerns.

The High House, left to Francesca by an uncle, is the family's holiday home. Significantly, it is in a remote spot, out of sight of the nearby village, close to the mouth of a river and looking out onto marshland that stretches down to the sea. When Caro is 14, Francesca gives birth to Caro's half-brother, Pauly. When Pauly is six months old, in the context of worsening climate emergencies, Francesca and Caro's father decide to return to full-time campaigning. They leave the family home quite suddenly, abandoning Pauly to Caro's care. We witness Pauly's searing distress at his mother's abrupt disappearance:

> That night, Pauly wouldn't sleep. He stood at his bedroom door, his face wet
> with tears and sweat, and howled as though he were in pain. (p.26)

One of the strengths of *The High House* is the author's ability to represent complex and mixed states of mind. Caro, on the one hand, resents being left to care for Pauly, and on the other delights in him and his adoption of her as his primary attachment figure. The net result of these conflicting emotions is a kind of *Schadenfreude* – a guilty pleasure in the distress of others. When Francesca returns for a break from campaigning, Pauly rejects her:

> I heard Francesca's hissed intake of breath. I heard her pause, turn, walk
> away, and I felt a sudden spasm of guilt. How warm Pauly was in my lap, how
> comfortable, how soft, and how it must have hurt Francesca then to be in the
> next room alone, and to have the truth confirmed: that it wasn't that Pauly didn't
> talk at all, but only that he didn't talk to her. (p.28)

A recurrent question in the text concerns the morality or immorality of Francesca's decision: '... that she should place the hypothetical, general needs of a population above the real and specific ones of her family' (p.26). Caro is unable to arrive at any lasting conclusion:

> This is the absurdity of it – that I couldn't forgive Francesca because she chose
> the world over Pauly, and now I can't forgive myself because I didn't. (pp.42–43)

Unbeknown to Caro, Francesca and her father's absences are not only for the purpose of campaigning but also to prepare the High House for Caro and Pauly to retreat to in the face of the inevitable future flooding of the area. In the village, Francesca befriends 'Grandy' and his grand-daughter Sally and shows them the supply of items she has stockpiled in the High House barn – row upon row of tinned food, boxed-up clothing and medical supplies, including a supply of morphine. Subsequently, Grandy has a fall while Sally is away at university. Francesca persuades Sally to return and move with Grandy into the High House, where they will look after the house and tend the vegetable garden as paid retainers.

Three or four years on, in a dramatic development, Caro's father calls her from the east coast of America, where he and Francesca are attending a conference, to tell Caro to take Pauly immediately to the High House. Leaving the train at the end of the line, Caro goes into the village pub and learns from the television news that a storm has 'ripped open' the hotel where Francesca and her father were staying and that they are both feared dead. Hours later and completely exhausted, she arrives at the High House carrying Pauly on her back. Sally and Grandy are there to greet her and the two narrative strands converge.

For a long time, Sally and Caro have a difficult relationship. Caro rages against her abandonment; Sally resents Caro's intrusion and is envious of her close relationship with Pauly. 'Grandy' is consistently kind and compassionate, a steady figure who consistently offers containment (Bion, 1962) when emotions run high. The dynamic changes as Pauly grows up and no longer needs to be looked after. Caro becomes both physically and mentally fragile. Her skin reddens and cracks, she suffers from chilblains that must not be allowed to become infected, she has frequent headaches and is unable to sleep. We are given to understand that her early experiences of abandonment and bereavement, along with being prematurely catapulted into a parenting role, have taken their toll. Sally softens towards Caro and, together with Pauly, cares for her, both physically and emotionally. Both women struggle with survivor guilt, which emerges and re-emerges in different contexts and remains unresolved:

> [Caro] What option is there, in the end, for the few of us who have survived but to be the unforgiveable, and the unforgiven? All those who might have lived instead of us are gone, or they are starving, while we stay on here at the High House, pulling potatoes from the soft earth. (Greengrass, 2021, p.43)

> [Sally] 'We should have done something. … We should have tried.'

> 'Tried what?' asked Grandy, and I knew he was right, but still it didn't rinse us clean from blame. (p.83)

The High House is a book in which the climate and ecological crises are recognised as being closely intertwined, symptoms of the wider malaise of seeing ourselves as separate from and superior to the rest of nature. One of its strengths resides in its lyrical descriptions of the marsh and the creatures that inhabit it. Pauly spends much of his childhood out on the marsh, falling under the spell of the wide watery landscape and in close communion with its fellow occupants:

> I remember the birds, and how it seemed to me that we hovered on the edge of understanding, and that they were only waiting for me to be still enough before they would come close to me and speak. (p.183)

We are also invited to vicariously experience the pleasures of growing and harvesting food. This is an area where Grandy's many decades of caring for the land come into their own, while the young people delight in their increasing skill and understanding.

The work is shown to be hard and often repetitive, yet we also come understand the rewards of a life lived close to the land.

Time passes and floods engulf the nearby village and, in all probability, other places along the coast. There is no external source of news, but Caro and Sally see increasing numbers of people passing by in the distance in search of sustenance and shelter. They are faced with a conundrum. They know they should take people in, but they cannot feed and house them all, and giving away their location would threaten their survival. As the novel draws to a close, the theme of isolation comes to the fore. Grandy dies, leaving just the three of them. Caro reflects on the nature of their reprieve:

> We are only here because Francesca couldn't bear the thought of Pauly drowning, but the High House isn't an ark. We aren't really saved. We are only the last ones, waiting. (p.276)

The final word is given to Pauly, as he ponders the probability of being the last of the group to die:

> I think it will feel very cold. I think it will feel very empty... The last of us will not be buried. The last will lie here forever, in the High House, which is our sanctuary and will be our grave. (p.277)

We are left to ponder the meaning of survival in isolation, with no succession in sight. As Chasseguet-Smirgel (1990) wrote: 'One comes to see that it is not so much the nature of the act that counts but its meaning.'

Reflections

Situations arise where refusing to take on board the reality of change and act accordingly becomes a matter of life or death, as is now the case in relation to the current climate and ecological crisis. Stephen Grosz (2013) describes how, in the 9/11 attack on the World Trade Center in New York, many people in the South Tower ignored the fire alarms and what they had just seen happen in the North Tower. They continued talking on the phone, or stood around waiting to see what others would do. Some of them went into meetings. They could have made it out if they had acted immediately. Instead, they perished in the fire. Grosz comments:

> We are vehemently faithful to our own view of the world, our story. We want to know what new story we're stepping into before we exit the old one. We hesitate in the face of change because change is loss. (Grosz, 2013, p.123)

Our fear of change, our reluctance to leave the comfort of the familiar, together with the strong urge to look away from distressing and threatening situations, lie behind the defence of disavowal, where the reality is not so much denied as accepted but kept out of mind. In our identification with Lizzie, Sylvia, Francesca, Sally, Caro, Pauly and Grandy, we may each hope to find inspiration in our struggle to remain engaged and to bear witness.

References

Armitstead, C. (2021, June 26). Stories to save the world – the new wave of climate fiction. *The Guardian.* www.theguardian.com/books/2021/jun/26/stories-to-save-the-world-the-new-wave-of-climate-fiction

Berry, W. (1990). *What are people for? Essays.* North Point Press.

Bion, W. (1962). *Learning from experience.* Heinemann.

Cardinal, M. (1984). *The words to say it.* Macmillan.

Chasseguet-Smirgel, J. (1990). On acting out. *International Journal of Psychoanalysis, 71,* 77–86.

Cohen, M. (2003). *Sent before my time.* Karnac.

Freud S. (1911). Formulations on the two principles of mental functioning. In J. Strachey (Ed.), *The standard edition of the complete psychological works of Sigmund Freud, Vol. X11* (pp. 218–226). Hogarth Press.

Freud, S. (1915). Mourning and melancholia. In J. Strachey (Ed.), *The standard edition of the complete psychological works of Sigmund Freud, Vol. XIV* (pp.239–258). Hogarth Press.

Greengrass, J. (2021). *The High House.* Swift Press.

Grosz, S. (2013). *The examined life.* Chatto & Windus.

IPCC. (2022). *Sixth assessment report.* IPCC. www.ipcc.ch/assessment-report/ar6

Klein, M. (1952). *Envy and gratitude.* Hogarth.

Liggett, W.A. (2018, December 11). *Dan Bloom interview: Creator of 'cli-fi'.* [Blog.] https://williamliggett.com/2018/12/11/dan-bloom-interview-creator-of-cli-fi/

Music, G. (2014). *The good life: Wellbeing and the new science of altruism, selfishness and immorality.* Routledge.

Oatley, K. (2016). Fiction: Simulation of social worlds. *Trends in Cognitive Science,* 20, 618–628.

Offill, J. (2020). *Weather.* Granta Books.

Plotnitsky, A. (2014). The thinkable and the unthinkable in psychoanalysis and philosophy: From Sophocles to Freud to Derrida. *The Undecidable Unconscious: A journal of deconstruction and psychoanalysis,* 1, 53–84.

Rustin, M. & Rustin, M. (2002). *Mirror to nature.* Karnac.

Stone, J. (2022, July 15). Tory MP says 'cowards' taking precautions in heatwave are 'snowflakes' and everything wrong with Britain. *The Independent.* www.independent.co.uk/news/uk/politics/john-hayes-heatwave-snowflakes-cowards-b2124023.html

Watkins, D. (2022, April 13). Global catastrophes also threaten to destroy hope. Letters. *New Scientist,* p.32.

Weintrobe, S. (2021) *The psychological roots of the climate crisis: neoliberal exceptionalism and the culture of uncare.* Bloomsbury.

Breaking the silence: An integrative psychotherapy model for working with eco-anxiety

11

Pedro Oliveira

At a point when we absolutely need the psychotherapeutic professions to come together regarding climate-based mental health concerns and climate-oriented action, denial within the profession and ideological differences about our preferred therapeutic models can still block us from attending to our clients' needs in relation to climate and ecological crisis. Here I present, with the generous permission of and my gratitude to its subject, a case study to illustrate how I work with eco-anxiety by drawing from a range of different therapy models to best address climate-based concerns in the therapy room.

Silence, responsibility and conflict-based symptom formation

Sandra covers her face with her hands as she looks at me from the screen. Our Zoom session has just begun and I am unsure whether she is expressing shame or something else. I offer a comment, trying to acknowledge her body language. I tell Sandra that today she seems to be covering her face a lot while talking to me. I ask her if she is aware of that gesture of protection. I wonder what it might be saying about her current emotional state. Sandra is, in her own words, protecting herself from the world and also protecting herself from me, as part of the world that connects her to the climate crisis. After nearly seven months of meeting her weekly to offer therapy, I have now become deeply attuned to Sandra's emotional states around the crisis.

Sandra is someone who is in touch both with the deep point of suffering of today's world and the climate and ecological emergency running through it, and with the imagination of the future of this world as the crisis deepens. As a short cut, she is having the (entirely appropriate) reaction to the crisis that is today called 'eco-distress' or 'eco-anxiety' (Royal College of Psychiatrists, 2021). Like anyone who lets anxiety about our ecological present and future descend from their mind to their body (i.e. give themselves permission to experience these feelings somatically), Sandra occasionally moves between anxiety *per se*, in its most common presentations, to other emotions, such as anger, guilt, grief and despair.

Another way of framing it is that Sandra is failing to stay successfully with 'disavowal' as a defence (Hoggett, 2022; Weintrobe, 2021); her bodily consciousness is being disobedient by simply refusing to conform and disconnect from the crisis. It is as if the part of her mind that wants to know and feel where we truly are in relation to the crisis is rebelling and beginning to dominate the part of her mind that bows to social conformity and is trying not to acknowledge the reality of where we are. While this happens, Sandra is becoming less and less able to comply with the set of complex social rules encouraging us to stay quiet about the crisis, particularly in our interpersonal relationships. Paradoxically, it is precisely this incapacity to conform that makes her reaction 'normal' and appropriate. She is, literally and metaphorically, failing to repress it. And, paradoxically, there is hope in that failure, for Sandra and for everyone else. It carries the potential of becoming what the renowned Buddhist, activist and ecologist Joanna Macy refers to as 'active hope' (Macy & Johnstone, 2012; see also Chapter 9 of this book).

While images of the climate and ecological emergency are all around us these days, engaging in an in-depth conversation about it among circles of families and friends still carries an element of taboo. Conversations around the topic are not always easy to start or maintain within one's close circle (Leiserowitz et al., 2021). An interpretation linking compassion and anxiety suggests that Sandra is awakening to a desire to care for the world more, or to care for the world differently (Hickman, 2020). Simultaneously, from an existential stance, we can think of Sandra's current position in the world as someone struggling with responsibility avoidance (Yalom, 1980). Inside of her, there is a conflict between trying to step up to a sense of responsibility for the world she belongs to, while another part is wondering if it's still possible to stay oblivious to it all. Conflicting feelings of this sort often give rise to a sense of impotence and paralysis towards the triggering crisis (Lertzman, 2015). As the part of her mind that wants to know seems to have more power than the part that wants to hide behind its defences, Sandra often finds that her body is in flight or fight mode. Stuck in the paralysis that generally follows responsibility avoidance, and aware that this is not just about her future but about the future of her child too, Sandra is drenched in guilt.

Individual and social awareness, even when disconnected, are intrinsically linked. As Sandra unravels, she becomes, on a micro-scale, a metaphor for society – for what the cognitive anthropologist Eviatar Zerubavel has called 'socially constructed silence' (2006). For Zerubavel, imposing silence around a topic or topics is never a solitary act. Denial begets co-denial; there is always more than one person involved in the act of silencing. We only need one person to speak up to break the silence, but several are involved in maintaining it. Over time, silence shapes not only what we talk about but also what we are able to perceive. Perception and language become symbiotic. Conversely, what we are able to talk about within our group of intimates in turn influences what we can perceive. Unravelling in the face of social silence on a sensitive topic, such as the climate crisis, is not substantially different from the unravelling happening inside Sandra. Different parts of her mind are trying to break through the silence and her body is becoming an ally to the part wanting to speak out.

Social silence and taboo tend to walk together. Silence in intimate relations around a taboo topic, uncomfortable as it feels, dangerous as it is at this point, is a consciously negotiated endeavour. As Zerubavel mentions, silence can function as meta-silence; human groups can impose a silence without explicitly agreeing to do so. One of the key points when working with Sandra, and others with the same clinical presentation, therefore involves helping her map her network of relationships to show where silence around the crisis is happening (who is silent?) and how it is happening (how are they silencing what is really going on with the world's climate?). My second line involves helping Sandra make sense of her defences, emotions and associated cognitions around the crisis. This involves helping her to listen autonomously to her emotions and thoughts about the crisis and note their fluctuations on any given day. And last, we need to attend specifically to her feelings of guilt, paralysis and impotence, and help her articulate how she wants to be in relation to this crisis: who can she be and how can she act at this specific point in her life?

If I am to bring all the threads together, it would be hard to stay with one therapeutic model; an integrative approach is needed. Psychoanalysis is needed for helping Sandra to map her defences around the crisis, exploring and understanding her emotions at both conscious and unconscious levels. Alongside, a Gestalt approach also contributes to a psychoanalytical integration in a multidisciplinary therapy frame (Bednarek, 2019). Systemic psychotherapy is useful in helping the client make sense of their relationship network and how that network is operating a socially constructed silence. Finally, third-wave cognitive models like acceptance and commitment therapy (ACT) are useful in helping the client go beyond their emotional avoidance and define who they want to be in relation to the crisis.

But at this point in time, as a profession, integrating different models in response to the climate and ecological emergency is not what we psychotherapists offer – inside the therapy room, for the most part, silence is still speaking louder than words.

When it comes to silence around the crisis, the interplay between the individual and society is not substantially different from what happens in the therapy room. Opening the topic of the climate crisis in the therapy room and working with it consistently over the course of the therapy raises complex doubts and dilemmas for the therapist, which suggests a need for further training for the profession (Silva & Coburn, 2022). Without such training, the therapist's difficulty in creating space for their own powerful feelings concerning climate crisis can lead to a disconnection between therapist and client. Clues to the client's eco-anxiety may simply not be named and acknowledged for what they are (Macagnino, 2022). Adopting anthropological language and evoking Latour, by not having worked through their own feelings around the crisis, the therapist themself can take up a position of someone who perpetuates silence in the therapy room, in order not to create social disruption: in other words, the therapist themself can become a 'quietist' (Latour & Porter, 2017).

Sandra is, of course, one of the brave ones. She has started therapy with the explicit request to explore her anxiety around climate-related issues. Where Sandra sees fear, guilt and anxiety, I see courage trying to emerge. Sandra is already familiar with the term 'eco-anxiety' and broadly what is meant by it. She is setting herself the difficult task of creating a space for the myriad feelings contained in this notion to flow in and be felt, but there is an internal conflict going on. By doing this, she is going beyond dealing with the climate crisis as a rational construct; she is letting the reality of it sink right through her, down to bodily level. Coming to therapy is about dealing with the dread of what both her body and the part of her that wishes to connect with reality are trying to say at this point. Conflict then ensues; it is as if 'society', also contained inside her, is trying to shut her up.

Client types: Challenging absolutes

As someone who is awakening to the crisis, Sandra is different from most other kinds of clients and how they respond to the climate crisis in the therapy room. Not all clients require an integration of different models, simply because not all clients have managed to bring themselves to the place of truth and vulnerability that Sandra is trying to reach. In my clinical work so far, the resulting constellation of emotions suggests a typology. There is the apathetic client who simply does not want to relate to the crisis, inside or outside the therapy room. In them, apathy and fatalism sometimes co-exist. The belief that humans are done for and that it is too late for any kind of meaningful action leaves the client in a protective cocoon, defended against uncertainty. Occasionally, this client takes refuge in the problems of interpersonal relations, as if such problems are somehow unaffected by our failing ecosystems. This nihilism stemming from a fatalist position towards climate and society is unlikely to be challenged by the quietist therapist. Alternatively, they may focus exclusively on an expressed sense of nihilism in interpersonal relations and leave the topic of climate crisis unexamined, thereby colluding with the client's defensive behaviour. By contrast, the climate-aware therapist can suggest a link between the nihilism expressed by the client towards interpersonal relations and their nihilism around the climate crisis, taking the client into a space where they can decide to accept or refuse the invitation to consider how much of their experience is conflating the climate crisis with the interpersonal.

Other clients may drop hints about climate anxiety while conveying a sense of ambivalence about discussing the topic. Possibly they may simply not know if the climate crisis is a topic that can be discussed in a therapy session (Macagnino, 2022), or they may be using the therapist as a continuation of their internal repressive processes. In the latter case, the therapist becomes analogous to a consciousness that fleetingly registers the evolving danger of the crisis without truly facing it – an extension of not-knowing. From a psychoanalytical perspective and borrowing from Wilfred Bion (1962), the therapist who does not respond, validate and acknowledge these anxiety cues in the repressive client is leaving out 'selective facts' that could otherwise bring together different aspects of the client's experience.

Another typical client I see emerging from my clinical work is the sacrificial type, often found in activists. Sacrificial dispositions have been mapped out in therapy models such as schema therapy (Young et al., 2003). In climate psychology, as well, activists have been a subject of both theoretical concern (Hoggett & Randall, 2018) and applied mental health work, developed by groups such as the Climate Psychology Alliance (CPA). In relation to the climate crisis, the sacrificial disposition involves a neglect of one's personal needs in the service of climate-crisis activism and involvement in protest organisations. Despite the welcome emphasis on self-development and personal and spiritual care in movements such as Extinction Rebellion, which can be seen in their regenerative practices towards mental health and wellbeing (Harms, 2021), climate activism – like most activism – can still lead to burnout. In this situation, external and internal factors coalesce. People in activist organisations often feel they must keep going, seeing what they do in terms of a higher mission. Set against the urgency of the crisis, self-care is relegated to a lower priority or regarded as some kind of privilege or self-indulgence (Conner et al., 2021). Working with activist clients individually, therefore, is not about mapping the social silence around the climate crisis but about mapping the social silence around wellbeing, mental health and self-care, especially where these aspects are not prioritised in the culture of the activist organisation. Schema-oriented work around sacrificial schemas can be particularly useful here, and more so if, in their own developmental history, in the systemic game of their family relations, the activist has previously occupied a self-sacrificial role. Equally, systemic therapy may have an important role in families where the parental subsystem is enacting the apathetic and/ or repressive roles and the activist is isolated with their concerns. Both in family therapy and individual therapy, where the therapist has started their emotional work around the crisis, therapist self-disclosure regarding the climate crisis can be an important ally to the client.

In the therapy room, both with the individual and with the family, therapist self-disclosure can open a gateway through their defences. The therapist may model a *both-and* strategy in which feelings of distress about the crisis co-exist with other kinds of less threatening feelings about the world and interpersonal relations. The therapist can position themself as somebody who is *both* worried about the crisis *and still* able to engage meaningfully with the current world. What is being modelled here is the capacity to simultaneously hold an awareness of the crisis without letting it take over the whole of one's emotional life. It may be particularly helpful for clients who are too afraid to experience sadness about the crisis for fear of drowning in paralysing grief. Noting hints of climate anxiety expressed by the client in the session, the therapist can also acknowledge them and check with the client if they would like to open up the topic, thereby validating the therapeutic setting as one where climate-crisis talk is possible. Through this, the therapist is inviting the client to co-hold the existential responsibility of opening up the topic.

Last, with the client who has dropped various hints about climate anxiety in several sessions, the therapist may trace bridges between the disparate remarks, with a view to helping the client clarify their narrative, feelings and beliefs about it. Here, the view is substantially different from Bion's 'no memory, no desire' (1962). As we face the greatest threat known to humankind, the work is also about getting people to mobilise, to break out of paralysis, for the sake both of their own mental health and that of the world around them. This necessary movement from paralysis to action means that therapeutic models mostly structured around insight, contemplation and understanding, although fundamental, are insufficient, given the urgency of our situation.

For clients like Sandra, people whom I call 'awakeners', the first work of contemplation is to help the client map their own defences towards the crisis. In the face of the threat of annihilation of all humankind, it is unlikely that either of the two people in the therapy room, therapist or client, have shed most of their climate and ecological crisis defences. The work here is to explore which defences the client desperately needs in order to maintain some sense of stability and sanity and which ones they are willing and able to release at this point. Such explorations are possible provided the therapist themself is educated about the different forms such defences can take and has mapped their own climate and ecological crisis defences.

The 'ultimate saviour' – someone or something that pushes away the threat of death and annihilation – is a common constellation of phantasies explored in existential psychotherapy with clients facing near-death experiences (Yalom, 1980). As the world gets more and more populated with images of natural catastrophes and writings on the existential threat that humankind faces, ideas about the capacity of human scientific knowledge to keep the world in a state of business-as-usual abound. The client may already have realised the limits of science in the face of the size of the crisis, and that realisation will have generated further anxiety, which must then be contained by other defences. So, in trying to substitute for a defence that is now failing, the client may have increased their splitting defences in another direction – for instance, by rigidly dividing human beings into 'good people' and 'bad people' with respect to the climate crisis. In short, the softening of certain defences is likely to involve the hardening of others.

This is the case with Sandra. As we work with her feelings of isolation, we explore where her sifting and splitting of people into 'good' and 'bad' originates from. Together, we identify that the splitting also stems from her experience of the Covid-19 pandemic and feelings of distrust around other human beings and the possibility of catching or transmitting the disease. In this case, instead of seeking to change the rearrangement of her defence map, the work becomes to get her to notice where she stands at this point in time. Paul Hoggett's comprehensive listing of climate and ecological crisis defences is invaluable here (Hoggett, 2022).

In my work with Sandra, I try not to assume what the crisis means for her. I know that she is the mother of a young child. At the beginning of therapy, I put a fair amount of care into my first attempts to explore her views around the future of her child. As Sandra talks about her feelings around the climate crisis, I search for what is most meaningful to her. What is Sandra concerned about? The loss of biodiversity? Climate justice? The future of her child? All of these? How does she think the crisis will impact her and others around her? More importantly, is it possible that her core beliefs about the crisis and the feelings associated with them are subject to fluctuations? Are they influenced by external events (such as the approaching summer, likely days of severe heat and possibilities of wildfires)? Are they influenced by habits and behaviours (such as watching the news versus not watching the news)?

The goal at this point is twofold: learning about Sandra's beliefs about the crisis and increasing her awareness of situational triggers and shifts and fluctuations in her feelings. With paralysis being so common among people in the early stages of embracing and creating internal space for eco-anxiety, learning to notice fluctuations is about learning to see that there are shifts, even where paralysis creates an illusion of an immovable, all-occupying terror. By bringing these oscillations in how they feel into their awareness, it becomes possible then to be more specific and to ask the client what action may be possible for them on a given day or week and point out that they are not in fact stuck in a binary of acting versus not-acting absolutes: there are windows where it is possible to act, to do. Increasing the awareness of these fluctuations is also fundamental to practising *both-and* statements. The gargantuan dimension of the climate crisis easily leads one to feel that all emotional space has been occupied and there is no room for anything else except dread, terror or uncontrollable anxiety. Mindfulness, in its applications to the psychology of depression and anxiety, is particularly useful here (Segal et al., 2002). By teaching the client some basic techniques of breathing and meditation, it becomes possible to invite them to increase their awareness of the peaks of anxiety and/or despair while simultaneously creating space for other feelings.

For clients like Sandra who are bringing up a child in a less than stable world, the climate crisis makes it hard to stay present with one's child in the everyday business of daily life. Alongside, there may be guilt or a self-punishing comparison with parents who just don't seem to be bothered about the climate crisis, or not to feel it as much or with the same intensity. For Sally Weintrobe, the 'culture of uncare' surrounding the climate and ecological crisis, and the neoliberal beliefs whence it derives, is characterised by a sense of exceptionalism (2021). Exceptionalism is the belief that you are somehow different, special, not like everyone else, and therefore will be saved from the oncoming societal collapse and climate chaos, or will rise above it.

Despite accusing society of being uncaring towards the crisis and uncaring about her daughter's future and the future of the next generations, Sandra finds herself sometimes idealising those who don't seem to care as much as she does. These people seem to manage to remain more present for their families than she can be when anxiety strikes. From this, guilt and self-devaluing follow. Sandra starts seeing herself as someone who, unlike others, is just not able to let it go. In such moments, by dint of violent introjection, she wishes she could assume the societal indifference that she criticises in others. Sometimes, she criticises the therapy itself as either not helping or doing more harm than good by bringing to consciousness what others are managing to ignore.

Therapeutic impasses of this kind make sense within a Bionian understanding that such an attack on knowing is driven by the desire to not-know (Bion, 1962). Interpretations of what is happening in the moment can be fed back to the client by stating simply that maybe today (emphasis on fluctuation) they are going through one of those times when staying with the crisis is just too hard. The therapist can then move with the client to an exploration of possible triggers, while researching what else is happening in their lives. If the client is consciously able to experience a peak of climate sadness in a particular moment in the session, it may be possible to complete the therapeutic movement with a *both-and* preposition. Here are some examples of questions that the therapist can ask that can be fed back to the client in a *both-and* structure:

- While the client is experiencing sadness, what is happening in their body? How is sadness expressing itself? Can the client describe it out loud? Are there any other emotions happening simultaneously? What is happening to their breathing?

- While sadness is happening, is there room for other feelings? What would it take, when playing with one's child, to be able to name and acknowledge that sadness while creating space for other feelings and experiences? Can the client still focus their attention on their child and their play while holding the space for the sadness, as it happens?

- What happens in their body when more than one feeling is happening simultaneously? Can they describe it out loud? What helps to create space for more than one feeling? Can they describe it in their own words? How can they best use breathing to slow down feelings and help to create space?

The goal at this point, more than dissecting feelings or trying to root them in a constellation of causes, is acceptance. We are talking about a reality-based crisis, so acceptance is key. Particularly useful in this regard, beyond the psychological and therapeutic body of knowledge on the intersection of mindfulness and psychotherapy, is Tara Brach's work on radical acceptance (2004). Despite the secularity of psychology as a body of science, the distinctive flavour of Buddhist-influenced psychology, with its emphasis on free-of-judgement contemplation of feelings and emotions, is an invaluable resource for reality-based questions about such topics as climate crisis.

If the client is experiencing a peak of anxiety, particular caution is required in relation to classical models of psychoanalysis, CBT and family therapy. Both classical psychoanalysis and classical CBT tend to internalise interpretations of anxiety as stemming from the subject (in the former, from unconscious conflict; in the latter, often, from the catastrophising of bodily sensations). Family therapy, too, tends to locate the symptom in the interactional space between individual and family, excluding 'nature' in the process (Duncan, 2018). None of these models locates the anxiety in the space between human awareness and natural systems, where human awareness itself is regarded as a natural system. Despite the work of Gregory Bateson (e.g. 1979), nature still doesn't have a place in the family therapy room. Conceptualisations of nature within psychology have more often fallen under the heading of ecopsychology (Roszak, 1992) or, more recently, what we have started to call ecotherapy (practising therapy outdoors) and ecopsychotherapy (Rust, 2020).

As the world heats up uncontrollably and ecological systems become more disregulated, there is the possibility of reaching a tipping point within the psychotherapeutic professions, bringing eco-knowledge to the fore. If this were to happen, it would be likely to be met with active resistance by therapists and therapeutic organisations, akin to the resistance Sandra is experiencing from within herself. Therapists, due to their training and profession, can produce interpretations that overinternalise conflicts such as Sandra's, as a way of defending themselves from their own existential uncertainty around the crisis. And they can apply the same interpretations to colleagues who are refusing to keep silent on this topic. In this optic, therapists who raise the alarm on climate change may be represented by peers as struggling to contain their feelings, and thus behaving more like 'clients' in the client/ therapist binary.

Until such a change happens in the therapeutic professions, the client's autonomous experience of the external environment should be respected and acknowledged, rather than shut down as 'internalisation'. When the client is, for instance, experiencing anxiety in relation to a period of very hot weather, interpretations rooted in concepts of unconscious conflict or catastrophising of bodily sensations or family conflict are likely to be received as too anthropocentric and invalidating of the client's experience. Respect for the client's experience of the environment must be preserved, particularly in such moments. Sometimes what is needed is simply to create a safe space so that both therapist and client can sit and breathe through these moments of anxiety about the reality of climate disruption. In tandem with this, and learning from ecotherapy, mapping the client's own and family history in relation to 'nature' is helpful. Nature is, of course, framed here not as an external entity but rather as a constituent part of both client and therapist. Ideally, therapeutic encounters outdoors could be offered. But taking the client out to 'nature' is not enough; the therapist must also adopt a therapeutic model that makes sense to both them and their client.

Dialectical interpretations, the 'climate conjunction' and orientation to action

As in any process of therapy, enquiry about reactions and responses to the climate crisis will run side by side with researching the client's history, particularly when it comes to them learning how to handle depressive and anxious feelings. When we talk about her childhood, Sandra lets me in on some important information about how feelings of anxiety and depression were managed in her family. I learn that, in her family, you were expected to avoid talking about things that could not be 'fixed', so as 'not to worry people or bring them down'. As our sessions unfold, a parallel emerges with the climate crisis: Sandra is suffering silently for what 'cannot be fixed'. A particular challenge emerges in framing this information in the context of her background. Suggesting that Sandra is, as she was when a child, dealing with what cannot be fixed in silence and reacting accordingly, puts too much emphasis on her personal history over the reality of the climate crisis happening outside and around that individual history. There is a risk of over-personalising and therefore minimising her very real concern about the immensity of the climate crisis. On the other hand, to ignore the clear connection to her childhood risks minimising or obliterating Sandra as a thinking and feeling subject with a history. Such interpretations are better framed in a triple dialectical structure of thesis-antithesis-synthesis.

In the thesis (the first part of the interpretation), the therapist starts by reaffirming the reality of the crisis we are in:

Therapist: Let's start by repeating the obvious: the crisis is real and it's happening beyond you and your personal history.

In the antithesis (the second part of the interpretation), the therapist connects Sandra's reactions and responses towards the crisis with her personal history:

Therapist: You talk of the climate crisis as something that cannot 'be fixed'. When you tell me about growing up in your family, you mention that people would not talk about things that cannot be fixed, as that would increase anxiety in others unnecessarily. I am wondering whether you tend still to resort to silence around things that cannot be fixed.

In the synthesis (the third part of the interpretation), the therapist brings the two parts together in the form of a question:

Therapist: Is it possible that your silence towards the climate crisis is also something that you carry from your family of origin when it comes to keeping quiet about things that cannot 'be fixed'?

Hence, what we can call the 'climate conjunction' binds together awareness about emotion, cognition and defences (defensive map), possibilities for *both-and* emotion, and dialectically based interpretations (thesis-antithesis-synthesis). Starting from the climate conjunction, it becomes gradually possible to focus on the client's relational map and analyse their relation to socially constructed silence. As Joanna Macy stresses over and over again, eco-work cannot be a solitary endeavour (Macy & Johnstone, 2012); activating social networks, even in the context of individual therapy, is key.

Notwithstanding, bringing a component of orientation to action into mental health work with clients is not an immediate given. In line with the individualised, self-centred ideologies of industrialised societies, most therapeutic approaches focus on increasing the functioning and wellbeing of the individual client, or, at best, the nuclear family. Narrative and social constructionist approaches are perhaps a bit closer to challenging the situation in this regard. Perspectives of this kind actively encourage helping the client to question wider aspects of their identity (Gergen, 2001; White & Epston, 1990), but with the aim of liberating the client – individual or family – from hegemonic stories, rather than challenging the client into becoming an active agent in social change.

With eco and social collapse already moving at a fast pace in different parts of the world, to liberate the client from the weight of hegemonic narratives while leaving them a passive agent in the face of the environmental change needed for our survival as a species is, to put it mildly, falling short of ambition. Yet equally, one must bear in mind the limits of the therapeutic dyad. Dealing with the climate and ecological crisis within the confines of the therapy room, whether physical or virtual, is probably too big an ask of the 'psychological container' required for this task (Macagnino, 2022). Thus, breaking through social silence is the first step towards constituting the therapy client as an active agent. Here, as elsewhere, the personal is political: breaking through silence is, of itself, a form of engaged social action.

Looking to systemic psychotherapy, the work of Carlos Sluzki (2010) around personal social networks adds a valuable contribution. In this approach, the client is asked to position the people in their social universe (family, friends, work relations and community-based relations) in three concentric circles, each representing a particular level of intimacy (the closer to the centre, the more intimate the connection). Through this, a schematic representation of the client's social universe is achieved. The next step is to map the beliefs of the members of the client's social network towards climate talk and climate silence, particularly in the first, most intimate concentric circle: who is the client engaging with in conversation when it comes to the climate crisis?

Here are some inter-related questions that can emerge from these explorations:

- Why is silence happening in the first circle and what is the client's contribution to it? Are there specific people blocking the conversation? How do they manage to do that?
- Are there any significant connections between the client's personal history and climate silence happening in their network?
- Is intimacy of relations affected by climate silence? If so, in what way?
- Is the client willing to 'shake up the network' and break through climate silence? What might be the consequences if they do? What gains can come from breaking the silence? How would they choose to go about breaking the silence? Why?

Experiencing eco-anxiety is often riddled with deep feelings of isolation. The belief that no one else in their close network is experiencing anxiety about the climate and ecological crisis or experiencing it to their level and intensity is common. By acting out this belief in isolation, the client, unbeknownst to themself, may be participating in forms of behaviour that reinforce the silence and keep them isolated. Breaking through climate-based socially constructed silence counteracts isolation both from others and from parts of oneself. Awakening beyond disavowal, however, is far from easy. Psychotherapy has a fundamental role in assisting the process, while encouraging the client to find balance and adopt wellbeing and self-care strategies, both individual and mutual with their personal social network. As the current recommendations on eco-anxiety show, beyond individual and family attempts at carbon reduction, participation in collective action is key to maintaining one's mental health (Royal College of Psychiatrists, 2021). In Sandra's case, by engaging with her personal social network and reflecting on it, it becomes possible for her to start disclosing her status to her family as someone seeking climate-aware psychotherapy, to initiate more conversations about it with work colleagues and eventually to join in action around environmental concerns.

With the client who is willing to work through climate silence and able to operate within what I am calling the climate conjunction, orientation to action becomes possible, or more possible than before. With regard to mental health issues, the therapist should attend to possible psychopathological co-morbidities that may need addressing first, before the client is strong enough to engage in collective action. At the stage of orientation to action, social construction therapy models and ACT are particularly useful. Using social constructionist models, the therapist and client can reflect on the client's identity and who the client wants to be in relation to the climate crisis. In relation to identity, the therapist would start by asking the client to represent who they are in terms of their main identities or identity facets (e.g. mother, daughter, spouse, co-worker, friend and so forth). Starting from this representation, therapist and client then explore what is possible for the client to be (or do) in relation to the crisis through these different parts of themselves. Here are some examples of questions the therapist might ask:

- As a mother/friend/daughter/partner, how are you currently approaching your concerns with the climate crisis with your children/friends/parent(s)/partner? Is there anything you would like to change here? What specifically? Why would you like to change that? How would you go about that change? What kind of help do you need to make that change and how could you ask for it?

- How are your concerns about the climate crisis expressed in the kind of work you do? How else could these concerns be expressed in your work environment? What sort of actions could you propose or engage in?

- What gives you the feeling of belonging to a community or a place? What kind of groups do you engage in that give you the feeling of belonging to a community or place? How are your climate concerns expressed in these groups? Would you change something? Why? Who could help you make that change and how could you go about it?

Choice points, found in ACT, are useful in helping to structure a commitment towards action (e.g. Doherty et al., 2022; Harris, 2009). By drawing two arrows pointing in opposite directions, the client is invited to represent their commitment in terms of behaviours and actions (*'moves'*) that bring them either closer to who they want to be (*'towards moves'*) or further away from who they want to be (*'away moves'*). With value-orientation being fundamental in ACT, 'towards moves' are framed in continuity with desirable value orientation, acting as reinforcers as the subject gets closer to where they want to be. Conversely, when it comes to 'away moves', the therapist works with the client to identify the behaviours, conduct and particularly patterns of thought or feeling that are keeping the person in paralysis. Learning to observe one's thoughts without identifying with them (cognitive defusion), as contemplated in ACT theory, is of paramount importance. *Both-and* statements are particularly useful in getting the person to move towards desirable action. Can the person feel anxiety *and still* participate in a climate march? Can the person acknowledge what in their history makes it harder to break through uncomfortable silences *and still* speak up?

In my own practice I have found that, although working with values can be useful in matters relating to career or interpersonal relations, it tends to become overwhelming or overly abstract in the face of the enormity of climate and ecological crisis. To help the client respond to the crisis in terms of their representation of the main aspects of their identity both helps to contain the anxiety and limits what is possible for the client to do or offer at present to what is realistic. Commitment extends to the self-care required throughout the process of opening oneself up to action. An illustration comes from Sandra's reaction to peaks of hot weather. In her anxiety about heatwaves, Sandra resorted to checking the weather forecast several times a day, which in turn further increased her anxiety. Part of the commitment we established around this trigger is that Sandra would have to start voicing aloud to herself a clear intention before checking the weather report again (for instance, 'I am checking the weather report to know what clothes my child should wear tomorrow'). It also involved her committing to resist impulsive urges and sit with uncomfortable feelings.

For a while, Sandra checked the weather forecasts less frequently and her associated anxiety reduced. But even when she defaulted to checking the weather report more frequently again, we have learned to talk about it in the therapy space as a signal marking a temporary increase in her eco-anxiety. We then proceed with mapping associated triggers and strategies. This is likely to be as much as we can do when working with a reaction to a reality that is very much located 'outside' the client. Learning to map the build-up of eco-anxiety in oneself as it unfolds is both grounding and, for lack of a better term, empowering.

Concluding remarks

Climate activists sometimes talk of tipping points in human action; contrary to the belief that we need everyone to change simultaneously, we may only need a significant percentage of society to change for a tipping point to happen. At present, as extreme weather events gradually become an accepted part of our everyday lives, a tipping point in the therapeutic professions is urgently required. In this chapter, by using a clinical case as an example, I have tried to illustrate how I draw on several different therapeutic models in the service of promoting climate-related mental health and helping clients move from paralysis to action. I call this model 'eco-integration', in that it combines different clinical models (psychoanalysis, systemic psychotherapy and ACT), with information from clinical experience and knowledge gained from the fields of ecopsychology, ecotherapy and ecopsychotherapy. As with other multi-modal forms of therapeutic intervention, more than simply offering a different form of analysis, the model presents itself as a distinct kind of synthesis. Training for therapists in this model is currently being considered, as well as its application as a form of psychologically orientated climate action with groups of non-therapists.

Bringing therapists together in pairs or groups to reflect on their defence maps, map their personal social networks and formulate their choice points in relation to the climate crisis can, potentially, go a long way towards helping therapists identify, contain and work with clients' climate feelings in the context of the therapy session. Extending training on the model may contribute to the tipping point we so urgently need in the therapeutic professions. It may also contribute to what Roszak (1992) once called the 'ecological unconscious' – that is, helping this concept move from a place of psychological abstraction into everyday mental health practice.

References

Bateson, G. (1979). *Mind and nature: A necessary unity.* E.P. Dutton .

Bednarek, S. (2019). Is there a therapy for climate-change anxiety? *Therapy Today, 30*(5), 36–39.

Bion, W.R. (1962). *Learning from experience.* Karnac Books.

Brach, T. (2004). *Radical acceptance: Embracing your life with the heart of a Buddha.* Random House.

Conner, J.O., Crawford, E. & Galioto, M. (2021). The mental health effects of student activism: Persisting despite psychological costs. [OnlineFirst]. *Journal of Adolescent Research.* https://doi.org/10.1177/07435584211006789

Doherty, T., Lykins, A., Piotrowski, N.A., Rogers, Z., Sebree, D.D. Jr. & White, K.E. (2022). Clinical psychology responses to the climate crisis. In J.G.G. Asmundson (Ed.), *Comprehensive clinical psychology,* (2nd ed.) (pp.167–183). Elsevier.

Duncan, R. (2018*). Nature in mind: Systemic thinking and imagination in ecopsychology and mental health.* Routledge.

Gergen, K.J. (2001). *Social construction in context.* Sage.

Harms, A. (2021). What kinds of activism do regenerative cultures fuel and how might we research them? *Social Anthropology, 29*(1), 238–240.

Harris, R. (2009). *ACT made simple: An easy-to-read primer on Acceptance and Commitment Therapy.* New Harbinger Publications.

Hickman, C. (2020). We need to (find a way to) talk about… eco-anxiety. *Journal of Social Work Practice, 34*(4), 411–424.

Hoggett, P. (2022). Climate change: From denialism to nihilism. In W. Hollway, P. Hoggett, C. Robertson & S. Weintrobe (Eds.), *Climate psychology: A matter of life and death* (pp.15–41). Phoenix Publishing House.

Hoggett, P. & Randall, R. (2018). Engaging with climate change: Comparing the cultures of science and activism. *Environmental Values, 27,* 223–243.

Latour, B. & Porter, C. (2017). *Facing Gaia: Eight lectures on the new climatic regime.* Polity Press.

Leiserowitz, A., Maibach, E., Rosenthal, S., Kotcher, J., Carman, J., Wang, X., Marlon, J., Lacroix, K., & Goldberg, M. (2021). *Climate change in the American mind: March 2019.* Yale Program on Climate Change Communication/George Mason University Center for Climate Change Communication.

Lertzman, R.A. (2015). *Environmental melancholia: Psychoanalytic dimensions of engagement.* Routledge.

Macagnino, T. (2022). *Why aren't we talking about climate change? – Defences in the therapy room.* (In press).

Macy, J. & Johnstone, C. (2012). *Active hope: How to face the mess we're in without going crazy.* New World Library.

Roszak, T. (1992). *The voice of the Earth.* Simon & Schuster.

Royal College of Psychiatrists. (2021). *Our planet's climate and ecological emergency: Position statement PS03/21.* Royal College of Psychiatrists. www.rcpsych.ac.uk/docs/default-source/improving-care/better-mh-policy/position-statements/position-statement-ps03-21-climate-and-ecological-emergencies-2021.pdf

Rust, M.J. (2020). *Towards an ecopsychotherapy.* Confer Books.

Segal, Z.V., Williams, J.M.G. & Teasdale, J.D. (2002). *Mindfulness-based cognitive therapy for depression: A new approach to preventing relapse.* Guilford Press.

Silva, J.F.B. & Coburn, J. (2022). Therapists' experience of climate change: A dialectic between personal and professional. [Early view]. *Counselling & Psychotherapy Research*, 1–15.

Sluzki, C.E. (2010). Personal social networks and health: Conceptual and clinical implications of their reciprocal impact. *Family Systems and Health*, *28*(1), 1–18.

Weintrobe, S. (2021). *Psychological roots of the climate crisis: Neoliberal exceptionalism and the culture of uncare*. Bloomsbury Publishing.

White, M. & Epston, D. (1990). *Narrative means to therapeutic ends*. Dulwich Centre.

Yalom, I.D. (1980). *Existential psychotherapy*. Basic Books.

Young, J.E., Klosko, J.S. & Weishaar, M.E. (2003). *Schema therapy: A practitioner's guide*. Guilford Press.

Zerubavel, E. (2006). *The elephant in the room: Silence and denial in everyday life*. Oxford University Press.

12 | Deep adaptation coaching in a time of planetary meta-crisis

Matthew Painton

In 2017 I suffered a crisis of grief and anxiety – something that, with hindsight, I call 'larger-than-me reality distress'. For approximately six months there was a continuous scream of anxiety in my belly that, on the worst days, prevented me from getting out of bed, let alone being able to coach anyone. This anxiety was accompanied by overwhelming grief and a loss of hope for humanity, the biosphere and the future – a dread realisation that 'this is not going to end well'. I did not have the language to articulate what I was experiencing – the threat and doom I saw everywhere I looked. That exponential growth on a finite planet must lead to collapse sooner or later was old news to me. The thing that changed was not new information but my relationship with reality: I became unavoidably sensitised to the 'actually-existing planetary meta-crisis' in an entirely new and somatically involved way.

The trigger for my collapse event of 2017 was the death of my father, which disrupted my defences and destroyed my carefully constructed, mostly unconscious compartmentalisation against large-scale planetary reality. At that time I had no one to talk with, I did not want to distress or try to convince my loved ones, and those I did try to share my distress with thought it was all down to grief for my father (which was slight by comparison). I am grateful that I found my way to the Deep Adaptation Forum, a virtual community of people who gathered to try and make sense of current reality through the 'prism' of collapse, after reading the 2018 'Deep Adaptation' paper by Professor Jem Bendell (2020).

Figure 12.1 is the first of several 'experiential maps' that I use in coaching deep adaptation and training other coaches and therapists. Like mandalas, these maps are intended to represent and help explore complex, deeply existential and metaphysical aspects of self, systems, reality and awareness. They are employed to help make coherent somatic and conceptual sense of the meta-crisis, in order to transmute compound reality-distress into adaptive and virtuous pathways. They also help us keep track of the process and identify where it most needs to go.

Figure 12.1: Transjective larger-than-me reality distress

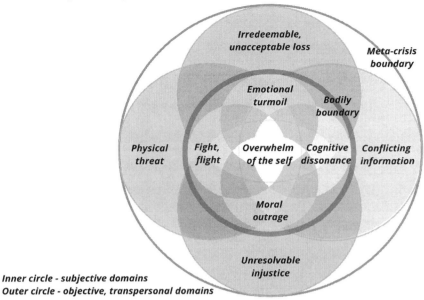

Figure 12.1 is a representation of compound larger-than-me reality distress. The outer circle represents objective, transpersonal aspects of the systemic meta-crisis; the inner circle represents the qualities of distress that bring us into a subjective, somatic and cognitive relationship with those transpersonal and systemic aspects. So the model is 'transjective'. Each subjective quality of distress identified in the inner circle arises in a particular sub-domain, or faculty, of embodied awareness. Together these faculties give rise to 'the self' – the awareness at the centre of being. The four sub-domains of the self are the sensibilities that both enable us to evaluate our eco-social environment and afford us our integral self-awareness, which is the fifth domain at the centre of the diagram. The sub-domains are the emotional/relational, the mental/informational, the ethical/discriminatory and the somatic/physical. Each domain, or faculty, discerns its own 'landscape' of relevance and concern beyond the body and has its own somatic qualia within the body. Ordinarily, the faculties of awareness give rise to a stable sense of reality at large and self-aware identity at the centre of being. The concerns and qualities of distress shown here are evolutionarily adaptive. The function of distress is to draw our conscious attention to matters of concern beyond (and within) the body so that we can get to grips with them. However, at a time of unprecedented, actually occurring meta-crisis, threat perception and somatic distress in all domains at once can easily compound to overwhelm the self *and* our sense of reality, or cause us to dissociate or become reactive in ways that make matters worse.

In my case (and for many of my clients), existential concern, threat perception and escalating distress in all domains at the same time led to the overwhelm and collapse of self – collapse of the stable identity and awareness at the centre of my being. My subjective micro-crisis presenced, mirrored and embodied the actually existing macro-crisis at large, all at once. The overwhelm at that time meant there was no longer any separation between 'me' and 'the meta-crisis', causing me to lose my grip. It also gave rise to the rational but unbearable realisation that, whatever 'normality' is, it is irrational, unsafe and precarious, and not to be trusted. This caused my perception of normality to alter and become a source of perpetual and seemingly unresolvable existential threat.

At that time, the only means I had to dampen down the runaway feedback loop of overwhelming reality-distress was to dissociate and distract – to 're-externalise' the planetary crisis and regulate my distress by focusing on the simple tasks of day-to-day living. Since that acute crisis phase, I have come to make sense of things and to conduct my life and my work as a coach as if every living being on Earth is entangled and immersed in a scientifically verified, planetary-scale, transformational meta-crisis, of which the long-predicted and self-evident symptoms are civilisational and environmental collapse. I now understand that most people of the global north are, as I was, not only unwilling but also physiologically and cognitively unable to be 'somatically present' to the facts about large-scale planetary reality and to internalise them and somatically respond 'as if' they are real. Most people here remain avoidant, distracted and compartmentalised, even while suffering the effects and being cognisant of at least some of the information. This is a dissociated, sanity-preserving, but maladaptive condition that externalises and defers the meta-crisis, guaranteeing even more consequential and dire outcomes later on. Unfortunately, there is every incentive and opportunity to compartmentalise against large-scale reality. We do so for the sake of our sanity and because we literally cannot afford to suffer the facts and make change, since we are obliged to survive and make our way in reality as it is, no matter how dysfunctional and incoherent that reality is 'at large'.

I now coach individuals, other coaches and therapists and groups who, like me, are trying to navigate the compound reality-distress described in Figure 12.1 – people who are no longer willing or able to compartmentalise, separate, externalise and defer, and so are suffering intense larger-than-me reality distress in their personal lives and every domain of their being.

From the collapse perspective, civilisational and ecological exhaustion is a well-verified present reality to which we must adapt, rather than an uncertain and avoidable future possibility. From a transformational perspective, we must embrace a 'post-industrial' way of being – a very different way of 'being and doing human' – ideally with love and resourcefulness. I personally hold both perspectives (they are not incompatible) and would contrast them with the sustainability perspective. I now view the sustainability perspective as 'sincere but naïve', given the scientifically verified facts and trajectories. But from any perspective, to accommodate and integrate the macrocosmic facts about large-scale reality into present awareness, identity and behaviour change is a complex, difficult task and highly disincentivised by the intense existential distress the facts now entail. The non-negotiable planetary realities and imperatives are extremely unpleasant to metabolise and get to grips with. Crossing the 'collapse Rubicon' from 'avoidable future nightmare' to 'unavoidable present reality' was by far the hardest thing I have ever done, and I do not suppose the process will ever be complete. I can, however, testify that there is a potential for steady, centred composure and enlivenment on the other side. Nonetheless, for me and for many of my colleagues and clients, periods of engagement and enlivenment still cycle with rounds of grief and panic, distraction and avoidance. I have to consistently practise my coaching vocation and co-regulate my distress with others to avoid falling back into futility, despair or runaway reactivity.[1]

Deep adaptation coaching framework

The diagrams I use in my coaching work and show here illustrate the framework for a deep adaptation coaching process that enables people to metabolise and get to grips with the distress of the meta-crisis in each somatic/cognitive domain, in whatever ways it is showing up in their somatic experience and conscious awareness – as an emotional crisis, meaning crisis, physical crisis, moral crisis and/or as a metaphysical crisis of awareness and identity. The mapping process is designed to help manage and metabolise larger-than-me reality distress in each or any of the domains and to enable our innate capacity to transmute distress into wise, collaborative virtue and embodied, transformational enlivenment.

I prefer the broad term 'larger-than-me reality distress'[2] to 'climate-anxiety'[3] and 'eco-grief'. The latter terms are certainly valuable because they name and enfranchise significant and distinct aspects of the larger-than-me reality crisis. However, they do not describe or encompass the whole existential territory – the many emerging forms of distress that people are suffering in relation to civilisational and ecological precarity and disruption. There are many novel types and patterns of distress emerging, just as we might expect when normative reality no longer makes sense and can rationally and objectively be viewed as maladaptive, self-terminating, incoherent and delusional.

Realising that I was not yet ready or competent to coach the existential territory that I myself was suffering with, I initiated a collaborative project within the deep adaptation community to create a database and community of practice of collapse-aware therapeutic professionals.[4] This is a diverse group of professional practitioners who are also making sense of the world through the prism of collapse and adapting their professional practice accordingly to tend to the needs of others. I have had the extraordinary comfort and privilege of spending hundreds of hours in the (virtual) company of these professionals, circling, talking, listening, researching, practising and co-supervising, and it is their

---

1. Katie Carr and Jem Bendell (2020) have published a useful paper on group facilitation for deep adaptation: https://insight.cumbria.ac.uk/id/eprint/5792/1/Bendell_FacilitationforDeepAdaptation.pdf. Training in deep adaptation facilitation is offered via the Deep Adaptation Forum.

2. I am grateful to my friend and colleague Dr Nick Laurence for the term 'bigger-than-self reality distress', which he uses in his clinical psychology doctoral thesis (Laurence, 2022). At this time of writing, his thesis is not published, but he explores the concepts, methodology and practice on his substack channel: https://biggerthan.substack.com. From 2023 he and I will be offering training in the methodologies for coaches, therapists and facilitators.

3. www.climatepsychologyalliance.org/index.php/component/content/article/climate-psychology-handbook?catid=15&Itemid=101

4. https://guidance.deepadaptation.info. I also facilitate a 'Deep Adapation Pod' within the Climate Coaching Alliance. See www.climatecoachingalliance.org/local-communities

company and support that has enabled me to recover my composure sufficiently to formulate the coaching practice, or framework, that I outline here.

Traditionally, therapeutic and developmental professionals are highly skilled at helping individuals calibrate with their 'private' reality in all kinds of ways. However, most practices and processes leave large-scale reality as an unquestioned given, assuming that, however challenging, reality-at-large is mostly stable, ethical and rational, or at least inevitable. The nature of the underlying and manifest 'fabric of reality', the invisible web of norms, assumptions and relations, is usually assumed to be beyond the scope of engagement and the therapist's or coach's professional competency. In normal practice, the overarching presumption is that, with effort, insight and progress, an individual's future can be significantly better than the present. So the focus and emphasis of most professional practice tends to foreground the individual as the fulcrum for change, development and transformation, against an invisible and unquestioned background of normative eco-social reality. What we are not normally prepared or trained for is a state where large-scale reality itself is no longer rational, safe or dependable and is ceasing to function in a stable or predictable fashion, while undergoing an enforced, uneven, unjust and existentially perilous meta-transformation. How do we practise ethically if the reality in which we are immersed, which we embody, enact and 'collude with', is verifiably maladaptive, dysfunctional and in denial about the facts? What if we have come to understand that the future will be exponentially more challenging and precarious than the present, no matter what we achieve as individuals? This would demand a shift in the framing, focus, ethics, skillset and objectives of counselling and coaching practice. We explore these complex professional and personal issues in the deep adaptation guidance and facilitators communities.

I take the view that it is not in anyone's interest to be dissociated from the facts about large-scale reality or the grave implications that the facts entail, but nor is it in anyone's interests to catastrophise or to be overwhelmed. As practitioners, we are trained to be client-centred, to focus on the client's world and to disclose very little about our own worldview, opinions or concerns. However, this professional neutrality is not in fact 'neutral' if we are indeed immersed in an unfolding planetary meta-crisis or transformation event and colluding with denial. From this perspective, the uncertainty is about how quickly and in what fashion disruption and decline will unfold, not whether there is indeed a large-scale existential meta-crisis; we should all be well past that point by now. A practitioner cannot meet their client 'in reality' if the therapeutic space is not at least permeable to large-scale reality, its fragility and epic malfunction and the implications that the facts entail.

We must take every care to be sensitive to our clients' capacity to cope with personal, let alone large-scale reality, but the unfolding meta-crisis is going to enter into everyone's awareness one way or another, and probably sooner rather than later, as tipping points continue to be crossed. Reality cannot, should not and will not continue as it is now, so projecting current norms into the future as 'sustainability' is delusional, privileged and ultimately maladaptive. The planetary meta-crisis means that, as practitioners, our worldview matters, and we have a duty of care to our clients, and to all beings, to be honest. So, as a deep adaptation coach, I break the fourth wall,[5] and transparently disclose elements of my own worldview and existential and metaphysical assumptions, as well as my uncertainty and my embodied distress. I find I am increasingly working with therapeutic and developmental practitioners to enable them to do the work to transform their own practice similarly.

All my clients report that they have previously been unable to find anyone they can talk to, socially or professionally, who 'gets it'. Deep adaptation spaces are appreciated because people do not have to justify, tone down or explain their reality distress, and it becomes safe to surface, own, explore and engage with the full depth and extent of it. The skill and wisdom of the coach, therapist or facilitator is to allow our own distress to legitimise and validate the disenfranchised distress of the client, without amplifying or directing it or colluding with false certainties, naive optimism, paranoid conspiracy or unsubstantiated catastrophism.

Mapping the meta-crisis

The spectrum of large-scale eventualities that my clients are trying to internalise, metabolise and get to grips with spans rapid civilisational breakdown, a non-viable biosphere, an increasingly hostile or uninhabitable Earth environment, the prospect of violence, authoritarianism and conflict, and the possibility of human extinction. These extreme eventualities demand urgent, whole-person investment and community engagement. My clients are looking for spaces in which they can feel and explore these large-scale eventualities as if they were real and happening in real time, in order to make ethical, wise, deeply personal and possibly risky life decisions on the basis of what they discover. This is a somatic, deeply personal and existential process, which requires tools, practices and techniques for (co-)regulation and inter-personal development in each domain of somatic and cognitive awareness.

For practical coaching purposes, I have adapted insight and theory from the field of 4Es cognitive and psychological theory (Newen et al., 2018). The four Es stand for the embedded, extended, enacted and embodied fields of transjective (subject/object) awareness. This theory is a broad and interdisciplinary approach to cognition and psychology that asserts that the field of self-awareness is not confined to the brain, and that 'the self' is not constrained by the body. Rather, cognition is understood to occur throughout the body and the self and extend into the environment out of which it arises, in which it is embedded and which it enacts (creates, adapts and maintains).

Figure 12.2 depicts a 'map' of the self from a transjective paradigm that understands it to be an integral and self-organising (autopoietic) 'expression' of the reality that gives rise to it, rather than a separate, ephemeral 'Cartesian entity' that exists apart from its environment, merely as activity of the brain. In this model, 'sense-making' is the recursive, physiological co-processing and co-adaptation of the internal (subjective/embodied) and external (objective/co-arising) environment. In this mode of perception, the self is something that the whole system gives rise to, so that the boundary of the self and of self-awareness extends far beyond the brain and the physical body to include place, objects

---

5. Breaking the fourth wall is a term borrowed from the world of theatre, when an actor breaks convention and speaks directly to the audience.

Figure 12.2: The embedded, extended, enacted and embodied field of transjective awareness (4Es)

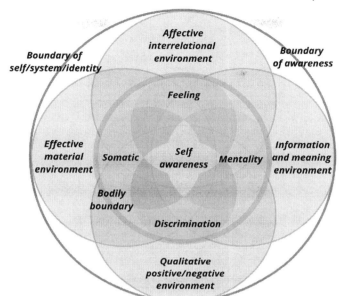

and other beings upon which we unconsciously depend and consciously identify as 'here', 'home', 'me', 'mine', 'us' and 'ours'. In this mode of sense-making, the 'self' accommodates and includes anything in present awareness with which we are consciously identified or knowingly dependent on, or to which we owe unconscious ontological allegiance, such as 'family', 'ecosystem', 'planet', or even 'universe'. This understanding and experience of self aligns with insights from all the sciences that everything is fractally entangled, interdependent, contingently co-arising, unitary and seamlessly interconnected. It also aligns with the insights from indigenous wisdom that the self is inherent to and an expression of the ecological environment to which it belongs, and the non-dual, axial wisdom traditions that the microcosmic self is an expression of the macrocosmic 'one'.

Figure 12.3 maps the stratified self from the transjective, non-dual model of reality. From this perspective, it is all 'self', all the way up and down, whether we are consciously aware and identified with it or dissociated from it. When exploring and coaching larger-than-me reality distress, it is enormously helpful and often revelatory for us to gain clarity as to which level of self and 'on whose behalf' our client is concerned and distressed – in other words, at which levels of self do they self-identify and feel concern, to which levels do they owe conscious allegiance, and at which levels are they othering, blaming and/or dissociating in their reality distress? The meta-crisis calls into doubt everything about meaning and normative identity, and this model of deep adaptation coaching helps to explore often unconscious and contradictory narratives and assumptions about who or what 'I am', or 'we are', and who is 'the victim' and who is 'the perpetrator' of the crisis.

The meta-crisis is presenced in awareness and appears very differently at different levels of identity awareness and allegiance and in each of the different cognitive domains. It can also be very helpful to define the 'planetary boundary' of the crisis

Figure 12.3: 'I am because we are' – the movable boundary of the experiential self and the outer boundary of the planetary meta-crisis

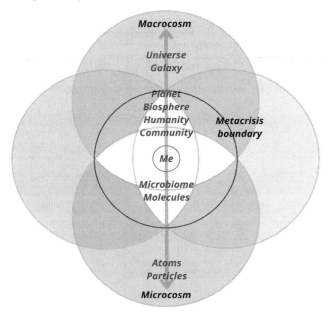

and explore deep time and cosmological reality – the even larger self/space in which the planetary crisis arises and unfolds. The universe is not, as far as we know, having a crisis and it can come as a great relief and a resource to remember that, and integrate it in our sense-making about the planetary-scale crisis and our role within it.

The maps allow us to be very precise about how and where and in what ways the meta-crisis is showing up, or being somatically presenced, in the extended 'body of self-awareness', and to explore both reality distress and reality arousal at different levels of scale, from different perspectives and in any or each cognitive domain.

For example, the coaching often explores the common narrative that humanity is an 'irredeemable perpetrator' and the biosphere is the 'innocent victim' that will be better off and get along just fine without 'us'. This narrative anticipates and accepts human erasure as a just or inevitable outcome by extending innocence, compassion, justice and allegiance to the biosphere while othering or dissociating us from our own humanity. It is a dissociative, irrational or fragmented trauma response, caused by collective shame in the personal being, and is especially common among environmentalists (among whom I count myself). It can all too easily lead to eugenicist and eco-fascist ideation. We have found that re-examining this narrative from a planetary or a cosmic/universal perspective can recover a compassion for and a re-identification with our innate humanity, which enables adaptive potential.[6] This deep adaptation model offers the opportunity to mindfully and somatically explore and integrate the highly structured,

---

6. 'Wider Embraces' is a group practice for mindful 'presencing' and sense-making from these wider perspectives developed by Stina Deurell and colleagues: https://wheelofwe.org/. I offer the practice alongside my one-to-one coaching and integrate it into the coaching much like 'parts work' or internal family systems work.

and often contradictory perspectives and narratives we each hold at the level of identity and self-awareness/awareness-of-self and that can be a substantial disincentive to wise action.

The phrase 'deep adaptation' conjoins subjective insight (deep) with natural history (adaptation). All the embodied forms of life to which the planet gives rise maintain, adapt and depend upon a prevailing 'consensus of all beings' – the Holocene – and all forms of life are adapted by it (natural selection). Humanity is unique in that we have the cognitive ability and cultural capacity to consciously and intentionally adapt the environment that sustains us, and the plasticity to thrive in highly varied eco-social conditions. It appears that, despite 'globalising', we have not integrated our objective conceptual knowledge about how the planet actually works with subjective and cultural awareness, identity and behaviour constraint, so we are currently in the process of smashing the Holocene consensus. However, adaptability, plasticity and collaborative virtue are hardwired into our physiology. Deep adaptation coaching assumes that discomfort, concern and distress are the drivers of biological adaptation and cultural evolution, and not something to be avoided, overridden or dissociated from. However, distress is inherently volatile; it can be transmuted towards coherent, intentional and collaborative adaptation (which we call virtue), or it can provoke incoherent, maladaptive reactivity, which makes things worse. This coaching seeks to discern, embody and enact the virtue that can arise in any and each of the cognitive/somatic domains of the self, as identified above.

Figure 12.4: Virtuous expansion and reactive contraction of personal and collective adaptational competencies

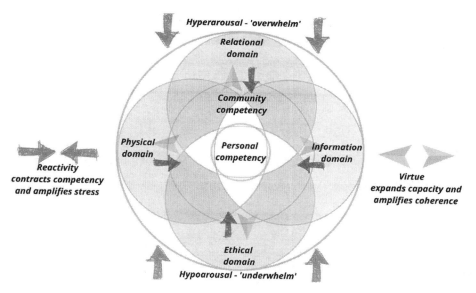

Figure 12.4 represents the 'what' of this deep adaptation coaching framework – the metapurpose, which is the expansion of personal and collective adaptational

competency (virtue) in any and each domain. Figure 12.5 represents the 'how', and names the respective virtues, competencies or vocation for each domain.

Figure 12.5: Mindful, somatic, meta-crisis-coaching and the virtue of each domain

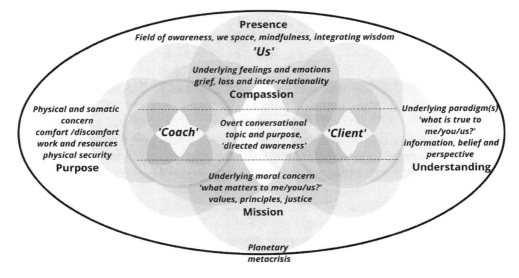

This framework presumes that the facts are non-negotiable and that every living being and community on Earth is uniquely situated and entangled within and enacting an epic transformational planetary meta-crisis, so that social and environmental stresses will cumulatively and exponentially increase for the rest of our lives and beyond. This is so, whether or not we realise and accept it and however we make sense of it through the prisms of collapse, or transformation or sustainability, or if we unconsciously react to it as if it were random misfortune or someone else's fault, or problem objectify it a 'puzzle' to be 'solved'. Metabolising and coaching collapse and meta-crisis is complex, distressing and multi-scalar, and the figures seek to represent this complexity so we can better co-navigate our sense-making spaces.

In the centre of Figure 12.4 are the circles of personal and collaborative competency, which are what the coaching aims to expand in any or all domains. The virtues that expand the circle of our adaptive competency in each domain are named in 12.5. 'Virtue' is an old-fashioned word: I do not use it in this context to mean 'personal moral accomplishment' or 'good character'. In this model, each of the virtues is an enabling skillset, deeply rooted in the physiology of somatic awareness, that can transmute distress into co-enlivenment and expand our personal and collective capacity to remain present and coherent and to mutually collaborate in wise co-adaptation.

Conversely, 'reactivity' is that which somatically contracts or collapses our inter-relational capacity and causes us to make things worse. Expanding the capacity to transmute distress towards adaptive virtue and away from reactivity in any or every domain, in whatever eco-social context we find ourselves, is the 'meta-purpose' of the coaching. What that looks like in practice and how it is languaged and articulated is unique to each client and to each eco-social community context. 'Vocation' describes the virtue or domain in which the client or community is most stressed, and/or competent, and/or called to serve and practically address. Some people and groups are predominantly caretakers (the virtue of compassion); some are primarily sense-makers (the virtue of understanding); some are called to ethics, justice and activism (the virtue of mission); some are called to practical and physical adaptation (eco-system regeneration and social permaculture), and some are primarily concerned with awareness, soul, spirit and the sacred (the virtue of presence). The meta-crisis simultaneously places stress on and demands adaptive virtue in all five domains of being, and at every level of scale. But it starts with 'me', in my body and my socio-cultural awareness. The model softens the boundary between personal and collective capacity because, in reality and at a time of existential meta-crisis, there is no hard and fast boundary between 'self' and 'other' or 'agent' and 'arena' – such perceived separation is a rapidly dissolving cultural artefact of the currently dominant physical-materialist paradigm.

Above and below in Figure 12.4 are the zones of dissociated *hypo*-arousal and reactive *hyper*-arousal. Hypo-arousal is 'pre-adaptational underwhelm': the familiar, dissociated, naive, distracted, unconscious, compartmentalised, habitual, medicated, complacent, depressed and distress-avoidant 'comfort zone'. Hyper-arousal is the state of reactive overwhelm and defensive narrow focus that can be explosive, hysterical, violent, delusional, paranoid, oppositional and defensive. Sustained or chronic hyper-arousal is physiologically costly and adaptively incompetent, or 'maladaptive'. It can be useful in the coaching to recognise and explore both conditions or tendencies in the client's own body and experience in order to identify practices that are appropriate to up-regulating or down-regulating our habitual pattern of arousal and stress response.[7]

I find that this master map is both useful for me to conceptualise and track the coaching territory and, more importantly, enables the client to proactively evaluate and map their distress, challenges, strengths and competencies and to identify their vocation and personal and community resources, so that the coaching can be directed to wherever it needs to go. Again, the theoretical explanation and formal language I use here is not the tender, intuitive and informal language of the coaching space, which elicits the client's own language, worldview, framing, priorities and wisdom. The figures are constantly evolving through use and feedback.

While we cannot predict with certainty the specifics of how meta-crisis and collapse will unfold, we can certainly anticipate the generalities. As the planetary meta-crisis accelerates and the large-scale norms and systems we are accustomed to rely upon become disrupted, all lives on Earth are going to become increasingly precarious and subject to accelerating, life-threatening and likely runaway change processes. Personal and collective adaptive competencies (virtue) will be at an ever-higher premium. We know that humans are capable of becoming violent and dissociated monsters or resilient and virtuous collaborators when circumstances are threatening, frightening

---

7. My friend and colleague Dean Walker has an extensive online body of work and facilitates a community of practice on the processes and practices of co-regulation, desaturation and reconnection against the meta-crisis: https://livingresilience.net

and unstable, so understanding the underlying dynamics is in everyone's best interests. Both our negative reactivity and our vocational skills and competencies can be identified and explored in each of the domains in Figure 12.4, so that the coaching can identify strengths to work with (vocation) and vulnerabilities to work on (reactivity).

Hyper-individualism, reactivity and paradigm distress

Larger-than-me reality distress can all too easily reinforce hyper-individualism. Individualistic and reactive responses to threats are predictable and understandable as threat and fear tend to be contracting and isolating. However, individualistic responses to our common predicament are inefficient, uncoordinated, rivalrous and maladaptive at scale (ethnic, national, regional). The complex planetary meta-crisis is not something the individual can bear, solve, metabolise or withstand alone, but that is precisely what the dominant social paradigm enforces on us. There is an enormous asymmetry between the scale of the planetary crisis and current personal, local and regional adaptive competency – an asymmetry that is inherently overwhelming to the (fragile) individual, our communities, institutions and our current explanatory framework.

In the global north, we have all been acculturated, conditioned and colonised since birth into a globalising paradigmatic reality that foregrounds the individual and backgrounds, dissociates, others and externalises many aspects of the interbeing that sustains, enables and resources us and is the far larger part of 'the self'. This tendency finds political, economic and ideological expression in neoliberalism. As a paradigm, neoliberalism foregrounds the materialist and individualistic dimensions of reality, and denies, backgrounds and suppresses awareness, identity and mutual behavioural constraint rooted in the actual reality of interbeing. The prevailing neoliberal paradigm selects for, normalises and advantages individualistic entitlement and sociopathy at every level of scale (as nationalism and human exceptionalism, for example). For many caring professionals and most of my clients, this is not really news. The rivalrous hyper-individualism and malign sociopathy that neoliberalism normalises and enforces can be seen as a creative and compelling transitional stage of human and civilisational development *and* as a delusional, dissociative and colonising cultural pathology. Either way, the intersection of hyper-individualism and physical-materialism that is neoliberalism is both a causal contributor and an accelerator of the planetary meta-crisis and is entirely inadequate for meeting the complex predicament it has created.

My clients tend to be chronically heartsick with regard to the failure of regional, national and international institutions – the 'system' – to even recognise, let alone get to grips with the planetary meta-crisis. I would urgently add 'paradigm distress' to the list of new but increasingly common forms of larger-than-me reality distress, alongside eco-grief and climate anxiety. Paradigm distress arises from the enforced obligation on us to participate and enact a dysfunctional, obviously self-terminating materialistic reality paradigm that we do not believe in – one that co-opts, obliges and conditions us to perform irreversible acts of self-harm. Paradigm distress, and the existential cynicism, dissociation and despair that it engenders, is real, legitimate and a commonly and deeply felt dimension of larger-than-me reality distress. But it is seldom recognised and very hard to articulate, and so it exists as an even more socially disenfranchised aspect of larger-than-me reality distress than eco-grief and climate anxiety. Deconstructing, justifying and formally articulating one reality paradigm and comparing it with another is laborious metaphysical territory that is mostly outsourced to academics. One of the ambitions of deep adaptation coaching is to enfranchise and embody the outrage, dissonance, cynicism and despair that arises as a result of chronic paradigm distress and to enable an exploration of self and reality from a different paradigm – one that reifies and resources us in the actual, regenerative reality of planetary and universal interbeing. So, in a sense, this is 'trans-paradigmatic' or 'inter-paradigmatic' coaching.

Self-as-system: The collapse of self and the virtuous expansion of interbeing

Figures 12.6 and 12.7 seek to represent in more detail the recursive collapse and expansion of 'the self' from the transjective paradigm. This allows us to explore crisis and collapse as something that is happening 'in here' as a subjective process, just as much as it is happening 'out there' in 'objective' reality. It offers the means of transformation and expansion rather than just reaction and contraction. Clients and groups bring their own circumstances, orientation, perspective, intuition, experience, language, insight, expertise, wisdom and understanding to the diagrams, generating all kinds of coachable 'grist for the mill' (and learning for the coach).

Figure 12.6: The collapse of the self into dissociated hyper-individualism

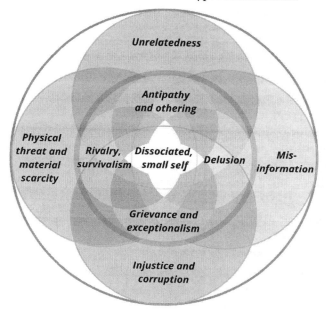

In this view, 'collapse' is the perpetual contraction of the 'circle of the self', set against an ever more distressing reality and that which becomes ever-more violently 'othered'. Loss and the breakdown of relationships provokes antipathy, trauma and unresolved grief, which further breaks down relatedness. Misinformation feeds cognitive dissonance and misunderstanding, which generates ever-more disinformation and delusion. Injustice and corruption provoke shame, blame, grievance and exceptionalism, by which our own immoral behaviour may appear evermore 'justified' and necessary. Physical threat provokes fight, flight and freeze, insecurity and hoarding of resources, which engenders narrowly self-serving, desperate behaviour and makes everyone less secure. Each of these is a recursive feedback loop in its own right, shattering the structures of mutuality and interbeing and contracting the self to ever smaller, 'entrenched' and ultimately fragile 'units'. This is our apparent destiny as existential stressors increase, unless we consciously and deliberately intervene with love and virtue.

Figure 12.6 is a representation of the recursive collapse of the self; it is what the fragmentation and contraction of reality looks like, feels like and behaves like, which clients can then map to their own experience, situation and insight. The evidence that these dire feedback loops are accelerating as stresses increase is all around us: depression, self-harm, polarisation, othering, alienation, disinformation, nationalism, ethnic tensions, authoritarianism, exceptionalism – narrowly self-serving behaviours and the fortification of boundaries between 'us' and 'them'. This is the unfortunate endgame of the physical-materialistic paradigm, which separates self from reality at large and guarantees the collapse of the large-scale civilisational structures and relationships that embody and enact that maladaptive paradigm.

Personally, I anticipate and fear reactionary, hyper-aroused eco-fascism more than I do ecological breakdown and climate chaos. Understanding the underlying dynamics of distress, self-contraction, dissociative trauma and fear-based hyper-arousal that feed, enable and justify eruptions of the human capacity for 'dissociative evil' has been a strong motivator for this coaching framework. We can all see it coming. The potential for genocidal eruptions of eco-fascism as civilisational structures collapse under the weight and momentum of their deeply embedded and embodied contradictions is predicted and predictable. Extreme violence is more or less baked into the paradigmatic, civilisational endgame; millions of us already feel this somewhere in the body of our awareness, and yet very few of us seem able or willing to talk about it, let alone behave as if it is real and happening now, so that we might do something worthwhile about it. This coaching seeks to 'enfranchise' and metabolise the fivefold distress in order to 'bring the meta-crisis inside' so that we can respond with collaborative virtue and expand and extend the inter-relational self wherever we are. The virtues reverse the contraction and collapse that happens in our own being and in our communities and they also happen to be enlivening and arousing because that is how our somatic physiology and cognitive awareness has evolved to work over millions of years – quite simply, embodying and enacting virtue feels good.

Figure 12.7 represents what everybody knows somatically and intuitively and has at least some experience of, even if they do not know that they know it overtly and conceptually. What is represented here feels inclusive, expansive, beautiful, truthful and undeniable when it happens. Each virtue creates a virtuous cycle – a self-expanding, recursively enlivening, coherent and generative, mutually beneficial feedback loop. From a metaphysical or transjective perspective, virtue is a transpersonal, mutually co-organising, anti-fragile and highly adaptive field dynamic that we embody and enact

Figure 12.7: The virtuous expansion of self as interbeing

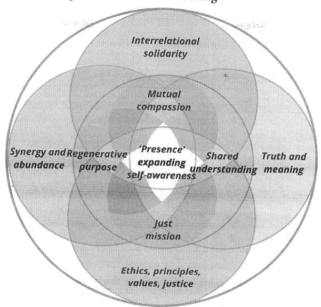

together, which extends, expands and enhances the coherence of 'the self' beyond the individual 'me'. In other words, the virtues enable us to withstand large-scale change and disruption with greater resilience. But we do not have to get metaphysical: each virtue is practical, vocational and instantly familiar as 'something positive that we do together'; something that brings us into closer relationship with each other and our common concern and interest, which benefits all beings without exception.

The virtues represent compelling and enlivening choices we can make about how to better participate 'with' (rather than against) what is unfolding, and arrest and reverse the processes of contraction, collapse and separation in our own being and our communities. Millions of people are already leaning into collaborative community virtue and creating 'islands of adaptive coherence' all over the planet. Each of the virtues is worth it for its own sake and magnifies and reinforces the others, and each ultimately works to widen the circle of coherence and alignment at scale, from the deeply personal to the local, regional and planetary. Virtue is how planetary interbeing actually works beyond the insidious paradigm of rivalrous individualism and material wealth extraction and the inevitable collapse that the paradigm guarantees. Is virtue enough to avoid catastrophe? No, it is already far too late for that. But how else shall we comport ourselves?

Local, regional and supranational institutions should be reifying the meta-crisis, sharing the burden of distress and engaging in appropriate and proportionate species-level adaptation and transformational change for the good of all life on Earth. However, our social architecture has been captured, optimised and incentivised over many decades by the prevailing neoliberal paradigm to promote human exceptionalism, rivalrous and regional advantage, individualistic hyper-consumption and the extraction and concentration of wealth. This means that the unbearable burden and responsibility for destructive, macro-level, systemic behaviours currently fall upon the individual and micro-level behaviour change. Consequently, most people do not even start to actually adapt, because the individual is obviously not the capable or sufficient locus of response and individual adapters are often placed at economic and social disadvantage. This is why the coaching pays a lot of attention to community, organisation and systems, not just the individual.

The clients who come to me tell me they are relieved to find virtual spaces and/ or a coach with whom they can begin to explore the full extent of their fear, grief and distress. But they are often entirely alone, at odds even with their closest loved ones, and must mostly start from scratch in terms of making contact with local and real-world, collapse-aware, adaptive communities. Connecting my clients with such communities of practice or coaching them to start their own is a critical part of this work and of the Deep Adaptation Forum, and it often begins with supporting them to 'have the impossible conversation' with their closest family and friends, who may be making sense of reality in very different ways.

The virtue at the centre of Figure 12.7 I call 'presence'. Presence is distinct but mysterious, something that many have tried to describe through the ages but no one seems able to define. It is almost always described as a paradox: for example, it might be said to be 'both full of itself and empty of self'. We may doubt the possibility of it when it is not present, but it is unmistakably convincing and transformative when it arrives. Presence arrives haphazardly and unbidden as 'grace' at peak moments of birth and death, joy and tragedy. But we can intentionally invite presence and practise 'presencing' through many means: through somatic, contemplative, mindful and meditative practices, through ritual or nature connection, and through virtuous action. Presence is a 'depth arousal', an unlimited resource and potentiality whereby we become both vessel and conduit for very much more than 'just me' – the individuated microcosmic self. Virtue is how we transmute presence into action. If we conflate presence with 'spirituality', then many become instantly 'allergic' or cynical. But in the collapse context, we could say that presence is our capacity to resource ourselves in the actuality of interbeing, from beyond 'just me' to both hospice and midwife larger-than-me reality.

We are each nested within, but not necessarily aware and 'present to', countless levels and layers of interbeing. The human body is a truly magnificent instrument through which the entire universe, the living planet and our common humanity can become present to self as 'the self', or we can remain oblivious to larger orders of reality, captured by the compelling spectacle and habitual demands of daily existence and outsourcing much of our sense-making to 'the system'. Consistent presence requires practice, especially at a time of large-scale disruption, existential threat and enforced transformational change.

My clients are trying to be consistently present to the prospect and actuality of social and environmental collapse within their own embodied and extended being. As a species, we have globalised but have not integrated or regulated our exponential technological power with our emerging knowledge about how life on a biological planet actually works, or how the universe actually works, indeed. So, we inevitably reach a transition point of disruption and large-scale failure that demands transformation if we are to survive. The distress that attends this epic predicament, and that might usefully draw our attention to it, also means it is increasingly hard to remain present, centred and available, because large-scale reality now threatens, offends and compromises us, demanding that we let go and enter the unknown. It takes practice to remain present and steady in the scale of our common predicament; it is much, much easier when we do it together.

Grief and acceptance

Finally, I want to describe the unbearable tension between acceptance and resistance, hope and futility and possibility and despair, which invariably surfaces in deep adaptation spaces. The wisdom traditions teach us that the basis of suffering is our naive and wishful resistance to impermanence and to accepting things as they actually are. When we are unable to accept how things actually are, when we are naively attached to permanence or to what should, could or ought to have been, we risk setting ourselves apart from and 'against' reality as it is, and we suffer as a result. A stubborn preference for the ideal over the actual means we can easily lose trust and break faith with reality as it is, and so cannot settle, resource or align ourselves with it. My understanding is that grief is the process of letting go of our most precious attachments, of coming into an emotional and somatic recalibration with how things actually are and so must be.

When it comes to planet Earth, the condition of the biosphere and the prospects for our civilisational future, there is very, very much to grieve for, to let go of and to accept in order to reconcile with the facts. It seems few people are in intimate, real-time calibration with and acceptance of the enormous and overwhelming loss of species, habitat and our familiar and complacent existence on a benign Earth. As hyper-individuated individuals, we are simply not big enough to fathom and accommodate the enormity of this loss and remain present to it. In collective processes of grief and acceptance, we can start to reconcile and resource ourselves in the actuality of the current moment, rather than wishfully, reactively and naively setting ourselves against it. By doing so, our suffering (futile resistance to what is) dissipates, and our capacity for realistic and virtuous engagement increases.

Acceptance need not be a passive, hopeless 'capitulation'. Deep adaptation is not the 'doomism' it is sometimes mis-characterised as or may appear to be from the outside. When we truly accept things as they are, an informed, active hope (Macy & Johnstone, 2022) arises to guide us towards the possible from the actual, from wherever we are now. The alternative is to hope and wish for or labour towards the impossible, based on how we would like things to be, or how we think they ought to be. When informed by acceptance, our resistance can be streamlined and well aimed from the actual towards the possible in whatever vocational and virtuous direction our best hope actually lies. My clients are struggling with epic and highly distressing uncertainty, doubt, futility, wishful thinking, acceptance, resistance and hope. So too am I. When the stakes are as high as they are now, this dynamic is excruciating and extremely difficult to accommodate and work through alone. Two people doing it together is infinitely easier than one person doing it alone, and groups are often much better than both.

Whatever existence is, it is truly strange, epic and mysterious – an enigmatic symphony, wrapped in a mystery, resting upon uncertainty and circumscribed by mortality. None of us were ever going to get out of this alive. This deep adaptation coaching seeks to transmute a portion of the dread, horror and distress into enlivenment and loving arousal, towards a fivefold growth in virtue and adaptive capacity, in the service of the unending evolution of planetary and universal interbeing, no matter what. What I offer and describe here is a framework for inquiry, I am constantly moved, amazed and enlivened by the wisdom my friends, allies and 'co-inquirers' bring to the process.

References

Bendell, J. (2018/2020). *Deep adaptation: A map for navigating climate tragedy* (Revised edition). IFLAS occasional paper 2. Institute of Leadership and Sustainability, University of Cumbria. www.lifeworth. com/deepadaptation.pdf

Carr, K. & Bendell, J. (2020). Facilitation for deep adaptation: Enabling loving conversations about our predicament. IFLAS occasional paper 6. Institute for Leadership and Sustainability, University of Cumbria. http://insight.cumbria.ac.uk/id/eprint/5792

Laurence, N. (2022). *Metabolising bigger-than-self distress through enactive nondual wisdom development.* Unpublished doctoral thesis. Massey University, Wellington, New Zealand.

Macy, J. & Johnstone, C. (2022). *Active hope: How to face the mess we are in with unexpected resilience and creative power* (Revised edition). New World Library.

Newen, A., De Bruin, L. & Gallagher, S. (Eds.). (2018). *The Oxford handbook of 4E cognition.* Oxford University Press.

13 Cultivating kinship through therapy

Yasmin Kapadia

We *are* our relationships. Ecological storyteller Sophie Strand (2022) writes: 'I am not a noun on an empty page. I do nothing alone.' The relationships between us and the worlds in which we participate are complex, rich and interweaving. When a person comes to me for therapy, their multiple ethnic and cultural heritages – transcultural, intergenerational – and individual histories and geographies come with them. They intermingle with all of those visible and invisible facets inside me. Who they have been to others, how they relate with the more-than-human world and with other humans who are different from them are in the space between us, as are my own relationships with other people and the planet. Who we will each become through our meeting and how we will affect the world are there in the mix as well.

Our relationships with one another – with other humans and with the other-than-human world – are central to both individual and collective healing. The therapeutic relationship is both a practice ground for and a microcosm of our relationships with the wider world. I agree with Vanessa Machado de Oliveira (2021) when she writes that, 'in order to make possible deeper engagements and better relationships we will need to reactivate capacities for sensing, relating, and imagining that have been deactivated within modernity'. Therapy is one potential vehicle for reawakening these capacities.

When 'someone' comes to 'me' for therapy, who (in the widest sense) is coming, who do they come to see, and what might we imagine our meeting to be in the service of? One fantasy of therapy could be as a process of what Gavin Van Horn (Wall Kimmerer et al., n.d.) terms 'kinning': remembering our belonging in a world of relations. Therapy could be about nurturing a sense of kinship between therapist and client, as well as between each of us and other (human and more-than-human) persons[1] beyond the therapy

---

1. I deliberately use the word 'persons' here as an equalising term. Our ecosystems, including oceans, trees, animals and mountains, are now beginning to be granted personhood status in law in various countries around the world in a bid to protect their rights not to be poisoned, exploited or eradicated, equal to those of human persons. The notion of the personhood of the more than human realm is also intrinsic to many indigenous languages. See www.garn.org/rights-of-nature

room. My own therapy practice aims to honour our fundamental interconnectedness (with each other and with all of life) at the same time as valuing our particularities and differences. In the intimacy of the therapy relationship, two fundamentally connected yet distinct and unique 'outcroppings of nature' meet (McGee, 2015). The dances we dance, the ways we relate, have consequences that ripple outwards. I want to explore what part therapy might play in attending to our relationships in this precarious time in global history.

How did we get here?

Donna Haraway and Anna Tsing (Mitman, 2019), among others, have proposed 'Plantationocene' as an alternative to 'Anthropocene' to name the epoch we are in, in recognition that it is not 'humanity' as a whole that has precipitated our modern-day climate and ecological crises but parts of humanity, who have abused both the other-than-human world *and* other humans. While it is still common to whitewash environmental narratives, I frame the climate and ecological crises firmly in the context of 500 years of brutal subjugation of indigenous, black and brown people through Western imperialism, colonialism, slavery and white supremacy. The industrialisation, extractivism, capitalism, consumerism and expansionism that have resulted in planetary destruction emerged from these foundations. The planetary crisis is a racist crisis (Williams, 2021), one that the black, indigenous and people of colour (BIPoC) global majority has done the least to cause, and yet who are impacted most. I aspire to provide a socially and ecologically concerned therapy that recognises the shared roots of environmental and racial injustices and addresses the ongoing manifestations of modern-day environmental degradation, colonisation and racism, within and outside the therapy room.

Psychotherapy was seeded in and grew from the same paradigms of thought as the rest of Western culture, through the European Enlightenment. This cosmology from which our profession emerged is ready for composting. I believe there are severe limitations in continuing to practise a form of therapy that is underpinned by Euro-patriarchal, white supremacist, materialist, individualist and racist assumptions about self and world in the context of the modern-day-climate, ecological cascade of related crises. In our hyper-individualised Western culture, there has been a crushing and silencing of indigenous wisdoms and traditional cultural knowledges. We live through the myth of separation (Eisenstein, 2013), enacting false hierarchies of mind over body, spirit over Earth, thinking over feeling, masculine over feminine, human over nature, and lighter over darker skin tones. We have lost sight of a world view and way of relating to one another and the planet based on the feminine principle and a deep knowing of our basic interconnectedness and interdependence with all of life. In my work as an integrative transpersonal counsellor, I come from a perspective that aims to re-member (re-embody) and reclaim forgotten ways of being and relating, and perhaps discover new ways, which are necessary and useful for the times we are in.

Deep adaptation for therapy

What it meant to 'be a therapist' in the time of Freud and Jung is very different from what is needed today. Countries, communities and individuals are adapting at varying rates (and with varying levels of urgency) to changing climactic conditions and impacts on their homes and livelihoods. Countries in the global south (whose peoples are predominantly black or brown), where the effects of climate change have already been catastrophically felt for some time, are having to adapt sooner and faster than richer countries (comprised predominantly of the global minority of white people), where the threat from climate change feels further removed, and where people and governments continue to turn a deaf ear to warnings from scientists (such as reports from the Intergovernmental Panel on Climate Change (2022)). The world of therapy (a predominantly white world) and the majority of therapists are comfortably embedded in a place of relative privilege, where denial and disavowal of existential threats to our earthly home are still (just about) possible. However, as I wrote in 2020:

> We cannot afford to continue hiding in the protected bubbles of our consulting rooms, carrying on with the business of counselling as usual and pretending the destruction of the world outside is not happening. There will be no therapy on a dead planet. (Kapadia, 2020)

The way I practise therapy is influenced by my growing awareness that there is only so long that the privilege of living here in the UK, cushioned by relative wealth, status and lighter skin colour, will protect me or future generations from ecological and societal breakdown. Deep adaptation[2] includes preparing *myself,* as a therapist, to be emotionally and psychologically ready for the conversations that are needed in order to lean into difficult truths with clients and colleagues (see also Chapter 12 in this book).

Using ordinary empathy and some imagination, I allow into my consciousness the realities of those already experiencing the consequences of inseparable climate and social injustices. I think about poverty, war, famine and migration in distant countries, and about the institutional and everyday racism, misogyny and homophobia, food and energy poverty, housing and energy crises, domestic and sexual violence, abuse and marginalisation here in the UK. I let myself feel the effects of ecological destruction on more-than-human beings such as other animals, plants and landscapes. Through letting myself imagine, feel and *know* these realities *as if they were my own,* I experience the need to *respond* to them very closely, and powerfully. This motivates me to prepare as best I can, in order to be of service to the human and other-than-human persons of the world in which I am practising therapy.

Without such preparation, I am likely to foreclose prematurely any potentially painful and frightening topics through being defended against them, thus colluding in our collective societal denial and disavowal. I realised some years ago that I would not be able to support my clients in processing existential threats to humanity and the rest of the planet, just as I would be unable to properly talk to them about racism or white supremacy, if I was too frightened or unwilling to face these issues in myself.

---

2. Sustainability leadership professor Jem Bendell's notion of 'deep adaptation' refers to the personal and collective changes that might help us to prepare for – and live with – a climate-influenced breakdown or collapse of our societies (Bendell & Read, 2021).

Through participating in organisations such as the Climate Psychology Alliance (CPA)[3] and Ecopsychology UK,[4] I sought the support of mentors and guides who have been facing into the realities of the climate and ecological crises for many years. Through the #BlackLivesMatter forum run by my counselling training organisation Re-Vision[5] and events organised by the Black, African and Asian Therapists Network (BAATN),[6] I met strong role models and found safe spaces in which to explore my ethnic identity and heritages, face my own internalised racism and practise having 'the race conversation' (Ellis, 2021). I started peer supervision with other therapists facing climate and ecological issues in our work, and joined another group for therapists of colour, exploring our experiences of training and working in the predominantly white world of psychology, counselling and psychotherapy. A group of BIPoC Climate Psychology Alliance members came together to support one another in our experiences of working in the largely white world of environmentalism. I also joined a mixed group of CPA members working to promote decolonisation and anti-racism within and beyond the organisation. In short, I realised that for the work of preparing myself to hold a therapeutic space for others in today's world, I needed groups and communities with shared values and goals. Nothing in nature works in a vacuum, and all the 'self-care' in the world would not enable me to do this work alone. Vikki Reynolds (2019) makes it clear:

> As individual workers, we cannot keep ourselves fabulous: we are meant to do this work together, and our sustainability is inextricably linked to our collective care.

Adaptation is an ongoing process. In our digitally hyper-connected modern world, it is impossible to claim ignorance as an excuse for complacency. As I continue to be exposed through the news, social media, the people I meet in my personal and professional life and my own direct experience to facets of the ever-more complex interweaving multiple crises faced by the different beings I co-exist with, I am forced to keep learning about and finding new ways of processing this emerging knowledge. I think therapy today demands an expansion of the meaning of 'continuing professional development', from understanding and working in new and better ways with the problems of individual clients' lives to engaging with, metabolising and finding useful responses to social and ecological problems, at individual, community and global levels.

Dancing between personal and global levels of suffering

Because we are so profoundly interdependent, I do not believe meaningful individual healing occurs separately from the healing of our collective human and more-than-human wounding (and vice versa). The personal level of therapy is intricately interwoven with, and inextricable from, the collective level. Rather than two atomised

---

3. www.climatepsychologyalliance.org

4. www.ecopsychology.org.uk/edge-of-the-wild

5. www.re-vision.org.uk

6. www.baatn.org.uk

Cartesian individuals working only on the client's individual problems, I conceive the two 'selves' in the therapy room as fractally connected parts of a self-organising universe. This wider framing allows the imagining of each therapeutic encounter as affecting the world on *all* levels – individual, societal, ecological and cosmic – whether we explicitly draw attention to this in the sessions or not.

In *The Dream of the Cosmos* (2013), Jungian analyst Anne Baring describes the way ancient cultures lived before the imposition of patriarchal hierarchies, believing in the myth of the Goddess and worshipping the divine feminine. Seen through this lens, the universe itself is conscious and all the (human or other-than-human) individuals interacting within it are expressions of a cosmic soul – a mysterious and sacred conversation in which we are all participating. I see all the moments in therapy, the process and the therapy relationship itself, as microcosms of the unfolding of this larger, living cosmos. There is a lot less for 'me' or 'my client' to actually *do* or get busy with in therapy when seen through this frame, rather than through the dualistic lens of separation. We are not there to heroically try to solve 'their' problems in a reductionist way, as if they were unrelated to anyone or anything else. The work is that of delicately sensing what is wanting to emerge through the therapeutic relationship and process, then humbly stepping out of the way to allow it to come through with grace, and trusting the process.

Every private, individual issue or experience that a client presents with in therapy has resonances with the larger whole to which we all belong. The things we speak about could be seen as dreams inside a social dreaming matrix (Long & Manley, 2019), each belonging both specifically to the individual dreamer and simultaneously to a collective web of meaning. Whether or not I explore these fractal connections explicitly with the client, privately or in supervision, does not matter – the links are there, infinite echoes of one another, as I 'create-discover' them (Burbea, 2017), and my consciousness of this affects the therapeutic process. The way I hear it, a client relaying painful experiences of sexual violation tells a story that is uniquely and distinctly her own and yet also linked to the stories of other women who have been similarly violated, and also to the raping of the body of the Earth. Because her body is part of the Earth's body, her healing heals a small but significant part of the Earth's wounding. 'Self-care' takes on a less individualistic meaning through this lens, since looking after oneself means taking care of a precious little piece of the world.

Sometimes people in therapy (especially activists) find it easier to engage with the collective and ecological levels of suffering than with their own personal wounding. They may be prepared to go to court to defend animal rights but not to speak up on their own behalf in relationships with other people. They may be outraged about climate justice issues but not about the mistreatment of their own childhood selves by their caregivers. I maintain a 'both-and' approach, supporting the passion that is there in such clients for others and for the planet, while also gently encouraging examination of their individual, personal, human stories. There is space in the therapy for different conversations about different levels of suffering at different times. The sessions weave in and out between focusing on personal and collective levels of wounding, allowing for the emphasis to contract and expand organically, like the dance of a breathing diaphragm.

In an ultimate sense, these different levels are not really separate or separable. Another way of sensing 'the self' is as intimately encoded within the whole of the cosmos, in visible and invisible, ever-changing, deeply meaningful yet unexplainable ways. This ancient, embodied, non-conceptual knowing of our fundamental belonging within Indra's Net[7] can be recovered through opening to our own direct experience of it. Through re-membering (coming back into membership) in this way, the false sense of separation between 'self', 'other' and 'world/cosmos' breaks down and we are freed from the isolation and imprisonment of Westernised ideas about 'me' and 'not me'. Therapy can be a space within which this re-membering can be cultivated, explicitly through nature connection and embodiment exercises, and also implicitly through the internalisation of a therapeutic relationship that embodies it. As a person gradually starts to see through the falsity of their disconnection from other beings and the whole of life, their basic sense of self-worth increases – not because they are special, or have done anything special to earn it, but simply because they exist and so are as worthy of respect and appreciation as any other part of nature.

Self-compassion and compassion for the Earth are intimately bound together. When we see the 'world as lover, world as self' (Macy, 2007), we naturally want to nurture and protect every part of it, including this miraculous little part inhabiting this human body and life right here. The capacity for relationships of kindness, care and concern for other humans, for non-human persons, and for ourselves (as a natural consequence of connecting with the rest of life in this way) is crucial in determining how we will respond to the immense challenges we face at this time in our global history, whether in the microcosm of our own lives or on a wider scale. Therapy is a place within which such relationships of care and concern can be fostered.

Relationship with time and working with natural cycles

The modernity from which our multiple world crises have been born worships gods of productivity, efficiency, certainty and control, promoting unfettered extraction of so-called 'resources' from the bodies and lives of both people and the Earth in the service of unlimited expansion and growth. This value system shows itself in the over-reliance on technological 'solutions' to the climate crisis, which reduce the perceived need to end consumption of fossil fuels and sacrifice the luxuries and comforts of our way of life in the global north. One symptom of this same singular orientation towards progress has been the growing emphasis on time-limited, 'solution-focused', quick-fix approaches to therapy, often the only 'choice' on offer to people on low incomes attempting to

---

7. To quote Francis Cook (1973): 'Far away in the heavenly abode of the great god Indra, there is a wonderful net which has been hung by some cunning artificer in such a manner that it stretches out indefinitely in all directions. In accordance with the extravagant tastes of deities, the artificer has hung a single glittering jewel at the net's every node, and since the net itself is infinite in dimension, the jewels are infinite in number. There hang the jewels, glittering like stars of the first magnitude, a wonderful sight to behold. If we now arbitrarily select one of these jewels for inspection and look closely at it, we will discover that in its polished surface there are reflected all the other jewels in the net, infinite in number. Not only that, but each of the jewels reflected in this one jewel is also reflecting all the other jewels, so that the process of reflection is infinite… it symbolizes a cosmos in which there is an infinitely repeated interrelationship among all the members of the cosmos. This relationship is said to be one of simultaneous mutual identity and mutual intercausality.'

access help through statutory services. From a linear, goal-driven perspective such as this, open-ended therapy is sometimes accused of being 'aimless', 'drifting' or lacking in focus and direction, inferring a value system in which it is always vital to know exactly what is going on, where we are and where we are heading. But, drawing on the poet John Keats' concept of negative capability (1817), which prizes intuition and uncertainty above reason and knowledge, and to paraphrase a quote widely attributed to James Hillman, I think that not knowing what the client and I are here for *is* what we are here for.

The cycles of nature always include fallow periods. Seeds and bulbs rest underground every winter before the first stirrings of visible growth in the spring. An ethic based on appreciation and respect for natural cycles values periods of inactivity or stasis as much as periods of obvious growth and development. In therapy as I have experienced and practised it, there is no ultimate 'goal' as such, and 'solutions' find us, or not, in their own time.

In the therapy I offer, I invite the emergence of a more spacious, less pressured relationship to time. The cool, smooth beach pebble in my pocket reminds me of the timeframe in which stardust coalesced into matter that hurtled through space, colliding to form this planet, and the pace at which tectonic plates deep beneath the Earth move to form the continents, and the time it takes for a stream to weather rock and carve a valley. Resting back into a geological perspective on time allows for a person's natural pace, modes, languages and rhythms to become apparent and be honoured through the work. Such an orientation could appear counter-intuitive, given the momentous and pressing nature of the tasks at hand, whether for responding to planetary catastrophes or to an individual's suffering when their life is in crisis. However, as Bayo Akomolafe (2022) has said, 'The times are urgent, let us slow down.'

Slowing down allows us to become more sensitive to, and ultimately more caring towards, both ourselves and our environments. The capacity to perceive our interdependence with the rest of the universe grows. It becomes possible to experience a wider range of feelings and sensations more deeply and be more reflective, less reactive, less habit-driven and more considered in our actions in the world.

With the slowing down that happened in the first coronavirus pandemic lockdown in the UK, when daily walks became popular, many people became familiar with the wildflowers, trees, butterflies, insects and birds (as well as human neighbours) in their locality, and began to follow the signs of the seasons changing for the first time. Lingering with our attention on such natural markers within therapy sessions, even if just momentarily, is grounding and fosters the cultivation of a deeper appreciation of the cycles of life in our bodies and in the rest of the natural world.

The medicalisation of distress

Many people arrive in therapy carrying a sense that the problems they are experiencing have originated inside themselves, as if they themselves were intrinsically 'broken' or 'bad'. This idea is encouraged by the hyper-individualism of the Western world. As psychiatrist Joanna Moncrieff (2022) explains, the public mental health system evolved alongside capitalism in order to manage the problems posed by people whose behaviour was too chaotic, disruptive or inefficient to make them useful participants in a labour market based on exploitation. The mental health paradigm privileges individualistic treatment and biomedical explanations for human distress – despite the abject failure in the quest to find convincing evidence of biological markers of mental disorders – over social determinants of health, such as material realities, issues of power, wealth inequality, disenfranchisement, and other forms of social disadvantage. The system is as institutionally racist as the rest of society: black people are four times as likely as white people to be detained under the Mental Health Act and 10 times as likely to be placed under a community treatment order (NHS Digital, 2021).

The problems that get called mental 'illnesses' or 'disorders' come from the same systemic issues of extraction (of human labour, in this case), exploitation and economic growth that have catapulted our planet into existential climate and ecological peril. Capitalism hurts people, communities and the planet in equal measure. For many people I work with, this framing comes as a relief. It gives them permission to put down the burden of being scapegoated by capitalism as they develop compassion towards the parts of themselves that are 'unproductive' or that have become distressed and overwhelmed as they struggle to fulfil the demands of living in the modern world or to fit into a society that is itself sick and broken.

Our intrapersonal relationships, between different aspects of the psyche and our relationships 'out there' in the world, mirror each other. Through therapy, we learn to develop a sense of seemingly 'internal' and 'external' kinship in parallel. Just as rising sea levels are a symptom of ice caps melting through global heating, the physical, mental and emotional symptoms that people present with in therapy carry important information about the processes underlying them, in both their own life and the state of the world. Rather than simply seeking to eliminate symptoms, they can be viewed as messages to be heeded. James Hillman (1990, p.18) writes, 'Symptoms lead to soul.' Much of therapy involves learning to listen to what is being communicated through a person's body, energy, thoughts, emotions, fantasies, dreams and unconscious behaviours. Clients learn to become sensitive to these messages and able to decode them, find meaning in them, and grow in kind and wise responsiveness to them. For example, gut problems, chronic pain, sleeplessness, emotional lability, anxiety, hearing voices, paranoia and relational difficulties could all point to overwhelming stress levels due to a person's current life circumstances or unprocessed personal or transgenerational trauma.

The symptoms an individual experiences might also be 'read' as messengers from the wider socio-economic-political-ecological-cosmic field. The difficulties a person encounters in their own life hold up a mirror to the problems faced by communities, societies and the planet. Symptoms may arrive on the shores of consciousness like asylum seekers making perilous journeys to the UK across the Channel in flimsy boats, carrying stories about famine, drought, extreme weather events, wars and conflicts, in which we in the global north are implicated. Our relationships to the parts of ourselves that are showing themselves in ways that disturb the status quo, making it impossible to blindly carry on with 'business as usual', often echo cruel, xenophobic, racist and Islamophobic British immigration policies of purposely creating a 'hostile environment', deterring boats, or threatening to exile desperate, displaced people to another country

4000 miles away. Through therapy, we can learn instead to listen, and to respond to the underlying parallel systemic issues that are causing our personal physical, mental and emotional symptoms, as well as causing such disturbance to human and more-than-human populations around the world.

Entering the territory in sessions

> Part of us already knows we are in a huge mess, but because we do not know how to sit with this knowledge, we tend to evade thinking about it. We prefer to avoid facing the facts out of fear that we will feel groundless and overwhelmed with anxiety and grief. However, unless we find a way to face this systemic shit together and learn to compost it collaboratively and to transform it into new soil, we will drown in it collectively. (Machado de Oliveira, 2021, p.84)

Some clients explicitly bring issues of climate and ecological breakdown and social justice into the therapy room. With others, there are points in our conversations that have the potential to open up as doorways for 'going there', if I view these as invitations to do so. A client may speak of childhood memories of camping or playing outdoors, their relationships with pets, holidays in beauty spots, gardening, or the birds they have spotted. They may speak about how much quieter and less polluted their local areas felt at the start of the pandemic when 'everything stopped'. Their attention may be drawn to a natural object or a picture of a landscape on the wall of the room. Or they may simply mention feeling disturbed by something they have been hearing about in the news. Inquiring a little more actively into these otherwise passing comments often uncovers a hidden tenderness and caring for other humans and for the more-than-human world, which they rarely voice or may not even have previously been aware of within themselves. The thread of such gentle inquiries can lead to disclosure or discovery of deeper concerns for the wellbeing of the planet, for other-than-human animals, other people, future generations or for the person's own future in a world that, at some level, they sense is unravelling. Therapy becomes a place where previously unconscious or silenced concerns can be spoken and where social taboos against entering this territory are removed.

As a therapist, I can model the possibility for entering into potentially difficult territory in sessions by voicing some of the things that come to my mind as we are speaking, rather than keeping silent. If a client is talking about the unseasonably warm winter weather, or the change in the way plants grow nowadays, I might mention the probability that these are symptoms of global heating that we are now beginning to feel close to home, here in the UK. In a conversation about refugees, I might comment on the difference in the ways those fleeing Russia's invasion of the Ukraine in 2022 were treated, compared with those from countries in the global south. I will explicitly invite exploration of the differences between me and a client in terms of gender and race.

Issues of climate breakdown and social and racial injustice are in the 'field', and they are being gestured towards in conversations all the time, if only peripherally. People living in our society today, including those who come for therapy, know at some level what is going on, even if they defend themselves from this knowledge through disavowal: 'living as if they didn't know' (Weintrobe, 2013). Like me, they are participating in the systems that create and maintain inequality, oppression and environmental degradation, and they are being affected, whether they are conscious of this or not. By speaking to these truths with sensitivity but also directly and openly, I invite these topics out of the shadows, making talking about them more ordinary, at least in the therapy space.

The sound of pennies dropping

While many people I meet are still clinging to denial and disavowal, for a growing number of people, the defences against the grim reality of global climate and ecological breakdown are starting to crack. Whether triggered by hearing about the latest IPCC report in the news (2022), witnessing environmental devastation first hand, watching David Attenborough's documentaries or studying the topic on a university course, the realisation of how bad things really are often comes as a shocking, rude awakening.

A person may quite suddenly begin to perceive their worlds and their lives in starkly new and different ways. Strong, often overwhelming feelings may accompany such epiphanies (Hoggett & Randall, 2018). Some people experience crippling anxiety, including apocalyptic visions of societal collapse, fear for their own or their children's survival, or terror at considering the prospect of human extinction. Some grieve vicariously for the suffering of other people and other species who have been killed or whose homes and livelihoods have already been destroyed through climate change-induced extreme weather events, such as wildfires, storms and floods. Some feel guilt at realising their complicity in creating the problem, entangled as we are in a culture of over-consumption and fossil fuel dependency, and helplessness or despair at not being able to fix or stop it. There may be anger, particularly from young people towards older generations, governments and corporations that have done little to safeguard their futures, or from the global majority of black and brown people, who may feel keenly the racial inequity in both the causes and consequences of these threats.

As one of my trainers, Joan Crawford, explains (2018), it is important not to pathologise these kinds of experiences, even though they can be deeply distressing and can negatively affect a person's mental health for a period of time. These are very normal, understandable responses to facing painful truths about our dying planet. There is nothing 'wrong' with them, and they can be usefully interpreted as information that the person having them, as well as others around them, needs to hear. Therapy can be such a deep listening space in which a compassionate relationship to such feelings can emerge, without the difficult messages they are carrying being swept under the carpet. I come alongside my clients in facing the enormous heartbreak of world pain, and we bear it together.

The distinct manner in which any 'eco-anxiety' manifests for any given person is very particular to them and is influenced by their geographical location, their social context and their own journey through life. The experiences of so-called 'eco-anxiety' may be very different for people embedded in different communities (Jaquette, 2021). People from the global south, those lower down the social ladder of power and privilege and those from black and ethnic minority communities in the global north experience ecological threats against a backdrop of having already faced existential threats to survival (such as slavery, colonialism and police brutality) for generations. Many indigenous communities have been awake to climate and ecological breakdown for much longer than the majority of the Western world; indigenous activists are being murdered and persecuted for defending the planet on behalf of us all.

Individual trauma might also be retriggered by opening to world-level existential threats. An individual's specific history of attachment wounding, childhood abuse and neglect, developmental trauma and trauma in adulthood, as well as their difficulties in navigating health, work, relationships or other aspects of their adult lives today, all interact with their realisations about and processing of social and planetary level crises. Such personal levels of suffering continue to matter in their own right, even after a person has realised the full extent of social, climate and ecological catastrophe. A person's individual and social problems continue to benefit from containment, care and processing within a therapeutic relationship, even while the world in which the therapy is taking place is on fire. William Merwin's poem 'Place' (1988) begins, 'On the last day of the world, I would want to plant a tree.' As a therapist, I might say, 'On the last day of the world, I would want to plant a seed of connection with another human being.'

Sometimes clients will say that they feel guilty for talking about their 'small' lives when they are aware there is so much else going on in the world, as if their own problems were insignificant in the grand scheme of things. But whatever matters to a person is worthy of kind attention. I want to learn more about the particular intricate texture of their experience, and to respond to whatever is pressing up in consciousness, whatever hurts at any given moment, at whatever level. Attending with compassion to the corner of the planet called 'my client', supporting the bringing home into warm relationship exiled sub-personalities and abandoned inner children, are all part of creating what Charles Eisenstein (2013) calls 'the more beautiful world our hearts know is possible'. The supportive holding of one-to-one therapy has also been necessary in many cases (including my own) for a person's capacity to grow sufficiently to even begin to touch the sides, let alone take in the tragedies and injustices of social and ecological realities.

Differences, boundaries and limits

Our fundamental interconnectedness is sometimes used as a way of viewing all beings as the same, fudging differences and attempting to exist as if we were one big, mushy, primordial soup. There can be a tendency to seek comfort and safety through sameness, affiliation, harmony and lack of conflict. However, any relationship needs 'two-ness'. Kinship involves allowing other humans, other creatures, plants, rocks, the atmosphere, their own subjectivities and their own perspectives – ones that are different from our own. We are all made of stardust and deeply interconnected, *and* we are also individuals, distinct from one another. The ability to discern and relate across differences is as important as remembering that we are all one. Our sense of interconnectedness with all beings needs to be grounded in another level of reality – that of very real power imbalances in a deeply unequal world. Power and difference between different groups of humans, as well as between humans and the more-than-human world, can be explored in the microcosm of the therapy space.

I am interested in how the human animals known as 'you' and 'I' come together in therapy, including how our differences in racial, ethnic and cultural heritage, nationality, social class, sex, sexuality, age, ability or disability meet. I want to see if we can name and talk about our differences, even if (especially when) it feels uncomfortable. I want to see what happens to the shame, fragility, fear and anger that may be evoked through 'staying with the trouble' (Haraway, 2016) as we face this discomfort together. This courageous endeavour grows the muscle of faith in the process of rupture and repair, reducing fear of conflict. Ultimately, this strengthens the therapeutic relationship and builds confidence in our capacity for mature relationships in the world outside of therapy.

Modernity's obstinate blindness and indifference to the environmental toll of unimpeded extraction and exploitation of so-called natural resources and human labour in the service of hyper-productivity and perpetual growth mirror the difficulties we can have in accepting and respecting boundaries. In my work as a therapist, holding firm, robust boundaries allows the person I am working with to confront their own finitude and develop a more grounded, response-able sense of themselves. The work of therapy includes facing into our human limits and mortality. Therapy can provide the wide, loving space needed to meet the grief that arises as we accept the facts of corporeality, temporality, impermanence, old age, sickness and death. Growing in consciousness of the Earth's climate and ecological distress expands the scope of grief work, from encountering our own personal fragility to appreciating the fragility of the very planet that sustains us and that we are a part of. Support through therapy can be helpful in learning to live within both our personal bodily and planetary limits.

Discerning your life's purpose/soul work

Therapy is a space in which it's possible to do the soul work of discovering one's unique position and role within the world and find meaningful ways to participate in responding to global (and local) destruction and injustices. Every person has gifts that are uniquely theirs to offer the world. When I am working with someone, I am always aware that there is a hole in the universe that only they can fill. The scale of a person's contribution to the larger whole is not what matters; heroic efforts to single-handedly save the planet are part of the problematic modernist way of viewing the world and our place in it that has resulted in the crises we are in. Different people are called to serve in very different ways, and the Earth needs them all. Some nurture houseplants and gardens, or take care of families, elders or neighbours; others clean beaches or parks, or help out in community groups, food banks, allotment projects, animal shelters or wildlife sanctuaries. Some teach children to love their environment, engage businesses or politicians, make art, or dance to express their passion and inspire others. Others do science, address conferences, or take part in various forms of campaigning and activism. Finally, some practise therapy and contribute chapters to books such as this.

References

Akomolafe, B. (2022, May 4). *Dr Bayo Akomolafe: On slowing down in urgent times.* [Audio podcast]. For the Wild. https://forthewild.world/listen/dr-bayo-akomolafe-on-slowing-down-in-urgent-times-encore-285

Baring, A. (2013). *The dream of the cosmos, a quest for the soul.* Archive Publishing.

Bendell, J. & Read, R. (Eds.). (2021). *Deep adaptation: Navigating the realities of climate chaos.* Wiley & Sons.

Burbea, R. (2017). *Aspects of the imaginal, Parts 1–6.* The mirrored gates: Rob Burbea's dharma talks. www.dharmaseed.org/teacher/210/?search=aspects+of+the+imaginal

Cook, F.H. (1973). *Hua-yen Buddhism: The jewel net of Indra.* Pennsylvania State University Press.

Crawford, J. (2018). Rediscovering our kinship with nature: Ecological issues in psychotherapy. In C. Robertson & S. Van Gogh (Eds.), *Transformation in troubled times: Re-vision's soulful approach to therapeutic work* (pp.118–136). Transpersonal Press.

Eisenstein, C. (2013). *The more beautiful world our hearts know is possible.* North Atlantic Books.

Ellis, E. (2021). *The race conversation: An essential guide to creating life-changing dialogue.* Confer Books.

Haraway, D. (2016). *Staying with the trouble: Making kin in the Chthulucene.* Duke University Press.

Hillman, J. (1990). *The essential James Hilllman: A blue fire.* Routledge.

Hoggett, P. & Randall, R. (2018). Engaging with climate change: Comparing the cultures of science and activism. *Environmental Values, 27*(3), 223–243.

Intergovernmental Panel on Climate Change. (2022). *Climate change 2022: Impacts, adaptation and vulnerability.* IPCC. www.ipcc.ch/report/ar6/wg2

Jaquette, S. (2021, March 2012). Climate anxiety is an overwhelmingly white phenomenon. *Scientific American.* www.scientificamerican.com/article/the-unbearable-whiteness-of-climate-anxiety

Kapadia, Y. (2020). The age of ecoanxiety. *Sussex Counselling and Psychotherapy News, 137,* Spring.

Keats, J. (1817, December 21). *Letter to his younger brothers, George and Thomas.* http://mason.gmu.edu/~rnanian/Keats-NegativeCapability.html

Long, S. & Manley, J. (Eds.). (2019). *Social dreaming: Philosophy, research, theory and practice.* Routledge.

Machado de Oliveira, V. (2021). *Hospicing modernity: Facing humanity's wrongs and the implications for social activism.* North Atlantic Books.

Macy, J. (2007). *World as lover, world as self: A guide to living fully in turbulent times: Courage for global justice and planetary renewal.* Parallax Press.

McGee, C. (2015). *Touching the earth.* Catherine McGee's dharma talks. https://dharmaseed.org/teacher/41/?page=13

Merwin, W.S. (1988). *Rain in the trees.* Alfred A. Knop.

Mitman, G. (2019, June 18). *Reflections on the Plantationocene: A conversation with Donna Haraway and Anna Tsing by Greg Mitman.* [Audio podcast]. Updated October 11. Edge Effects. https://edgeeffects.net/haraway-tsing-plantationocene

Moncrieff, J. (2022, March 26). The functions of the mental health system under capitalism. [Blog.] *Mad in America.* www.madinamerica.com/2022/03/mental-health-system-capitalism

NHS Digital. (2021). *Mental health act statistics, annual figures: 2020–21.* https://digital.nhs.uk/data-and-information/publications/statistical/mental-health-act-statistics-annual-figures/2020-21-annual-figures#

Reynolds, V. (2019). The zone of fabulousness: Resisting vicarious trauma with connection, collective care and justice-doing in ways that centre the people we work alongside. *Context, 164,* August. https://vikkireynoldsdotca.files.wordpress.com/2019/09/2019-context-uk-zone-of-fabulousness-reynolds.pdf

Strand, S. (2022). *The flowering wand: Rewilding the sacred masculine.* Inner Traditions.

Wall Kimmerer, R., Hausdoerffer J. & Van Horn, G. (n.d.). Kinship is a verb. *Orion: People and nature.* https://orionmagazine.org/article/kinship-is-a-verb

Weintrobe, S. (2013). *Engaging with climate change: Psychoanalytic and interdisciplinary perspectives.* Routledge.

Williams, J. (2021). *Climate change is racist: Race, privilege and the struggle for climate justice.* Icon Books.

14 | Solution-focused practice at the edge of despair: Nursing a planet in hospice

Fred Ehresmann

The latest report from the Intergovernmental Panel on Climate Change (2022) confirms that the jury is now officially in. Anthropogenic climate change is underway to such an extent that we are facing a species-wide challenge. Given the underwhelming international response from those with the power and resources to make a difference, this could result in catastrophic consequences. Theories abound, not only about how we have ended up in this mess and what needs to happen next, but also about what could happen should responses continue to be inadequate. For some, civilisational collapse and human extinction in the near term are inevitable (McPherson, 2020; Ozarko, 2018). For others, we are on the threshold of a major transformation of human consciousness, which represents the next evolutionary leap for our species (Patten, 2017). Between these two poles seems to be a range of positions and narratives. As a registered healthcare practitioner working in mental health nursing, I am still unsure as to whether we are talking about hospice nursing or midwifery with complications.

In any event, we as a species seem to be in the deepest of trouble. To use a medical metaphor, if our home planet were a patient, there would be a crash team, tubes, bleeping machines, an army of nurses and a small gaggle of specialist consultants on hand. What we have is planet Earth triaged onto a waiting list, with the paramedics trying to keep her going, and pushed up the list as a matter of urgency. (For a further exploration of the use of gender to describe planet Earth, see Young (2017).) While I have used a metaphor drawn from physical medicine, we know that where there is physical trauma, psychological trauma is often not far behind, and working with people who are experiencing psychological trauma is the bread-and-butter work of the mental health nurse (Isobel & Delgado, 2018; Menschner & Maul, 2016). We are all facing an international public health crisis (Harmer et al., 2020) and, as the recent Covid-19 pandemic has demonstrated, nurses from all disciplines are on the front line.

As a mental health nurse working with people who have been profoundly impacted by our climate and ecological crises, I am forced to ask myself, 'What does mental health actually mean in a context that is so unstable and where the future seems so bleak?' With the term 'eco-anxiety' entering the narrative, and the arrival of the Hogg Eco-Anxiety Scale (Hogg et al., 2021), people's genuine and valid fears for the future are seemingly being pathologised. Waiting in the wings are fledgling recommendations for the 'treatment' of 'eco-anxiety' (Bauden & Jachens, 2021). While some of the initial findings are promising and the absence of a pharmacological approach reassuring, the use of the word 'treatment' remains worrying. In my professional context, 'eco-anxiety' is the kind of term that gives an air of familiarity to an unfamiliar emerging phenomenon, thereby perhaps offering false reassurance to practitioners seeking to know how best to respond.

Joanna Macy (1995) more aptly uses the term 'environmental despair'. In subsequent writing – for example, Macy and Brown (2014) – this experience is not packed neatly into a pathological framework, but more eloquently and thoughtfully discussed from an eco-systemic perspective. The excruciatingly painful experiences of environmental despair are seen as a sign of healthy awakening to, and empathy for, the distress and suffering of a world – human and non-human – that is in freefall destruction. The suggestion is that each of us is as connected to each other and the whole entirety of life as our earlobes are to the rest of our bodies. This perspective seems to resonate with and expand on the eco-systemic model of child development proposed by Uri Bronfenbrenner (1979) and echoes the seminal work of Gregory Bateson (1979). More recently, social neuroscience has been playing catch-up, conceptualising the brain as a social organ, with Louis Cozolino (2014) poetically describing the brain as an ongoing, living sculpture of all of our relationships and experiences. We are all inevitably neurologically interconnected. Dan Siegel (2021), in coining the term 'Mwe', seems finally to be bringing social neuroscience in line with Joanna Macy's thinking. To sum it all up, do you see Patient Earth on the waiting list? That's us, in the 'planetary Mwe' sense of the word. Small wonder that our mental health has been taking such a battering.

Any self-respecting mental health practitioner, whatever their profession, can expect to undertake a full assessment, formulation and diagnostic process that will guide their intervention with someone who is experiencing mental health problems. The nature of these activities will be informed by their theoretical orientation. All this, and more, was shovelled into my enthusiastically curious mind during my training in the early 1990s. As the years rolled on, I became baffled and bewildered by the ever-growing number of theoretical orientations on offer, and the attempts, or not, to prove their efficacy via what, apparently, is the 'gold standard' of the randomised controlled trial. I will avoid wandering off down a side-route critique, save to recommend *The Heroic Client* (Duncan et al., 2004), which offers a forensic critique of the thinking behind the therapeutic enterprise.

To return to Patient Earth, languishing on the waiting list, there seems to be a similarly baffling array of framings and formulations as to how 'Mwe' ended up in such a pitiful state. We have a smorgasbord of conferences, workshops, webinars, Mighty Networks, Slack channels and, yes, books (apologies to the editors and my fellow authors) with new perspectives and theories emerging, refinements of pre-existing perspectives being made, debate, controversy and all the rest of it… and yet Patient Earth remains firmly, stubbornly, on the waiting list. I have worked for 30 years in the public sector, so the phenomenon of the waiting list is not new to me. In fact, it was the final straw that led to me abandoning so much of what I had been taught about mental health, mental ill health and its treatment. I needed a different paradigm with which I could approach the diverse and growing tidal wave of human suffering that I was facing in my work. Enter the solution-focused approach.

A brief and ill-disciplined literature search at the university where I teach turned up around 5000 publications on the subject, while an even sloppier Google search led to me throwing in the towel at 46 pages. There is clearly no shortage of descriptions and commentary on the approach. I recommend Guy Shennan's (2019) text as an excellent entry point for the newcomer, or Evan George's (2020) short video explanation. Having said that, I will take the variety of descriptions available as licence to add my own perspective, in the context of working with people for whom thinking and talking about our environmental crisis have been having a devastating impact on their mental health. This perspective has been heavily influenced by adaptations to the approach in the fields of end-of-life care (Simon, 2010; Bray, 2007), children's safeguarding (Edwards & Turnell, 1999) and suicide prevention (Henden, 2017). Clearly, in these sorts of scenarios, stakes and emotions are high, and having worked in all three areas, the credibility of this approach is enhanced by the effectiveness that I have observed and its flexibility and portability.

To elaborate further, drawing on an observation by Shennan (2019), there are two broad approaches to using solution-focused practice. I have used it in a formal and structured manner in 'clinical' settings in children and young people's mental health services, where referrals have been made and allocated and there is an expectation of 'therapy' being 'done'. I have also used it less formally in situations where there has been a need to respond more organically to people in crisis, without necessarily following a formalised and structured approach. My observation is that people who have come to talk about how information about the climate emergency is impacting them are in crisis. It is not so much that they have been experiencing the 'environmental despair' described by Macy (1995) but that this experience has been unexpected and unmanageable and has been having serious and multiple negative impacts on their lives. I will later attempt to offer practical insight into the solution-focused approach by using an example drawn from a conversation with a person to whom I am eternally grateful both for their allowing me to record it for publication and for being part of my own journey of learning about how best to respond to and live with what is unfolding. Their name and any identifying details have been changed to preserve their confidentiality.

First, I would like to offer my perspective on the solution-focused approach. This is derived in part from the work of Assay and Lambert (1999) and descriptions of the nature of the relationship between the person coming for help and the person offering help that are to be found in much of the literature on solution-focused practice (for example Ratner et al., 2012).

Assay and Lambert (1999) suggest that the person coming for help, in this case referred to as the 'client', accounts for 40% of the factors in therapeutic change, and the therapeutic alliance between this person and the person offering help accounts for another 30%. The actual model or techniques of therapy used account for a mere 15%, with remaining 15% being placebo. This is colloquially known as 'Lambert's pie' (Assay & Lambert, 1999). From Duncan and colleagues' (2004) perspective, the client is the hero of the story. From a solution-focused perspective, I would agree with Anderson and Goolisham's (1992) framing of the client being the expert. To expand further, the client has the knowledge, resources, creativity and, indeed, ingenuity to navigate the ups and downs of their life. The practitioner will therefore inevitably be located in a not-knowing and non-expert position. This idea of the practitioner not having any 'expert knowledge' seems to be a logical outcome of how solution-focused practice developed. It emerged not from any particular set of psychological theories about human behaviour or psychopathologies but from practice, as practitioners continually sought to ask themselves and the people they were helping how they might be more effective. Gradually developing out of solution-focused brief therapy, the solution-focused approach has no fundamental theory of personality or human development, no normative principles out of which diagnostic formulations can be made and, as such, no structure for analysing the causes of people's problems. In fact, Ratner and colleagues (2012, p.21) suggest that '*Attempting to understand the cause of a problem* is not a necessary or particularly useful step towards resolution.' (The emphasis is mine, for clarification.) I have found this stance to be particularly helpful as we all grapple with the magnitude of what has been happening in the world and where it is heading.

Professor Phil Barker (2004), one of mental health nursing's leading academics, has long contended that the project of helping people with their problems is both deeply relational and reciprocal. I suspect this was never more true than it is today. Having been personally deeply affected by environmental despair and engaged in an ongoing journey of discovery about living with and being informed by it rather than 'cure' or 'manage' it, my expertise comes less from study and training and more from lived experience. How does the therapeutic encounter work when the people within it are both 'helper' and 'helpee' and also, at the most fundamental human level, peers who are deeply affected by the same issues? I am forced to ask myself, 'What does it mean to be a therapeutic practitioner in our world today?' Perhaps the answer lies in an examination of the section in Lambert's pie labelled 'therapeutic alliance'. This is a concept that will be familiar to those working in counselling, psychotherapy and other helping professions, and one that has evolved over time (Ardito & Rabellino, 2011). Can there ever be a place for a first-person description from a therapeutic practitioner of their own experiences of reckoning with environmental despair? If so, where is that place, and does it belong at all within the therapeutic alliance?

The question 'What is solution-focused practice?' invites conceptual responses (what it is all about) and practice responses (how it is done). There is so much I could write about the former and some of that will emerge as I turn my attention to the latter. My starting point is Shennan's (2019, p.17) observation that:

... the solution-focused approach is a *question-based approach*. The solution-focused worker tries to find useful questions to ask, rather than answers or advice to give. (Original emphasis)

I will use a vignette from a recorded conversation with a client to illustrate how this might work, beginning with the start. Henden (2017, p.109), in his work with people who are suicidal (a potential consequence of despair), refers to 'the crucial first 10 minutes' in which the practitioner must establish a strong therapeutic alliance. Here's the beginning of my conversation with Mae – confidentiality, times and so forth having been established:

F: *So, what are your best hopes from us talking together, Mae?*

The wording of the opening question – as with all subsequent questions – is vitally important. I could have asked 'What brings you here?' or 'How can I help?', but I want to ask a question with the word 'hope' in it. This is a common opening question in solution-focused practice. It not only establishes a clear purpose and direction but also introduces the possibility of something hopeful happening for Mae, at least at some point over the next hour.

M: *I'm really feeling completely overwhelmed by the whole climate thing. Everything I read and hear is just so... horrible. It's, like, I haven't slept for ages. Most days I just want to curl up under the duvet and cry all the time... I feel like I'm no use to the kids... it's terrible. I went to my GP who told me that I've got depression and that I should see a counsellor. I'm not interested in taking pills – that doesn't solve anything. So, my friend Pete said that I should talk to you.*

Mae doesn't answer my question. This is common – some people will start by letting me know what they need me to know at the time. And I listen carefully in a very particular way, described by Lipchick (1988) as 'listening with a constructive ear'. My interpretation of what Lipchick is suggesting is that, when listening to someone's description of their suffering, rather than listening for information that will contribute to a hypothesis about them and their problem, the solution-focused practitioner is listening for strengths, resources and personal qualities in the quest to define the suffering as containing the seeds of some sort of achievement. Obviously, you can't see my nods, leaning in, facial gestures and other non-verbal signs of showing empathy. That said, here is my response:

F: *Sounds like things have been terrible – feeling overwhelmed by what you've been finding out about the climate thing, having kids to be thinking about as well, and then not feeling any use to them. What on earth gets you out from under the duvet and keeps you going?*

Here is an example of O'Hanlon's (1998) 'acknowledgement and possibility' principle. O'Hanlon rightly points out that acknowledgement of a person's suffering is an absolute prerequisite for introducing the possibility that there might be nuggets of gold to be found in there somewhere. I do this by summarising, using some selected words from Mae's description in my response in order to weave a co-created narrative. But the key in this particular response is in the words 'have been'. Placing these experiences in the past – on the shelf, if you like – creates some space in the present moment for this new narrative. Having placed the experiences in the past, and avoiding the assumption that they are happening here and now in the space between us, I want to shift my focus for a moment. The question is designed to gently invite Mae's attention to a possible nugget of gold and a hint of her own agency, given that she has been feeling overwhelmed. I am assuming that something has been getting Mae 'out from under the duvet' (where she would rather be, crying) and is keeping her going. My evidence, slim though it might be for some – but I'll take it – is that she is here talking with me now. I therefore place the question in the present.

M: *Well, when you've got three kids... you know... you've just got to keep going somehow...*

The casual 'you've just got to keep going somehow' is a response that I've heard so many times, and one that I have uttered myself. I want to invite a consideration of the enormity of what Mae is achieving. This is genuine – I have been finding co-parenting one child in these times challenging enough, but three...?

F: *Blimey... three?*

M: *Yep, and a dog! And no help. My husband died a few years ago, so it's just me and... and... this...* (starts to well up with tears, then starts sobbing)

F: *Yep... this...*

I am sticking closely to the O'Hanlon principle and staying with acknowledgement of 'this', echoing her 'Yep'. I need to add here that I experience a sense of kinship when Mae uses the word and I too start to cry. I have had my own version of 'this', but I have no idea whether my 'this' bears any relation to Mae's 'this', so I tread carefully. The 'not-knowing' position that I referred to earlier needs to come into its element right now. However, let's recap what I do know from what Mae has told me. She is a single parent with three children and a dog. Her husband died a few years ago. Something has launched her into finding out information about a topic that many people find it hard even to begin to engage with. The challenges of parenting three children alone, coupled with the overwhelming emotional impact of what she has been learning (which I do not even know is factual, by the way), have been significant. As part of the discipline of not knowing, I cannot make assumptions about the impact of her husband's death on her and her children (I do not know if he was the father of any of them, or the nature of his relationship with them). It might have been an abusive relationship and his death a relief. It might have been the complete opposite.

   From the perspective of many therapeutic approaches, there are so many questions to be asked and so much more information to be found out. From a solution-focused perspective, while I might agree with the first proposition, I would not agree with the second. The task of the question is not for me to find out more information. The question needs to be useful to Mae, right now, in this moment. As a solution-focused practitioner, I really do need to be aware of what my 'need-now' mind is up to. Everything that I have learned and practised about being completely present comes in handy, as my mind is desperate to go on a sightseeing mission. So, I wait, watch and listen, until Mae lets out a sigh.

F: *How are you doing? Need to get a tissue?*

You'll notice that there are two questions – I want to offer Mae a choice of an open or closed question, to decide for herself how she moves forward. Small experiences of agency in a conversation might be the beginnings of something.

M: *Nah... I'm alright. Fuck I needed that. Thanks.*

Now I'm curious – what did I do?

F: *Thanks?*

M: *Yep, you just let me cry and didn't interrupt or give me all that shit about* (in parody voice) *'Oooh... it's OK to cry. It's fine'. It's not fine – it's completely shit. Everything's so fucked up.*

F: *Okay, so one of your instructions for me is, 'When I cry, shut up and let me cry'?*

I deliberately frame my response this way as a clear indication of who is in charge – which is pretty much a cornerstone of solution-focused practice: the client is in charge, the client decides what is useful, and the client sets the agenda.

M: (Laughs) *I'm sorry, that sounds bossy... but actually, yes, that would be really helpful. I don't cry in front of the kids, and when I start crying around friends or family, they keep fussing over me, telling me I need to see my GP... so, I've just been holding it all in...*

Despite Mae's apology, I can sense the therapeutic alliance developing and know that she needs me to see and acknowledge her emotions as they arise. The subject of emotions has been an area of contention within, and misunderstanding from without, the solution-focused approach (Lipchick, 2002). However, Lipchick is very clear about the centrality of a concern for human emotions in our experience, which therefore should be incorporated into the approach. Echoing O'Hanlon, when practitioners listen and attend to their emotions and struggles, as well as their strengths and 'gold nuggets', people can make their own changes. Lipchick's perspective has been central in my take on using solution-focused practice in this particular context.

F: *Well, you are the boss here so thank you for being so clear about what you need from me. So, one of your best hopes from our talking together is...?* (I pause, searching for the right words).

M: *… for me to have a good cry!*

Mae finishing my sentence indicates that we do seem to have the makings of a good therapeutic alliance and the co-creation of a narrative in the present moment about her situation. Notice how I have returned to 'best hopes', but have framed her need to cry and be seen as one of her best hopes. I have done this because, as Shennan (2019) points out, when people come to talk, the assumption is that they want something in their life to be different. I want to invite Mae to consider what difference her stated best hope so far would make in her life in the future, outside of our conversation.

F: *Okay, so what might you notice yourself doing differently in your life if you could have a good cry?*

Three points here: the 'what difference…' question invites Mae to consider what she would like to be different outside the conversation once it is complete. The future is a primary focus in solution-focused practice. What I have found so fascinating in these conversations is that the approach brings this elusive place – which doesn't actually exist in reality and yet causes so much distress – closer to the present moment in a more manageable and bite-size way. The use of the word 'might' rather than 'will' or 'would' holds this future lightly and implies that possibility and uncertainty are close relatives and that their impacts can be nuanced and context dependent. The words 'notice yourself doing' contain some essentials of solution-focused language. The word 'notice' invites a shift in attention away from what might be problematic/distressing for a person and towards a future where there is a possibility of something that might be helpful to them. The word 'doing' is also key in that it assumes and introduces thinking about a person's agency into the conversation.

M: (Heaves a big sigh) *Mmmm… I'm not sure… that's a tough one… Ummmm… I don't know really…*

F: *Okay, that's a tough one… let's try another one. Who might be the first to notice you doing something differently after we've finished talking?*

Notice the pattern of my use of Mae's language as the building blocks for my next question. I have also made the question more specific to the present moment, as she seems to have had a good cry in the presence of an acknowledging witness. Also particularly important is the widening of Mae's field of vision. I had assumed that *she* might notice herself doing something. Part of the language of solution-focused practice involves drawing in outside perspectives, which invites Mae to step briefly outside of herself into the little bit of the future after the conversation.

M: *Ah… that'll be Rufus, our dog… poor thing. He gets such a raw deal. He's so lovely, with his big boo-boo eyes. Completely loyal, always on duty. And I've just been rotten with him. He needs a good cuddle… actually we could both do with a big cuddle. And a nice long walk. I'm always badgering the kids about him being their dog… he's* *nobody's dog! He's a member of the family, and I've completely forgotten him. He was Steve's idea, not mine. Then he offs and dies, leaving me with three kids and a dog. Poor old Rufus...*

I was surprised by this answer – and secretly delighted by its length and how Mae had suddenly launched herself into a conversation that seemed to me was really one with herself. I didn't want to interrupt, just to echo what struck me as standing out...

F: *A cuddle and a nice long walk with poor old Rufus...*

M: *Yeh... but when am I going to find the time to do that with three kids and a job?*

I am briefly thrown off balance by the word 'but' and momentarily concerned that Mae will talk herself out of her potential solution. I snap out of it quickly and just put my faith in the process that seems to have started in Mae's previous response.

F: *That sounds like a tough one...*

M: *Look, I don't want to be funny... this is really helpful... but can I just go and grab Rufie and take him out? I know that we're supposed to be talking for an hour, but the kids are parked and I've left myself time to recover because I was expecting to be in a right state after this. I had no idea that therapy made you feel better. I was expecting all sorts about my childhood and that... There's some lovely woods, Rufie loves them and I never get the time. I think it'll do me some good.*

I really wasn't expecting this at all! There was me thinking that we were just getting started, and Mae decides to go and take the dog for a walk. She's come up with the perfect plan to make the best use of her time and do something that she's realised might be helpful. Listening to the recording and reading back the transcript, I am still struck by her slightly apologetic tone, her asking for permission and her need to justify her decision. From my perspective, this is a beautiful example of someone finding their agency, creativity and connection with nature, all under her own steam. And I love that I can only speculate as to how this happened!

F: *I always book out an hour, but it doesn't have to take an hour. And it sounds like you've come up with a plan for the next steps forward.*

M: *Awww, that's great. Thanks. So, what happens now?*

F: *That's completely up to you, Mae. Everything from 'We're done here...'*

M: *We're definitely not done here... do I book in another appointment?*

F: *If you think that would help, that would be fine.*

M: *When do you suggest?*

F: *Remember, you're the boss, you've just come up with a great plan for the next bit of time ahead. What do you think?*

M: *I think... I think... I think I need to get out of the house with Rufie more. Maybe take the kids with me if I can't get out on my own. I'm always getting the oldest to do it and take the other two so I can have some peace and quiet. Mmmm... Rufie and me... Rufie, me and the kids. Would it be okay if I give it a go and come back in a week's time?*

Mae is wanting to try something that she might find useful. We agree to email to arrange a time to meet again so that she can fetch Rufus and go out to those woods. We meet a further five times, during which Mae builds on what she discovered in our first conversation and goes on to draw on her experiences of navigating herself and the children through the uncertainty, Steve's death and subsequent grief afterwards to work out, in her words, 'how we're all going to live our lives in a world that's crumbling around our ears'. In many ways, Mae's experience seems to echo that of all the people with whom I have had the privilege of exploring ways of living life 'with the blinkers ripped off', as one young person described it. The solution-focused approach privileges resourcefulness, creativity, agency and personal expertise. Through the use of questions, it aims to invite people to direct their attention towards these qualities and consider ways in which they might be mobilised. The expertise of the practitioner lies in being present, not knowing, and listening carefully for the seeds of the next question that lie in what the person has just said.

Closing reflection

For this jobbing mental health nurse, some 25 years ago, the solution-focused approach offered a portable, flexible and pragmatic way of being able to support people to navigate their way through psychological crisis and find some solid ground under their feet. When, four years ago, at the age of eight, my youngest daughter told me of a planet that is dying and her fears that she would not live to experience either adolescence or adulthood, this prompted a deep psychological crisis in my own life that continues to reverberate to this day. That conversation was unlikely to end with the words 'Don't worry, everything will be fine.' In fact, that conversation is ongoing as she stands at the threshold of the adolescence that she feared would be stolen from her. It's been hard work, sitting on my hands, resisting the urge to explain, analyse, make suggestions and generally try to make things better.

I will close with one of my daughter's favourite questions to ask of me:

'Imagine it's quite a few years in the future – as far ahead as you like – and whoever is still here, well... they're sitting around of an evening talking about how they managed to get this far. They're looking back and talking about now, and you and me and all the others who want to do something. And they're being grateful – very grateful. Imagine that you could listen in to what they're saying about you and what you did... how would you like that conversation to go?'

Thank you for reading this far. May you find your way of getting through the dark days and doing what there is for you to do.

References

Anderson, H. & Goolisham, H. (1992). The client is the expert: A not-knowing approach to therapy. In S. McNamee & K.J. Gergen (Eds.), *Therapy as social construction* (pp.25-39). Sage Publications.

Ardito, R. & Rabellino, D. (2011). Therapeutic alliance and outcome of psychotherapy: Historical excursus, measurements and prospects for research. *Frontiers in Psychology, 2,* 270–281.

Assay, T. & Lambert, M. (1999). The empirical case for the common factors in therapy: Quantitative findings. In M. Hubble, B. Duncan & S. Miller (Eds.), *The heart and soul of change: What works in therapy* (pp.23–55). American Psychological Association.

Barker, P. (2004). *The tidal model: A guide for mental health professionals.* Routledge.

Bateson, G. (1979). *Mind and nature: A necessary unity.* Hampton Press.

Baudon, P. & Jachens, L. (2021). A scoping review of interventions for the treatment of eco-anxiety. *International Journal of Environmental Research and Public Health, 18,* 9636–9654. https://doi.org/10.3390/ijerph18189636

Bray, D. (2007). A tailor-made psychological approach to palliative care. *European Journal of Palliative Care, 14*(4), 141–143.

Bronfenbrenner, U. (1979). *The ecology of human development: Experiments by nature and design.* Harvard University Press.

Cozolino, L. (2014). *The neuroscience of human relationships: Attachment and the developing social brain.* W.W. Norton & Co.

Duncan, B., Sparks, J. & Miller, S. (2004). *The heroic client: A revolutionary way to improve effectiveness through client directed, outcome informed therapy.* John Wiley & Sons.

Edwards, S. & Turnell, A. (1999). *Signs of safety: A solution and safety approach to child protection casework.* W.W. Norton & Co.

George, E. (2020, June 24). *What is solution-focused practice in 2020?* [Video.] https://www.youtube.com/watch?v=JBMNhKWM7q4

Harmer, A., Eder, B., Gepp, S., Leetz, A. & van de Pas, R. (2020). WHO should declare climate change a public health emergency. *BMJ, 368.* https://doi.org/10.1136/bmj.m797

Henden, J. (2017). *Preventing suicide: The solution-focused approach.* John Wiley & Sons.

Hogg, T., Stanley, S., O'Brien, L., Wilson, M. & Watsford, C. (2021). The Hogg Eco-Anxiety Scale: Development and validation of a multidimensional scale. *Global Environmental Change, 71,* 102391–102401. https://doi.org/10.1016/j.gloenvcha.2021.102391

Intergovernmental Panel on Climate Change (IPCC). (2022). *Climate change 2022: Impacts, adaptation and vulnerability. Sixth assessment report.* IPCC. www.ipcc.ch/report/ar6/wg2

Isobel, S. & Delgado, C. (2018). Safe and collaborative communication skills: A step towards mental health nurses implementing trauma informed care. *Archives of Psychiatric Nursing, 33*(2), 291–296.

Lipchick, E. (1988). Interviewing with a constructive ear. *Dulwich Centre Newsletter.*

Lipchick, E. (2002). *Beyond technique in solution-focused therapy: Working with emotions and the therapeutic relationship.* Guilford Press.

Macy, J. (1995). Working through environmental despair. In T. Roszak, M. Gomes & A. Kanner (Eds.), *Ecopsychology: Restoring the Earth/healing the mind* (pp.240–260). Counterpoint.

Macy, J. & Brown, M. (2014). *Coming back to life: The updated guide to the Work That Reconnects.* New Society Publishers.

McPherson, G. (2020). *Extinction foretold, extinction ignored.* [Blog.] Nature Bats Last. https://guymcpherson.com/extinction_foretold_extinction_ignored

Menschner, C. & Maul, A. (2016). *Issue brief: Key ingredients for successful trauma-informed care implementation.* Centre for Healthcare Strategies, Robert Wood Johnson Foundation. www.chcs.org/media/ATC_whitepaper_040616.pdf

O'Hanlon, W. (1998). Possibility therapy: An inclusive, collaborative, solution-based model of psychotherapy. In M.F. Hoyt (Ed.), *The handbook of constructive therapies from leading practitioners* (pp.137–158). Jossey-Bass/Wiley.

Ozarko, D. (2018). *Beyond hope: Letting go of a world in collapse.* Deb Ozarko Publishing.

Patten, T. (2017). *A new republic of the heart: A guide to inner work for holistic change: awakening into evolutionary activism (sacred activism).* North Atlantic Books.

Ratner, H., George, E. & Iveson, C. (2012). *Solution-focused brief therapy: 100 key points and techniques.* Routledge.

Shennan, G. (2019). *Solution-focused practice: Effective communication to facilitate change.* Macmillan.

Siegel, D. (2021). *IntraConnected: Mwe (Me + We) as the integration of belonging and identity.* W.W. Norton & Co.

Simon, J. (2010). *Solution-focused practice in end-of-life and grief counselling.* Springer.

Young, A. (2017). Latest scientific discovery drops bombshell – 'Mother Nature' is biologically male – Ruminations on the value of care as sustainable organizational practice. *Gender, Work and Organization, 25*(3), 294–308. https://doi.org/10.1111/gwao.12185

PART 4

Holding hope for children
and young people

15 Feeling okay with not feeling okay: Helping children and young people make meaning from their experience of climate emergency

Caroline Hickman

There is growing understanding of the impact on mental health that follows increasing awareness of the climate and biodiversity crisis (Pihkala, 2020), with concern often centred on how this is affecting children and young people (Lawton, 2019; Hickman, 2019a; Hoggett, 2019).

It would be a mistake to try to directly compare children's distress with that felt by adults in relation to the climate crisis: children and young people think and feel differently to adults about it, not only because their defences can be shaped differently but also because they have grown up with an awareness of the vulnerability of the planet. This can leave them feeling misunderstood and dismissed when talking about their despair, as it does not always feel understandable to adults (Hickman, 2019b). This chapter explores imaginal and creative ways to listen to the experiences of children and young people and support them to navigate these difficult times, using a 'climate change emotion' model adapted from Fisher's transition curve (2000).

Children and young people are undoubtedly suffering severe emotional and mental distress because of climate change – knowing about it, witnessing it, experiencing its impact, and fearing for their increasingly uncertain futures. They are suffering from trauma and prolonged psychological and physical stress; they have symptoms of depression, grief and anxiety; they feel betrayed, abandoned and dismissed by the people in power they expect to protect them (Hickman et al., 2021). They are suffering from moral injury, or institutional betrayal, because of government failure to act on climate change. They feel uncared for, unprotected and abandoned by government inaction; they do not need further betrayal by political, social, educational, legal or mental health systems. They need their distress and pain to be understood, validated, taken seriously and acted on.

Children are also more at risk psychologically because they have not developed the adult psychological defences that might temporarily numb them to the injustice they are facing or their fears about the future. They are more easily traumatised, and their trauma can have long-lasting effects on their physical and mental health. Indeed, climate change is now recognised as an Adverse Childhood Experience (ACE) (Nelson et al., 2020). Research shows that trauma in infants and young children can alter brain development, nervous system regulation and stress responses, leading to increased risk of chronic physical health conditions, auto-immune disorders, self-harm and suicide. The impact can be seen through psychosocial factors such as poor academic achievement, low life satisfaction and difficulties building and maintaining long-term relationships in adulthood (Hughes et al., 2017). Adverse childhood experiences can be direct, such as exposure to traumatic events (wildfires, floods or extreme heat) or indirect, such as witnessing the harm caused to others in news reports showing animals and people fleeing wildfires or listening to stories told by survivors of traumatic events (Lawrance et al., 2021; Obradovich et al., 2018).

The psychological process of 'othering' children and young people is key to understanding how adults can struggle to comprehend young people's perspectives and feelings about climate change (Hickman, 2019b). We need to see climate change through their eyes, understand it through their minds, feel it through their hearts, and sense it through their experience. Using adult psychological models to understand the child's experience may leave the child disillusioned and feeling misunderstood. Six years ago, a 10-year-old boy became frustrated with me during a research interview. He said:

> You just don't get it, Caroline, none of you adults really get it. You think you do, but you don't. You grew up thinking polar bears would be there for ever, but I am growing up *knowing* they will go extinct. It's different for us. It's personal, this is being done to us. But we're not the ones doing it.

I have been listening to children and young people's complex feelings and increasing distress about the climate and biodiversity crisis since 2017, through my research at the University of Bath (Hickman, 2019c, 2020), for 10 years as a psychotherapist in private clinical practice and through climate psychology and eco-anxiety workshops and talks with young climate activists in the UK and internationally in Brazil, the Maldives, USA, Sweden, France, Nigeria, Canada, Spain and Portugal.

The qualitative research referenced throughout this chapter comes from my own research (Hickman, 2019a). Influenced by Romanyshyn (2013), who encourages researchers to play with the imaginal landscape of the work, I used a range of creative research methodologies including art, theatre, personification and storytelling. I created seagull puppets with children and then interviewed the puppets about climate change. I spray-painted (using organic chalk paint) a baby humpback whale onto a school playing field and then planted 2500 crocus bulbs into the outline to create stories with the children about climate change, the impact of warming seas on whales, biodiversity loss and extinction. I worked with youth theatre groups and had 60 children enacting climate change. I have stood in grass fields, on cliff tops and in woods, talking with children, and I've collected hundreds of stories and drawings (Alderson & Morrow, 2011; Kay et al., 2009).

Following the rapid development of the climate school strikes in 2018, I started to notice a change in the way that young people were talking with me about the climate crisis. While they continued to talk about their fears and anxieties about the worsening state of the planet and the effects of climate change on animals and the environment generally, they also began to make strong links to a broader global injustice, and to express frustration and incomprehension with governments' failure to listen to scientists and take urgent action (Hickman, 2020; Hickman et al, 2021). It was clear that the school strikes were giving young people an external focus for their concern, a community through which they could deepen their understanding, and space in which to express their anger, show it to the world and create a collective voice that could reach a global audience. At the same time, they were often struggling with difficult feelings, and I was asked by groups of young people to provide workshops on eco-anxiety. I found myself in these workshops saying things like:

> You are not mad, your feelings make absolute sense. No, we can't get rid of uncomfortable feelings, but we can transform them, change our relationship with them, find their meaning and use them to nourish sustainable activism.

I framed this as internal activism and inner emotional biodiversity. Imperfect names, but useful constructs.

The climate change emotion transition curve (based on Fisher, 2000) grew out of a need for depth psychology models that could be understood and taught in workshops for children and young people. The model is introduced here to help understand children's emotional engagement with climate change, the process that many go through, and the usefulness of a containing model in which all feelings have their place.

Children and young people are increasingly speaking out about their frustration and despair at the lack of action being taken to address the climate and biodiversity crisis. Inspired by the Swedish environmental activist Greta Thunberg, the largest climate strikes in global history saw 4500 school strikes across 150 countries in the 2019 Global Week for the Future, with millions of children and young people taking part. Research published in 2021 reported 'an explosion' in anxiety in young people over the past 10 years (Slee et al., 2021), and in 2020 a YouGov poll in the UK reported that 70% of 18–24 year olds were more worried about climate change than they were a year before (Friends of the Earth, 2020).

Young people showing concern and care, speaking out about their fears and taking action could be argued to be a healthy psychological response to the growing climate crisis. As the following quote from a 14-year-old school striker shows, for many children and young people the school strikes were saving them from psychological distress, not harming them. They were the only thing left for them to do to try to have their feelings about the climate crisis heard and validated:

> People don't understand, for me there is no choice, I have to do something, anything to make people understand that the damage being done to the planet is being done to me. It is personal. It is hurting me. Going on strike has saved

my sanity and my life, and people need to understand that'. (Research interview, female, age 14, UK)

Fisher's transition curve

My adaptation of Fisher's curve (2000) offers a visual model that can help children and young people think about the unthinkable and make sense of the range of feelings they are experiencing. It potentially acts as a container without pathologising feelings. It presents a visual framework that shows that the emotional journey is not linear or causative but involves a more cyclical process, with starts and obstacles, diversions and distractions. It is not a staged developmental model; nor is it a complete map. However, it can be helpful in validating a holistic emotional narrative that allows space for all feelings and shows that they have their place in meaning-making (Hollis, 1996; Randall, 2019). One limitation is that it can look rather two dimensional (see Figure 15.1), and I suggest it could be better imagined as a spiral, with repeated deepening cycles, rather like a Slinky. In workshops, young people have found it helpful as a visual representation of their range of feelings, leading to the emergence of a non-shaming narrative that has helped change their view of themselves, their mental health and life more generally.

Figure 15.1: Climate-change emotional transition curve (adapted from Fisher, 2000)

The journey downwards – from blissful unawareness to anxiety, disbelief and terror

Eco-anxiety (Davenport, 2017; Hickman, 2020; Ray, 2020) is increasingly recognised as a congruent, meaningful and healthy emotional response to the worsening ecological crisis (Ojala, 2012; Nugent, 2019; Pihkala, 2020), and children and young people are feeling this acutely and painfully:

> I just feel scared all the time, so scared of the future, of today, of people, of everything now. (Research interview, male, age 12, UK)

This anxiety has understandably drawn attention in part because of the increased and very real environmental threat it is connected to, but it would be a mistake to just focus on the anxiety without understanding how it connects with a range of other complex emotional responses.

In moving from a state of relative unawareness to anxiety as they start to become aware of the multiple ecological threats facing the planet, the young person can descend or fall from anxiety into feelings of fear or terror. These can, in turn, trigger the psychological defences of denial, disavowal (Weintrobe, 2021; Tollemache, 2019) and sometimes a naïve hope that someone will act to save the planet, or something will be done to halt or mitigate the worst impacts of climate change. These hopes are often presented as fantasies of rescue, usually projected onto adult authority figures such as parents, scientists or the government (Hickman, 2020).

> When I learnt about climate change, I just couldn't believe that no one seemed to be doing anything fast enough. I just couldn't wrap my head around it, why were the newspapers not full of it, why were people acting normal, when I just found out at school that the planet was being destroyed, by us?! (Workshop participant, male, age 19, UK)

This descent can feel terrifying, and is often accompanied by an emotional experience of chaotic feelings, abandonment, disillusionment and disbelief that these previously trusted adults were now failing to protect them:

> What I couldn't get was that my parents were not talking to me about this stuff. Where were they?! (Workshop participant, female, age 16, US)

Why were parents not at the very least openly talking with young people about it?

> I felt like I was going mad – every time I started to try to talk to my parents, they told me to stop worrying. Were they mad? How could I stop worrying? I had just found out that the planet was in serious trouble. (Workshop participant, female, age 14, US)

What is significant here is not just the personal emotional experiences of anxiety and terror, but also the social and relational loss of faith and trust in adults:

> I feel so stupid, why did I ever trust them? Have they been lying to me all my life? (Workshop participant, male, age 16, Brazil)

The experience of eco-anxiety and terror, then, is not simply fear of environmental destruction and collapse, but greater distress due to the failure of governments to act to halt and repair this destruction:

> Just watching them call a climate emergency and then fail to do anything else to stop things from getting worse, I feel as if all my trust in adults has been trashed. Do they think we're stupid? (Research interview, male, age 17, UK)

Some young people told me that they felt that their parents or the government had betrayed or abandoned them, that they felt their futures had been sacrificed.

Defences and denial

During the descent into the despair and depression, there can be a loss of connection with others, sometimes characterised by withdrawal:

> I just can't bear to be with people or talk about anything. It's like I can't think or feel anything. (Research interview, male, age 20, UK)

Disillusionment and loss of trust in previously trusted others is also common – usually expressed as loss of faith in adults and the government. If defences against this fear and loss and anxiety are activated, this can serve to guard against or mitigate this loss, and perhaps divert from the descent. The child or young person can preserve the relationship with the adult by unconsciously using the defences of denial, disavowal, rationalisation, splitting or displacement (Weintrobe, 2013, 2021). This presents a complex unconscious dilemma for the child, however, as their knowledge about the climate crisis will have to be driven into the unconscious but may re-emerge unconsciously when the defences are breached:

> Every night at the moment I'm dreaming of my family starving, I can't feed my cat, the river is flooding so we can't get out to get food. It's terrifying. (Research participant, female, age 17, US)

Or it may simply bubble up to the surface over time. The anxiety may be 'acted out' unconsciously through another form of anxiety, such as developing a phobia or anxiety about school or social relationships. In the model, the defences act to preserve the security of the relationships and defend against the fear of ecological breakdown, but the price paid is to stay unaware of the anxiety and possibly feel disconnected and shut off from loved ones:

> My friends laugh at me and tell me I've disappeared into my climate bubble. I just want to cry. They don't understand how scared I am, I'm so scared I can't talk. (Research participant, female, aged 15, UK)

Nearing the bottom – loss of control, powerlessness, disillusionment and betrayal of trust

I found that many young people struggled with a loss of emotional control as their anxieties grew and deepened into despair, often accompanied by feelings of betrayal at the seeming indifference of others:

> What's the point in talking with them? They just don't get it, they're happy to be ignorant. (Research participant, male, age 19, UK)

Attempts to talk with friends could be met with a further denial or dismissal, which is often particularly painful when this reaction is felt from friends:

> I couldn't face school. My friends sat in the same classes as me, but they didn't care. I ended up on my own in the break, crying, while they talked about stupid things. (Workshop participant, female, aged 17, US)

Loss of connection and the sense of belonging with a peer group can be especially painful for young people, especially when felt alongside a loss of faith in adults to take the steps needed to act on climate change. Many young people spoke of their disillusionment; the things they had believed in, old certainties about the security of the world and security in previously reliable relationships, were being lost to them:

> It's as if my world changed overnight, I lost trust and faith in everything and everyone.' (Research participant, female, aged 13, UK)

Hitting or sinking into rock bottom – depression, hopelessness, collapse and despair

The bottom of the curve is hitting 'rock bottom', depression and psychological collapse. Young people talked about sometimes retreating to bed for days, giving up all idea of going to school or college or university. Nihilism and hopelessness could take over their lives:

> I just didn't see the point, I was afraid of the future, I had no future, and the future I could see was a nightmare. It was better to not have a future than to have that nightmare. (Research participant, male, aged 20, Brazil)

Emotional collapse was sometimes mirrored in a social collapse of relationships, belief and hope in any version of their own or others' futures. Some focused their fears on the possible future that their younger siblings faced; others worried about the global injustice and plight of children in other parts of the world. Many young people talked about depression and despair as they struggled with a disillusionment and loneliness that they feared others could not understand. At this point it would not be unusual for them to also stop speaking and eating, in part from an attempt consciously to act to reduce a personal carbon footprint and as a depressive response to the hopelessness; eating and living just became too hard to imagine or engage with.

I stayed in bed for weeks, there was no point in getting up more than I had to. (Research participant, female, aged 17, UK)

One 15-year-old described how he would 'act' as if he cared about himself and his life to deflect attention from his worried parents:

They want me to be okay, so I act as if I'm okay, but I'm not. I just can't bear their questions when I just don't think they really care, because the world doesn't really care about us, does it. If it did, it would do something, wouldn't it? (Research participant, male, aged 15, UK)

The turning point

From this place, there are different pathways. These can be summarised as mainly inwards or outwards in direction: inwards towards internalised anger, blame, shame and guilt; outwards towards a more externalised anger and then grief, understanding and compassion. It would be a mistake, however, to frame this in binary 'either/or' thinking. There is a powerful mixture of feelings that seem to compete, but falling into binary thinking at this point would be unhelpful and risk the young person thinking there is a 'right' or 'wrong' way to emotionally respond. I have observed that there can be some feelings of vulnerability and uncertainty at this point, which may trigger further defences – a temptation to 'get back to normal' and push feelings away:

I just wanted to feel better. I wanted my old life back. I wanted to believe that climate change wasn't real and it had all been a bad dream. I wish it wasn't real. If this is how my life is, then I don't like it. (Research participant, male, aged 14, the Maldives)

Internalised anger, blame, shame, and guilt

I just hated myself for not having woken up sooner. I was ashamed for my stupidity for all those years. (Research participant, male, aged 14, UK)

For some young people, there was a tendency towards self-blame and even self-hatred and self-harm. They struggled to understand how they had not seen the state of the planet sooner and directed their feelings of anger inwards at themselves:

I couldn't enjoy anything. My friends went out to the country for the day, and I just couldn't do it. I felt so guilty – the fuel for the car to get there just wasn't worth it. (Research participant, male, aged 19, UK)

Some expressed shame about their privilege at having a comfortable home and food 'when other people are dying because of what we have done or failed to do' (Research participant, male, aged 14, UK).

Many talked about not being able to enjoy anything – loss of ability to play or see any joy, hope or purpose in life. A few talked about feeling suicidal from their frustration, anger and hopelessness: 'At least that would be doing something wouldn't it' (Research participant, male, aged 16, US). Some young people considered suicide as a way to reduce the world's population and their impact on the climate by reducing their own carbon emissions; others thought about suicide as an objective and rational solution in the face of social collapse because of continued political inaction:

> If the government doesn't care about our futures enough to take action, then killing myself seems to be a reasonable alternative to living with these lies and hypocrisy. It's the lies I can't stand. (Research participant, male, aged 19, UK)

Compassionate and passionate anger, grief and a different understanding

> I just realised I had to do something to make up for all the injustice, all the unfairness, I still feel guilty, but at least I'm doing something now, it helps, a bit. (Research participant, male, aged 17, UK)

If young people were able to find a way to direct their anger in more of an outwards direction, rather than towards themselves, this rage and passion could further transform into what was often perceived as more 'positive' action – a determination to challenge global climate injustice. As young people engaged in activism and school strikes, they started to feel less alone and more empowered. Sometimes they were inspired by the action of others: 'I just felt better listening to Greta. She inspires me. She knows how we feel' (Research participant, female, aged 14, US). Sometimes they found a community of others who felt similarly: 'I didn't feel so alone or mad after I joined the strikes' (Research participant, female, aged 20, UK).

Empathy from and with others and anger at injustice and unfairness that is embodied in the climate crisis globally helped to balance or reduce the guilt, shame and distress. Young people started to support the development of more feelings of understanding and compassion for themselves:

> I still feel bad about it all, but it's not all my fault. I'm only 12, other people should feel worse than me, shouldn't they? (Research participant, female, aged 12, US)

Feelings of sadness for the planet, for animals and for others were often felt as reparative in that they connected young people with feelings of eco-grief and solastalgia, which relieved some of the despair and painful isolation that could be felt in the depression:

> I feel bad for the koala bears. (Research participant, female, aged 12, US)

> I feel sad for the fish. My friends are dying, my friends the fish are dying and I feel sad. I want to help them, I want to do something good to help them. (Research participant, male, aged 15, the Maldives)

In turn, this led to a more emotionally integrated understanding of the role the individual person can play in taking action, but now this was clearly located in a psychosocial and political framework that held awareness of the role of the individual alongside the need to address social and economic and global inequalities more broadly.

I noticed an awareness and growing resistance from some young people to the experience of being 'othered' (Ghidina, 2019; Mavronicola, 2019), and a renewed determination towards empathy. Young people felt frustration at being blamed for creating anxiety in other young people and spoke of anger at the marginalisation of their concerns:

> I just don't get how we are being attacked for speaking out about injustice. To blame children for this is totally twisted and unfair. It's nuts, insane, we must really be getting to them to attack us like this. (Research participant, male, aged 16, UK)

Some were inspired by prominent activists such as Greta Thunberg and the way they dealt with personal attacks and criticism in the media:

> Did you see the stuff they print about Greta? It's abusive. Just because she makes them feel bad about what they haven't done to fix the problem, they treat her like that. She's amazing the way she doesn't take it from them. (Research participant, female, aged 15, US)

But others were scared that they would be mistreated or bullied themselves:

> Sometimes I'm scared to speak out now at home or at school. I heard someone say that [Greta Thunberg] should be shut up for good. That's wrong, she's just a kid. (Research participant, male, aged 18, Brazil)

Mavronicola (2019) identifies how 'us' and 'them' narratives can exaggerate the perceived danger of the 'other' and condone their marginalisation – a phenomenon seen in some press reporting of youth climate strikes and of Greta Thunberg in particular. But I also saw young people counter this fear with empathy and a belief that, by being criticised in this way, they were starting to achieve something positive. This was a powerful reframing.

Acceptance, realism, radical hope, imagined futures

> I realised that I could do something to help, so I started striking, writing letters, making a fuss, that made me feel better, at least I was doing something (Workshop participant, female, aged 16, US)

A combination of acceptance of the reality of the ecological crisis and radical hope (Adams, 2019; Hoggett, 2019) gave some young people the belief that their actions could make a difference. As they developed this integration of complex feelings of despair, frustration, anger and action, they also became more able to imagine a future self and, from this, a future version of the planet grounded in a sense of moral justice and fairness. This aligns with Verlie's (2019) arguments about 'bearing worlds, learning to live-with climate change'. Psychologically, anger becomes integrated with depression, leading to a more emotionally balanced, resilient and sustainable form of activism that is less vulnerable to burnout and disillusionment. This is a 'both/and' psychological position, rather than a splitting into 'either/or'. The climate crisis is both awful *and* there is a lot we can do, rather than the splitting into either despair or naïve optimism.

> I know it will be hard, but I decided it was worth trying to do something. Even if we fail, at least we tried. (Workshop participant, female, aged 16, UK)

Beginning to image a future self was crucial in this process. Moving towards a future, seeing themselves occupying a future, even if the details were uncertain, was part of the young people's move upwards, outwards and forwards, out from the despair. Many of them did not hold a confident view of their own future but seemed able to tolerate increased uncertainty alongside some belief that they could have a role in shaping their own and others' lives – a sense of radical hope. I noted an increased ability to tolerate and understand the complexity of their feelings, especially their ambivalence towards authority figures and greater tolerance of the multiple uncertainties of the ecological crisis (Gillespie, 2019).

The emergence of hope in this stage is important, and it is complex; there are many versions of hope and they need careful differentiation. Ojala (2015, 2020) has drawn a distinction between constructive hope and hope based on denial. However, Verlie (2019) links hope back to anxiety and uncertainty and the importance of grieving in order to go on to learn to live with climate change, not in a passive relationship but in an active entanglement. Ozarko (2018) proposes living with presence rather than hope, as this presence leads to acceptance, peace and liberation. I have named the concept of radical hope as important in this model, but defining this precisely is complex. I would suggest, in practice, encouraging individuals to define this construct in their own way, in order to create some sense of safety for themselves amid the uncertainty and insecurity.

Empowered agency, action, resilience and wisdom

These transformed relationships with their feelings led to other changed relationships. Some young people talked about feeling more connected to themselves and to others, and about finding a renewed faith in human nature. Some talked about having a greater empathy for animals and younger children, more understanding of global injustice and more determination to try to make a difference. Many talked about having learnt a lot from going through the downwards journey:

> I hated feeling so down, but now I'm feeling stronger I can see that it was good for me to feel so sad. At least it was real, and another time I might not feel so scared. (Research participant, female, aged 17, UK)

Some were able to recognise that they were likely to go through a number of cycles of feeling down, and sometimes had already done this, as they found ways to integrate their knowledge about the climate crisis with the need to live with this knowledge rather than split into denial or collapse into despair:

> I decided it is a rollercoaster and I just need to learn to hold on and not panic when it goes off again. (Workshop participant, female, aged 16, US)

Jung (1969) identified that, by holding the tension between opposites and allowing both to exist, a new understanding and wisdom can emerge. Some young people found that they were able to tolerate the binary feelings of optimism and pessimism, hope and hopelessness once they found they were likely to feel both (Pihkala, 2017). Randall and Hoggett (2019) identified in their research with adult activists that, when the activists were more able to manage these complex opposing emotions, they were more able to engage in realistic action. So too, in the words of one of my young research participants:

> I stopped bouncing around like a ball in a pinball machine and started to feel okay with not feeling okay, if you know what I mean? (Research participant, male, aged 12, US)

In conclusion

Listening to some young people reflecting on COP26 in November 2021 in Glasgow, I heard how failed, betrayed and abandoned they felt because of collective inaction on climate change. They said to me:

> We're on our own with this now, COP just abandoned us. Caring about climate change and the futures of children and young people can itself feel like a suicide mission sometimes. It's hard to keep going, we pay a high price for caring. But we don't want to escape from these feelings; they are the only thing that makes this suffering meaningful. This hurts because we care.

Looking under the surface requires us to be curious, to use deep listening (Hoggett, 2019), show respect for all forms of emotional expression (Hickman, 2020; Pihkala, 2020; Weintrobe, 2021), show humility towards feelings (Hollis, 1996) and develop climate-aware psychological models that can help us to navigate these unprecedented challenges (inner and outer) in the world today. The adapted Fisher (2000) transition curve that I developed through psychosocial research and workshops with young people offers us a practical and visual tool to help children and young people map and learn to navigate their own emotional journey. It reduces the risk of their eco-anxiety or depression being pathologised as a mental health problem and, at the same time, deepens adult understanding of the complexity of eco-anxiety in children and young people.

In recent years there have been arguments about activism being 'a cure' for eco-anxiety. This is concerning from a depth-psychology and psychosocial perspective as it suggests that eco-anxiety needs to be treated or cured. It places this emotional experience within a medical model framework when, in fact, as discussed above, it should be seen as an entirely congruent and emotionally healthy response to the external reality we are facing (Hickman, 2020; Wray; 2020, 2022; Pihkala, 2020). Also, worryingly, this approach risks trying to take an emotional short-cut from the anxiety at the start of the transition curve straight over to action, avoiding the descent and journey through despair, depression, loss and grief. A depth-psychology approach (Hollis, 1996; Hoggett, 2019; Weintrobe, 2013, Lertzman, 2015, 2019; Randall, 2019) would argue that it is this very descent, depression and experience of grief and loss that gives meaning to the experience of waking up to the climate crisis. This is where emotional resilience is shaped and nurtured. It an important journey if we are to get under the surface of the feelings and make a space where eco-anxiety and fear can move into relationship with agency and action – through eco-compassion, eco-empathy, eco-community and eco-awareness (Hickman, 2020), not by avoiding them. This argument also assumes that eco-anxiety is entirely conscious and can therefore be 'dealt with' by an equally conscious leap across into activism. The risk here, however, is that this is an attempt to avoid, run away from, flee or escape the anxiety, uncertainty and accompanying vulnerability, which may be disavowed or denied and pushed into the unconscious (Weintrobe, 2021), rather than accept, value, respect and sometimes transform it.

Transformation involves making space for and being able to tolerate vulnerability and uncertainty as a healthy part of life. Life today involves multiple uncertainties that have not been faced on this scale before, so of course this is threatening. But if we adopt a more global perspective, we will see that vulnerability and uncertainty are familiar everyday experiences for many communities in the world who are on the front line of the climate crisis: Bangladesh, India, Brazil, the Maldives, and the Philippines. If we frame eco-anxiety as an opportunity to deepen global empathy and fight for climate justice, it might become part of the healing needed, rather than something to be feared and fixed. It is a sign of care, and young people should feel proud that they care.

Haraway (2016) argues we should learn to 'stay with the trouble' of living and dying together on a damaged Earth in order to build more 'liveable' futures for all young people. Inevitably, it may be troubling for adults to see through children's eyes, to feel their betrayal and abandonment, especially as many adults do, of course, also care deeply. Psychological defences of rationalisation, minimising, disavowal, sublimation and excessive consumption can all be used to help navigate the sometimes tough world we are living in, but these tactics can silence children's experiences (Weintrobe, 2021; Hickman, 2020). Generally, children will not have needed to develop these defences so strongly, which is why they are so attuned to the hurt of global climate injustice. For children, it can be felt as a moral injury (Weintrobe, 2021) to be misunderstood emotionally and not have their inner experience of eco-anxiety and distress validated. Hickman and colleagues (2021) found that, globally, 48% of children and young people had been dismissed or silenced when they tried to talk about climate change. By getting under the surface of eco-anxiety and climate distress, by seeing through children's eyes, we could and should change this. Today.

As a final note, in case you were left wondering, yes, this model could be equally supportive to understanding climate anxiety and distress in adults.

References

Adams. M. (2019). *Ecological crisis, sustainability, and the psychosocial subject: Beyond behaviour change*. Palgrave Macmillan.

Alderson, P. & Morrow, V. (2011). *The ethics of research with children and young people: A practical handbook*. Sage.

Davenport, L. (2017). *Emotional resiliency in the era of climate change: A clinician's guide*. Jessica Kingsley Publishers.

Fisher, J.M. (2000), Creating the future? In J.W. Scheer (Ed.), *The person in society: Challenges to a constructivist theory* (pp.428–437). Psychosozial-Verlag.

Friends of the Earth. (2020, January 21). *Over two-thirds of young people experience eco-anxiety as Friends of the Earth launch campaign to turn anxiety into action*. [Press release]. Friends of the Earth. https://friendsoftheearth.uk/climate/over-twothirds-young-people-experience-ecoanxiety-friends-earth-launch-campaign-turn

Ghidina, M. (2019). Deconstructing victim-blaming, dehumanization, and othering: Using empathy to develop a sociological imagination. *Teaching Sociology, 47*(3), 231–242.

Gillespie, S. (2019). Researching climate engagement: Collaborative conversations and consciousness change. In P. Hoggett (Ed.), *Climate psychology: On indifference to disaster* (pp.107–128). Palgrave Macmillan.

Haraway, D.J. (2016). *Staying with the trouble: Making kin in the Chthulucene*. Duke University Press.

Hickman, C. (2019a). Children and climate change: Exploring children's feelings about climate change using free association narrative interview methodology. In P. Hoggett (Ed.), *Climate psychology: On indifference to disaster* (pp.41–60). Palgrave Macmillan.

Hickman, C. (2019b, October 11). A psychotherapist explains why some adults are reacting badly to young climate strikers. *The Conversation*. https://theconversation.com/a-psychotherapist-explains-why-some-adults-are-reacting-badly-to-young-climate-strikers-125079

Hickman, C. (2019c, September 15). I'm a psychotherapist – here's what I've learned from listening to children talk about climate change. *The Conversation*. https://theconversation.com/im-a-psychotherapist-heres-what-ive-learned-from-listening-to-children-talk-about-climate-change-123183

Hickman, C. (2020). We need to (find a way to) talk about… eco-anxiety. *Journal of Social Work Practice, 34*(4), 411–424.

Hickman, C., Marks, L., Pihkala, P., Clayton, S., Lewandowski, E., Mayall, E., Wray, B., Mellor, C. & Susteren, L. (2021). Climate anxiety in children and young people and their beliefs about government responses to climate change: A global survey. *Lancet Planetary Health, 5*, e863–873. www.thelancet.com/action/showPdf?pii=S2542-5196%2821%2900278-3

Hoggett, P. (Ed.). (2019). *Climate psychology: On indifference to disaster*. Palgrave Macmillan.

Hollis, J. (1996). *Swamplands of the soul: New life in dismal places*. Inner City Books.

Hughes, K., Bellis, M.A., Hardcastle, K.A., Sethi, D., Butchart, A., Mikton, C., Jones, L. & Dunne, M.P. (2017). The effect of multiple adverse childhood experiences on health: A systematic review and meta-analysis. *Lancet Public Health, 2*(8), 356–656.

Jung, C.G. (1969). *The archetypes and the collective unconscious*. Princeton University Press.

Kay, E., Tisdall, M., Davis, J.M. & Gallagher, M. (2009). *Researching with children and young people: Research design, methods and analysis*. Sage.

Lawrance, D.E., Thompson, R., Fontana, G. & Jennings, D.N. (2021). *The impact of climate change on mental health and emotional wellbeing: Current evidence and implications for policy and practice.* Briefing paper no. 36. Grantham Institute. https://spiral.imperial.ac.uk/bitstream/10044/1/88568/9/3343%20Climate%20change%20and%20mental%20health%20BP36_v6.pdf

Lawton, G. (2019). I have eco-anxiety but that's normal. *New Scientist, 244*(3251), 22. www.sciencedirect.com/science/article/abs/pii/S0262407919319141?via%3Dihub

Lertzman, R. (2015). *Environmental melancholia: Psychoanalytic dimensions of engagement.* Routledge.

Lertzman, R. (2019). New methods for investigating new dangers. In P. Hoggett (Ed.), *Climate psychology: On indifference to disaster* (pp.25–40). Palgrave Macmillan.

Mavronicola, N. (2019) *Security and human rights* (2nd ed.). Bloomsbury Publishing.

Nelson, C., Bhutta, Z., Harris, N., Danese, A. & Samara, M. (2020). Adversity in childhood is linked to mental and physical health throughout life. *BMJ, 371*, m3048.

Nugent, C. (2019, November 21). Terrified of climate change? You might have eco-anxiety. *Time Magazine.* https://time.com/5735388/climate-change-eco-anxiety

Obradovich, N., Migliorini, R., Paulus, MP. & Rahwan, I. (2018). Empirical evidence of mental health risks posed by climate change. *PNAS, 115*(43), 10953–10958.

Ojala, M. (2012). Regulating worry, promoting hope: How do children, adolescents, and young adults cope with climate change? *International Journal of Environmental & Science Education, 7*(4), 537–561.

Ojala, M. (2015). Hope in the face of climate change: Associations with environmental engagement and student perceptions of teacher's emotional communication style and future orientation. *The Journal of Environmental Education, 6*(3), 133–148.

Ojala, M. (2020). To trust or not to trust? Young people's trust in climate change science and implications for climate change engagement. *Children's Geographies, 19*(3), 284–290.

Ozarko, D. (2018). *Beyond hope: Letting go of a world in collapse.* Ozarko Publishing.

Pihkala, P. (2017). Environmental education after sustainability: Hope in the midst of tragedy. *Global Discourse, 7*(1), 109–127.

Pihkala, P. (2020). Anxiety and the ecological crisis: An analysis of eco-anxiety and climate anxiety. *Sustainability, 12*(19), 7836.

Randall, R. (2019). *Climate anxiety or climate distress? Coping with the pain of the climate emergency.* [Blog.] Rosemary Randall. https://rorandall.org/2019/10/19/climate-anxiety-or-climate-distress-coping-with-the-pain-of-the-climate-emergency/

Randall, R. & Hoggett P. (2019). Engaging with climate change: Comparing the cultures of science and activism. In Hoggett, P. (Ed), *Climate psychology: On indifference to disaster* (pp.239–262). Palgrave Macmillan.

Ray, S.J. (2020). *A field guide to eco-anxiety.* University of California Press.

Romanyshyn, R.D. (2013). Making a place for unconscious factors in research. *International Journal of Multiple Research Approaches, 7*(3), 314–329.

Slee, A., Nazareth, I., Freemantle, N. & Horsfall, L. (2021). Trends in generalised anxiety disorders and symptoms in primary care: UK population-based cohort study. *British Journal of Psychiatry, 218*, 158–164. doi: 10.1192/bjp.2020.159

Tollemache, R. (2019). We have to talk about… climate change. In P. Hoggett (Ed.). *Climate psychology: On indifference to disaster* (pp.217–238). Palgrave Macmillan.

Verlie, B. (2019) Bearing worlds: Learning to live-with climate change. *Environmental Education Research, 25*(5), 751–766.

Weintrobe, S. (2013). *Engaging with climate change: Psychoanalytic and interdisciplinary perspectives.* Routledge.

Weintrobe, S. (2021). *Psychological roots of the climate crisis: Neoliberal exceptionalism and the culture of uncare.* Bloomsbury.

Wray, B. (2020, 5 August). *Why activism isn't *really* the cure for eco-anxiety and eco-grief.* [Blog.] Gen Dread. https://gendread.substack.com/p/why-activism-isnt-really-the-cure

Wray, B. (2022). *Generation Dread: Finding purpose in an age of climate crisis.* Knopf.

16 | Changing the world in one generation: Raising children to grow resilience amid climate and social collapse

Jo McAndrews

We cannot protect our children and young people from the impact of the climate crisis, but we can protect them from being alone with it.

A few years ago, a colleague attended a schools conference on the environment. This is what they told me. The participants included pupils from Year 5 (aged 9–10) and Year 13 (aged 17–18). The first half of the conference comprised a range of talks by different climate-engaged speakers, including one particular talk that was very hard hitting about the catastrophe of the climate crisis. After the speakers, there were workshops for separate age groups. In a Year 5 workshop of 60 pupils, one girl spoke up immediately: 'I'm really scared that I am going to die.' The workshop facilitator was not prepared for this. She had 60 children in front of her and a plan to stick to. She replied, 'Oh well, you're not going to die immediately so don't worry about that.' She then moved on with her workshop plan, leaving the girl feeling dismissed and exposed, and all the others who had similar fears to that girl but had not spoken got a clear message to keep their feelings to themselves.

I am telling you this story not to shame that particular facilitator but to illustrate an experience that is happening every moment of every day: the experience of a child's feelings being dismissed by an adult who just doesn't know how to respond and who doesn't have enough support themselves. This behaviour reflects an abandonment of the needs of children to find safety in the adults around them. The whole world is now in trouble, and it is desperately urgent that adults do better by the children and young people in our care and across the world.

We are facing catastrophic climate and social collapse, which I am convinced is because our cultural systems of power and domination have separated us from the land, from each other and from our own true nature, especially our imaginations, our emotional intelligence and our body awareness. These are the most basic conditions for mental health, thriving and the ability to meet change with collective flexibility and strength.

This is a time for rethinking everything we thought we knew, a time to tell a different story and to tread a new path.

How did we get here?

There is no such thing as an individual human. We have evolved over millions of years as beings who depend on close relationships in order to survive and thrive. We are utterly dependent on each other for our birth, development and life-long functioning. Everything we do is in the context of the communities we live in and their beliefs about what is important.

We have evolved with an exquisitely fine-tuned capacity to take each other in, not just through our senses but through a complex network of nervous system cells and processes that can tell us in a fraction of a second whether we are safely held by others or scarily alone. This biological interbeing develops as we grow to include our emotional and social world and the architecture of our most sophisticated thinking and imagining. Darcia Narvaez has devoted her career to studying the deepest and most anciently rooted needs of our 'evolved nest' (Narvaez & Bradshaw, 2023).[1] She describes how each species on Earth has evolved a specific set of conditions for the optimum development of their young. When any form of life is deprived of those conditions, it cannot develop to its potential. Think of a lion cub, born in a zoo to a mother who was taken from the wild. The cub has no memory of running with the pride over the vast savannah, but every cell in its body feels that something is wrong. It cannot flourish.

To be fully human, we require early and extended dependence on one primary carer, with a whole community of others supporting that relationship, in the environment of the particular bit of land that is home, giving us an experience of unconditional belonging. When we are deprived of that, we are living in a state of trauma, unable to find consistent regulated states where we have choice about our actions and feel connected with the intricate network of life that we are part of.

Children are utterly dependent on the adults in their lives in order to grow and thrive. This is one of the marvels of human development. We are born so vulnerable and helpless, and yet, over a long childhood, nurtured by the community around us, we grow extraordinary capacity and skill in living in the culture and on the land that is our home.

> Young children experience their world as an environment of relationships, and these relationships affect virtually all aspects of their development. (National Scientific Council on the Developing Child, 2004/2009)

This truth has been hidden from us in a culture that prizes independence over nurturing and behaviour over emotions. Daniel Siegel, who calls the current research known as interpersonal neurobiology 'the new science of kindness', argues that the most dangerous idea in the history of humanity is that people are individuals.[2] It is this catastrophic idea that has led to the runaway growth of systems of separation. Current

1. https://evolvednest.org
2. https://drdansiegel.com/interpersonal-neurobiology

neuroscientific study supports this – both Louis Cozolino (2014) and Stephen Porges (2009), for example, have researched the inherent biology of connection that shows that we develop and function in connection with others. Polyvagal theory (Porges, 2009) has mapped the autonomic nervous system and its exquisite attunement to the people around us, although, along with most Western scientific models, it has yet to acknowledge the importance of the natural environment in human development. Although this neurobiological research has revolutionised modern understanding of human nature, it is not new wisdom. The truth of our interbeing has been held in cultures around the world who still live in indigenous relationship with the land, or who have managed to preserve their knowledge in the face of colonisation by European invaders, who have stolen their land, culture, language and the heart of what it is to be fully human.

The project of separation has been so successful that we have allowed, or been forced to watch, our planet being devastated to the point where the survival of most life is threatened.

Having trained as a psychotherapist many years ago and devoted my career to supporting children's mental health, I am now utterly convinced that we cannot know anything about a child without acknowledging the context they live in: their family, their school and, most importantly, the culture that they are immersed in. These systems of thinking and power are often invisible to us, as water is unknowable to a fish. The most accurate and concise description of these interlocking systems that are the water we swim in is described by bell hooks as 'imperialist white-supremacist capitalist patriarchy' (hooks, 2004, p.29). Each of these words is worth exploring in more depth than I have space for here, but at their heart, they describe a system of oppressive power that allows some people greater access to resources and autonomy than others.

These systems of separation and domination that have spread across the world through the colonising of land and people have deprived children of their basic needs for healthy growth. We have become like animals in captivity, knowing that something is wrong but unable to remember, or never having known, freedom. One of the gifts of human evolution is the ability to adapt to whatever culture and land we are born into. We are amazingly flexible. Most of our development happens after we are born, so that our bodies, hearts and minds are shaped by our experiences, most strongly in our relationships and in the physical experience of home. This flexibility means that we can learn to live in a world that does not meet our needs for warm, responsive care from a network of supportive adults, at least one of whom holds us close and delights in our very existence. We can learn to live without it, but it costs us dearly.

The impact of separation culture has been so strong that we have learned to devalue and even mock these essential human qualities of body awareness, emotional intelligence and imagination, describing those who express them as touchy-feely, arty-farty, flaky, tree-huggers, hippies, snowflakes, idealistic, cloud-cuckoo land, cry-babies, over-sensitive, childish and naive. Colonising cultures have discredited the peoples who remain connected to these human qualities as primitives and savages. Maybe this rejection of our precious human gifts helps us to bear the pain of losing them; maybe it reassures us that all is well in the hostile world we are living in.

Children are an often-unacknowledged group whose voices and needs are marginalised in our industrialised cultures. They are denied even the most basic rights for safety and protection. The way we raise children in Westernised cultures of separation and domination does not meet their basic human needs for warm and long-term care and belonging. We are parented and educated out of our whole humanity into separate, productive, consumer beings who accept the separation because we do not see anything else on offer around us. Once we have adapted to our birth culture, it is very hard to see any alternative to our ways of seeing the world. In most primary-school classrooms, questioning the behaviour charts on the walls is like questioning the walls themselves. Cultures where babies are trained to sleep separately from their family members believe that it is outrageous and dangerous to share a bed.

Living and working in the UK, I see that mainstream parenting advice is focused on training babies and children into independence: how to sleep train, potty train, stop them being a fussy eater… so many ways that children are taught not to trust in or believe their own bodies: 'That didn't hurt', 'Don't cry', 'You are just tired'. They move from there into pre-school groups, whose targets for their tiny charges include 'school readiness', which means learning how to obey instructions. School brings a committed focus on doing what you are told: 'Sit still', 'Stand up', 'Play now', 'Stop playing now'. Children are taught that they need permission to go to the toilet and that they have no right to control their own bodies, or even their thoughts. If feelings of distress bubble up into agitated behaviour, they are punished with humiliating exposure. Most teachers are utterly unaware of the pain they are causing with their behaviour charts and have never questioned their use. Parents often feel uncomfortable about their child's experience but are reluctant to question the school, or if they do, there is no way of changing the system, which has the weight of authority behind it. Of course, there are many lovely teachers and forward-thinking head teachers who work hard to make their schools places where communities of children can thrive. But they are the exception, and they have to expend a lot of energy holding the government policies and control at bay in order to protect their cultures of care.

If you are bristling at what I am saying, if you think that I am being over-critical and extreme, I would like to invite you to notice that discomfort. It is hugely uncomfortable to question things that we have always taken for granted, that we participate in, that we want to protect because it keeps our worldview whole. I have regular experience of being with groups of adults who sit calmly through conversations about global climate change and social collapse yet get very agitated and defensive around the suggestion that we should stop punishing and rewarding children's behaviour.

Yet I persist in saying these challenging things because I believe that our children need better, and this need has become noisily urgent in the face of the climate emergency that is guaranteeing them a very different future from the one we are preparing them for.

Counselling and psychotherapy, along with other body-, emotion- and mind-based therapies, attract and support those of us who have rediscovered the importance of empathy, listening and feeling: the power of being seen, heard and understood in our deepest experience. Often, we are drawn to these professions in search of our own healing. Our culture has directed listeners and healers into becoming a professional class with clinical training that takes years and much time and money to acquire. We have subcontracted out our emotional lives and our mental health. And our capitalist models have created scarcity and inequality in accessing that professional help. One in six children and young people in the UK have a probable mental health disorder (NHS Digital, 2021). The UK House of Commons Health and Social Care Select Committee (2021) reported that only 40% of young people with a diagnosable mental disorder got any support for it. Publicly funded services have been decimated over the last decade, private therapists are fully booked with clients who can afford to pay, and those who can't are left with no support at all.

We know that children need warm, welcoming relationships in order to be well, yet the adults who spend the most time with children and young people – their parents, carers, family and educators – do not know how to offer this responsive, empathic care. They will often say, 'I am not a therapist' as a reason for not engaging with the child's feelings or distress. Teachers will say, 'I am not a social worker' when faced with a child who has problems at home. So many adults do not know how to respond to a child's basic needs to be seen, heard and welcomed because we did not have that experience ourselves.

Studies on climate anxiety are exposing the extent to which children and young people are feeling abandoned by the adults in their lives. A survey of 10,000 young people aged 16–25 in countries all around the world found that 84% were worried about climate breakdown (Hickman et al., 2021; see also Chapter 15 of this book). Half of those who tried to talk about it said they had been dismissed by others.

If you are thinking that I am describing a bleak and overwhelming picture, then I agree with you. I believe that we need to face these 'truths' together. I use inverted commas because I don't want to suggest that I am the holder of the truth. There is so much I don't know that I have never been exposed to because of my own cultural conditioning. However, the more I learn, the clearer it seems to me that this story of separation makes complete sense of the mess we are in and points to the ways forward. It is clear to me that we are in need of some strong response to the literal threat of mass global extinction of life, including human life. Writer and activist Naomi Klein says, 'There are no non-radical options left before us' (Winship, 2016). Once we embrace the urgency to get radical, a whole new world opens up. Getting radical means going back to the roots, remembering the basic needs of life on Earth, accepting that we have gone a long way down the wrong road and rethinking everything. It means questioning our deepest assumptions about how we live and being willing to change, in the knowledge that unimaginable change is happening right now, whether we choose it or not, and there is no possibility of going back. If we still have the privilege of choice about whether or not to engage with this, we need to face the fact that every moment we delay means more suffering and destruction for all those in climate-devastated areas who do not have that choice.

Getting radical means rethinking the way we work and joining movements of collaboration towards making the best contribution we can to changing the system to one that loves and protects connection and life.

How do we go forward?

Culture is created through the upbringing of children. The world we contribute to and create is deeply influenced by our childhood experience. We are born with ancient, evolved needs for warm, responsive care, and also extraordinary adaptability to meet whatever faces us in the culture we are born into. If we were to change how we parent and educate, we could change the whole world in one generation. I love the simplicity of this idea, and of course I also recognise the complexity. I would like to offer some ideas about how we can reconnect with our evolved needs for human and planetary health in order to take meaningful action in the face of the climate crisis and grow a generation of adults who are better equipped to face the changed world they have inherited.

Rebuild our co-resilience

If we are to meet the radical changes that are facing us, we need to reclaim our access to our body awareness, emotions and imagination and our belonging to the Earth. These are the core aspects of humanity that we can no longer allow to be taken from us. When we do this work in communities of adults, learning and practising a new way of being, then we can offer a more whole accompaniment to the children and young people in our lives. We can take our place in the village that welcomes and includes everyone and keeps the children's fire at its centre – the fire that symbolises the inclusion of children in all decisions made by the community, ensuring that a sustainable future is always at the heart of any action taken.

The word 'resilience' is of the moment. We need to be talking about it and yet it is understood in different ways according to the context. The type of resilience I am talking about is the strength and flexibility to change, adapt and thrive in the face of challenge. It is not about simply bouncing back. It is about growing ever deeper into connection with ourselves, each other and the natural world, knowing that we are not alone.

There is no such thing as a resilient individual. Humans have evolved to depend utterly on each other and on the natural world. For this reason, I use the word 'co-resilience', which better captures the depth of our dependence on each other.

Co-resilience is rooted in childhood, in the connection to safe adults that our children need in order to develop to their full potential and that our industrial cultures have forgotten, with devastating consequences. We see these consequences in soaring levels of mental distress among children, soaring social inequality, ecological devastation and climate change.

To face the challenges now and in the future, we need a new story – a story of change and reconnection with life, with all that enables us to be fully human. Co-resilience means that we are stronger together. It shows us a different way to bring up children – a more resilient, radical, respectful way. I firmly believe that this is where hope lies. How else will any of us have what it takes to face what is happening in the world and the certain and enormous change that we are part of?

Notice the water we are swimming in

This means understanding our world through a systems lens. It is clear that the way we live does not work, and that attempts to change it have, so far, not been successful. It is a courageous and empowering act to question our deepest beliefs and to recognise that we have been mistaken in much of what we think. It is an awakening that exiles us from the comfort and privilege of thinking that this is the only way to do it. It can be distressing to see the world through a different lens, to find ourselves out of step with the dominant culture. One question leads to another and unravels the story we have been holding.

Joanna Macy, the deep ecologist and activist, describes three stories of our time (Macy & Johnstone, 2012).[3] The first is 'business as usual'. This describes the dominant culture, the current economic, political, global and local systems that shape our everyday lives. For many of us, it is easy to see that our economic systems cause great suffering, but it can be less obvious that our schools are part of this too, or that our parenting is the training ground for children's disconnection from their essential selves. Macy's second story is 'the great unravelling'. This is the story of collapse and catastrophe, where we recognise the emergency we are in and feel the urgency of addressing it. In this story we can feel overwhelmed and helpless, tiny amid the huge complexity of the scale of it all. I think that facing climate crisis involves us getting immersed in this story for a while and that many children and young people are feeling abandoned and alone in it. We need to know about the third story as well, 'the great turning'. This is the story of change. It tells of how we can move into active engagement with others, finding new ways of seeing the world, taking meaningful action in good company and reclaiming our whole selves in the process. It is a story of active hope, of living according to our deepest values and knowing that our contribution is valuable even if we are unsure of the outcome.

Our young people need us to be engaged in this story of change and to accompany them in it. It is a strong call for adults to step up and it starts with questioning our beliefs about the world.

An important way to notice the water we are swimming in is to engage with decolonisation work. This work has been developed largely through anti-racist movements and climate justice thinking. When we look at the world through the lens of imperialist, white-supremacist, capitalist patriarchy (hooks, 2004, p.29) we start to realise that pretty much all of our thinking, our very language and each cell of our bodies have been shaped by these ways of seeing the world. Being willing to notice this is the first step to unravelling the web that holds us within its invisible threads. This work involves consciously learning about the experience of people of colour in the communities we live in, as well as listening to the wisdom and teachings of indigenous cultures. It involves reading, watching, listening to and talking about perspectives that are different to the mainstream white perspective.[4]

---

3. https://workthatreconnects.org/spiral/the-great-turning/the-global-context

4. For example, in the Radio 4 programme *Culture on the Couch*, broadcast in 2022, Ramaa Sharma reports on how standard psychological therapies are based on a white Western model that claims to represent 'universal' human experience but actually fails to understand or help people from ethnic minorities because of its emphasis on individualism. Resmaa Menakem (2021) has written about racialised trauma and the impact of racism on all of our bodies. Layla F. Saad has developed a process for acknowledging and challenging the impact of white supremacy, which she has now published as a book (2020). A resource list for white people looking to engage in decolonisation work can be found at https://starterculture.net/gateways/decolonising

Update our knowledge

This is a time for deep learning, for questioning our models and frameworks. There is so much important thinking and research that is showing us ways forward in our understanding: the sharing of ancient and profound wisdom by indigenous elders who have stayed connected with ways of living in harmony with the Earth and all life; the urgent calls of youth activists who are showing the way. There is evidence emerging from so many areas of scientific research that challenges the separation cultures. Interpersonal neurobiology is transforming our understanding of the importance of attachment and trauma-informed practice. It has ended the debate on nature versus nurture and the separation of mind and body. It is clear that there are no such divisions. Our binary thinking that one thing is 'better' than another is being disproved again and again.

When I was coming to the end of my psychotherapy training, the principal of my college started giving lectures about the neuroscience that was just emerging. I was relieved that I didn't have to learn about it as I had studied enough for my qualification and was full up with theories and models. I had a prejudice about the unfeeling rationality of science in the field of psychological wellbeing. I didn't want to engage with any more of it. My confidence in what I had already learned made me arrogant and closed to new ideas. Now I laugh at myself for that thinking. Polyvagal theory (Porges, 2009) and interpersonal neurobiology[5] have utterly transformed my understanding of how humans function, of the many layered experiences of trauma, and how the embodied nervous system is at the heart of healthy functioning. I feel as though I have been handed the keys to all the big questions about life, the universe and everything, and there is so very much more to learn.

I believe that we need to let go of therapeutic ideas that focus on the individual as separate from the systems they live in and that concentrate on treating personal pathology rather than question the dysfunctional systems that create suffering. I am thinking, for example, of all the neurodivergent or traumatised children who are seen by school counsellors or therapists with the aim of helping them fit into a system in which it is impossible for them to thrive. Imagine if we created a classroom where every child felt seen, heard and welcome, just as they are. What impact would that have on behaviour and learning? Luckily, we don't need to just imagine it; we can learn from education systems that are already based on child-friendly principles. There is so much information and evidence available that supports a different way.

Come home to our bodies

Humans are part of nature. We have complex biological needs and gifts that allow us to live in harmony with each other and with ourselves. Research on trauma over the past 30 years has made it clear that all psychological, emotional harm manifests in the physical body and that the most direct way to heal or even prevent trauma is through attending to the body's experience (see, for example, Rothschild, 2000; van der Kolk, 2014). Paying attention to our sleep, our food and our water intake are fundamental acts of care for the body. Movement and stretching, being outdoors, attending to our comfort – all of these

---

5. https://drdansiegel.com/interpersonal-neurobiology

activities deepen the care. We can reclaim even more of our body's wisdom by learning to notice the physical sensations around our emotions, our needs in relationship and our levels of consent in our interactions. Learning to say 'no' to what is not okay with us and asking for what we need is ongoing radical work in a culture that has denied us these things. There is privilege inherent in this. Not everyone has access to the resources needed for the most basic aspects of care. This makes it a political and social issue. Tricia Hersey, founder of the Nap Ministry, calls us to recognise that tending to our body's needs is a crucial step in changing oppressive cultures:

> The Rest is Resistance movement is a connection and a path back to our true nature. We are stripped down to who we really were before the terror of capitalism and white supremacy. We are enough. (Hersey, 2022, p.7)

Grow our emotional intelligence

Our capacity to understand, regulate and express our emotions is at the heart of our relationships. Our brains process emotions more quickly than thoughts and all our decisions are made on the basis of our emotional reactions. We have been led to believe that our thoughts are more important and influential, that being rational is the best way to be. In practice, being able to face and honour emotions and how we feel them in our bodies is the path to deeper wisdom, mental health and clarity about our actions. I have been part of many well-intentioned and visionary groups and communities who have stumbled and fallen over conflict between members and difficulty in processing the emotions that emerge through being in relationship with others. Being with and integrating our embodied emotions allows us to be more fully ourselves in connection with the world we live in. When we reclaim our own emotional intelligence, we can support the young people we live and work with, through empathic warmth and accompaniment. When we can find support to bear our own big feelings, we show children that we can also bear theirs, and instead of dismissing them, we can stay close.

Use our imagination

How can we hold hope or create change unless we can imagine what we are working for? We are in dire need of reclaiming the central role of the imagination in resilient change. What if we allowed children to play until they had had enough? What if we prioritised play, creativity, art and emotional skills in our education system instead of prioritising maths and science? What sort of adults would those children grow up to be? What if we could imagine a way of living that valued equality and inclusion, that saw all forms of life as precious? What if the land we lived on was commonly shared rather than privately owned? Can you even imagine a world like that? Rob Hopkins has devoted his work to reclaiming the imagination and asking, 'What if?' He believes that, in the context of climate change:

> imagination is the only thing we have that is – or could be – radical enough to get us through, provided it is accompanied, of course, by bravery, and by action. (Hopkins, 2021, p.13)

For many of us, our imagination has been dulled or even stolen by the culture we have grown up in. Let us attend to the work of reclaiming it, through play, creativity, conversation; whatever it is that wakes up our dreams of the world we long to live in. Then we can share with young people the ability to imagine a world where respect for and protection of all life is possible.

Change the way we bring up children and young people

This means doing everything we can to offer a warm, empathic welcome to children, to be on their side, to recognise their dependence on adults and to stand up as their advocates. It means offering them the environment of relationships that grows deep resilience for their whole lives.

A world that meets the needs of children becomes a world that has whole, healthy adults who know how to collectively protect life. Once we have really learned about what children need in order to grow healthily into their full potential, it is heartbreakingly obvious that our cultures of separation rely on denying those needs in order to maintain themselves, and that this has had tragic consequences for individuals and for the whole world. I believe there is a direct link between the broken attachments and unmet needs experienced routinely by children in industrialised, capitalist nations and the out-of-control destruction of life on Earth.

There are many changes we could make in the way we treat children. At the heart of this endeavour is recognising that children's needs are valid and important and, when they are met, thriving is the result. We do not need to train children into being adults, teach them how to behave and shape them into obedience. We do not need to control them for the sake of order and so that they will cope in the 'real world'. Children are utterly dependent on warm, responsive adults to create an environment of security that allows them to grow into their potential. This environment allows for the gradual development of behaviour regulation and responsible action.

If we prioritise the warm, friendly care of children and their need for relational safety and regulation, then the way becomes clearer. We can let go of the behavioural control systems that seek to train children into doing what we think they should do. We can learn to meet and welcome their emotional expression with empathy and curiosity. This approach is not possible when parents and carers are burdened and unsupported. Humans have not evolved the capacity to meet a baby's needs alone or in pairs. We need community support in ways that are hard for us even to imagine when we have not experienced it for ourselves or seen it modelled. When stressed parents receive acknowledgement of how much support they need and don't have, it is such a relief. Understanding that it was never supposed to be like this makes sense of their experience and struggle. So, even if we don't yet have the government policies and funding to give parents the support they need, we can at least acknowledge the severity of the attitudes and ideas that withhold such support.

I would like it to become unthinkable that we punish and bribe children in our homes and schools. This is a concrete change that would transform our understanding of how children thrive. It would open the way to a more accurate knowledge of who children are. Contrary to what we have been told, children don't learn to manage their behaviour through adult control. Distressed behaviour is not a choice, it is a biologically driven survival instinct. As children, we learn to regulate and control our behaviour as we grow alongside warm adult guidance and social norms. The belief that teenagers are inherently rebellious is a myth of our punitive culture towards children. When children are brought up with respect and non-violence, they grow into teenagers who still seek closeness and guidance from the adults around them, even as they become more focused on their peers and on taking risks to change the world they have inherited.

What are the skills needed to start this work?

This is huge work, and it is important that we have a sense of where to start. I would like to suggest some practices that will develop our skills in the direction of radical system change around parenting, education and the care of young people. These are:

Questioning our deeply held beliefs

We can learn skills of enquiry that allow us to step back from the story we are taking for granted, learning from others on this path and working together to unpick our certainty of our ways of thinking. Regularly asking, 'Is this true?' about our habitual ways of seeing the world develops the wisdom that there may be another way.

Building communities of connection

We need other people for this work, and we have not grown up with the relational skills of forming healthy groups where we feel welcome and belonging. So many groups fall apart because they focus on tasks over relationships or think that a longing for community is enough to make it work. We need to learn relational skills that make it possible for groups to function and thrive. These include listening and empathy, decision-making, dealing with conflict, purpose and meeting structure, among others. There are many people sharing wisdom and frameworks for forming and maintaining healthy groups.

Nurturing our creativity

What is your most available creative act? Start there. Maybe you would love to plant a whole garden? Start with one seed. If you long to be an artist, pick up a pencil and a piece of paper and start there. Do it regularly – do anything that tends to the imagination and the capacity to create something that expresses who you are. Play games, knit, carve spoons, sing, dance. It can be so hard to reach our creative self-expression when we are burdened with the heaviness of anxiety and worry for the world. It seems trivial or self-indulgent, when actually it is a practice of health and wholeness. Let's bring art and imagination into our professional practices too.

Growing our belonging in nature

Again, the skill here is to start small and practise regularly. Spending time outdoors is not a Sunday afternoon luxury. We need the fresh air, the birdsong, the warmth of the sun, the rain on our faces. We were born expecting this. To reclaim our whole selves and to allow children theirs, we need to know that we belong on the Earth, in a very real, practical way.

Learning and practising self- and co-regulation of our embodied nervous systems

I am so grateful for all those who are working to share simple, effective practices that allow us to tune into and regulate our nervous systems. This is the foundation of choice. When we are dysregulated by stress, we are unable to choose our response. We are thrown instinctively into survival responses of fight, flight, freeze and faint behaviour. Living in this time of collapse and crisis without a culture of care, many of us are in a state of trauma, at the mercy of our stress response. Simple embodied practices, including breathing, shaking, stretching, soothing and grounding, offer us effective ways of regulating ourselves and each other in the moment and also for the future as our nervous systems become rewired. These practices can become part of our everyday lives in our families and communities, instead of the inaccessible reserve of scarce therapeutic services.

Resonant empathy

This is an extraordinarily powerful skill for our inner healing and our relationships. Our human need for warm, responsive care means that we long to be seen, heard and understood, to know we make sense and belong in our community. When we practise resonant empathy, we show others that we are warmly curious about their experience and that we care enough to find accurate understanding of them. I am regularly blown away by the power of this when it works, and I am regularly heartbroken by how rarely adults are able to offer this to children and young people. A young person I worked with in a support group for youth activists said in wonder, 'It is amazing to talk to an adult and be believed!' Non-violent communication holds at the heart of its purpose resonant empathy of our own and others' feelings and needs. Sarah Peyton (2017) is one of the most inspiring teachers I have found of this particular skill.[6]

Counsellors and psychotherapists

I have focused a lot in this chapter on how people in any caring role can work to reclaim our own wholeness in order to bring that healing to others. I would like to end with some thoughts on how counsellors and psychotherapists specifically can contribute to the huge and exploding need for meaningful support of children, young people and adults in the context of this time of crisis.

I want to urge us all to:

1. Question our models and adapt our frameworks to include understanding of systems contexts and the impact of climate crisis as an unprecedented collapse of everything we know. Humans are not individuals and the pain we struggle with is not our own. We are holding our clients' suffering in the understanding that it is inevitable in the cultures we are part of and in the collapse we are witnessing. It is not just about their parents' mistakes or their habitual thoughts; none of us have

---

6. www.yourresonantself.com

what we need to live as whole people. This points the way to deep compassion and the recognition of the resonant accompaniment needed alongside structural change to really offer healing.

2. Bring our skills and understanding out of our therapy rooms and contribute to the development of community-embodied emotional intelligence. Share practices and skills with the everyday adults in children's lives so that most children and young people do not get to the point of needing specialised help. We need to de-professionalise the body and emotional literacy in our cultures so that it is not only available to the most desperate or the most wealthy.

3. Be part of growing cultures of welcome and belonging for children and young people so that future generations of adults will be whole. Challenge the way children are punished at home and in schools. Campaign against the teaching of punishment strategies to parents. Help get behaviour charts off the classroom walls. Challenge hostile language and action towards teenagers and show them that they are welcome and valuable. It sounds almost unbelievable, but just having an adult look directly at them and greet them with a smiling hello is outside the everyday experience of huge numbers of children and young people.

My strongest call to adults is to face what is happening in the world and step up to accompany our young people with deep empathy, care and clear action so that they no longer feel abandoned. We cannot protect them from what is happening but we can and must protect them from being alone with it.

Further reading

Dana, D. (2021). *Anchored: How to befriend your nervous system using polyvagal theory.* Sounds True.

Holt, J. (1991). *How children learn.* Penguin.

Knussen, J. (2018, September 2). 'Little people matter': Time to change our thinking on 'challenging behaviour' in the classroom. Ace-Ware Scotland/*The Herald.* https://aceawarescotland.com/wp-content/uploads/2018/09/ACE-Aware-Media-Herald-02092018.pdf

Kohn, A. (1993/2018). *Punished by rewards.* Houghton Mifflin.

Levine, P. (2010). *In an unspoken voice: How the body releases trauma and restores goodness.* North Atlantic Books.

MacCartney, M. (2018). *The children's fire: Heart song of a people.* Practical Inspiration Publishing.

Zeedyk, S. (n.d.). *Connected baby: Bringing the science of connection to life.* https://connectedbaby.net

References

Cozolino, L. (2014). *The neuroscience of human relationships: Attachment and the developing human brain*. W.W. Norton & Co.

Hersey, T. (2022). *Rest is resistance*. Octopus Publishing.

Hickman, C., Marks, E., Pihkala, P., Clayton, S., Lewandowski, R., Mayall, E., Wray, B., Mellor, C. & van Susteren, L. (2021). Climate anxiety in children and young people and their beliefs about government responses to climate change: A global survey. *The Lancet Planetary Health, 5*, e863-e873. 10.1016/ S2542-5196(21)00278-3

hooks, b. (2004). *The will to change: Men, masculinity, and love*. Simon & Schuster.

Hopkins, R. (2021). *From what is to what if: Unleashing the power of imagination to create the future we want*. Chelsea Green Publishing Co.

House of Commons Health and Social Care Select Committee. (2021). *Children and young people's mental health*. UK Parliament. https://publications.parliament.uk/pa/cm5802/cmselect/cmhealth/17/ report.html

Macy, J. & Johnstone, C. (2012). *Active hope: How to face the mess we're in without going crazy*. New World Library.

Menakem, R. (2021). *My grandmother's hands: Racialized trauma and the pathway to mending our hearts and bodies*. Penguin.

Narvaez, D. & Bradshaw, G. (2023). *The evolved nest: Bringing parenting back to nature*. Penguin/ Random House.

National Scientific Council on the Developing Child. (2004/2009). *Young children develop in an environment of relationships*. Working paper No. 1. (Updated and reprinted October 2009). Centre on the Developing Child, Harvard University. https://developingchild.harvard.edu/wp-content/ uploads/2004/04/Young-Children-Develop-in-an-Environment-of-Relationships.pdf

NHS Digital. (2021). *Rate of mental disorders among children remained stable in 2021 after previous rise, report shows*. NHS Digital. https://digital.nhs.uk/news/2021/rate-of-mental-disorders-among- children-remained-stable-in-2021-after-previous-rise-report-shows#:~:text=Mental%20Health%20 of%20Children%20and,2%20in%202020%20and%202021

Peyton, S. (2017). *Your resonant self: Guided meditations and exercises to engage your brain's capacity for healing*. W.W. Norton & Co.

Porges, S. (2009). The polyvagal theory: New insights into adaptive reactions of the autonomic nervous system. *Cleveland Clinical Journal of Medicine, 76*(4), s86–s90.

Rothschild, B. (2000). *The body remembers: The psychophysiology of trauma and trauma treatment*. W.W. Norton & Co.

Saad, L.F. (2020). *Me and white supremacy: How to recognise your privilege, combat racism and change the world*. Quercus. http://laylafsaad.com/meandwhitesupremacy

Sharma, R. (Presenter) (2022). *Culture on the couch*. BBC Radio 4. www.bbc.co.uk/programmes/ m0015vcc#:~:text=Journalist%20Ramaa%20Sharma%20explores%20how,help%20people%20 from%20ethnic%20minorities

Van der Kolk, B. (2014). *The body keeps the score: Mind, brain and body in the transformation of trauma*. Penguin.

Winship, M. (2016, February 4). Naomi Klein: 'There are no non-radical options left before us.' *Salon*. www.salon.com/2016/02/04/naomi_klein_there_are_no_non_radical_options_left_before_us_partner

17 | Climate crisis as emotion crisis: Emotion validation coaching for parents of the world

Andy Miller

I coach parents and teens whose relationship bond has frayed over climate and related existential crises like disease, racism, poverty and the many ills of capitalism. I coach in many traditional cultures and use those learnings to land on my own truth, which is that personal development is grounded in the evolving stories we tell ourselves, about ourselves, in community. All these stories start with emotion, as does the initial response of every human being to climate crisis. My coaching guides parents and children into liminal spaces deep in their bodies and deals with big emotions at the intersection of stories old and new. We spend time with trees, listen to their wisdom, apply their strengths to self and share emergent narratives to re-shape each family's journey through existential crisis. I bring nature into the coaching equation to inform, align and connect emotions, values, belief, purpose and behaviour. We use vivid guided imagery to illuminate and bring clarity. We immerse ourselves in recent troubling events to change problematic emotional states, create meaning and guide behaviour. This informs our 'mind's eye' as to our who, why and how.

Let's start with an extract from a narrative-based coaching intake interview. We'll begin with a teenage activist who chose to express their feelings through a theatrical presentation of a spoken-word poem they had written. This is followed by their parent's description of a related, emotionally triggering event they called a 'letter to self'. They are fictionalised amalgams that I have created from dozens of such encounters:

Teenager:

I am a tree. Somewhere beyond the figurative. No, I'm not on mescaline. Never touch the stuff. I am pure. I am a tree. The swirling warm-misty fog barrelling in from the Pacific touches my leaves like a lover. My perfection enables my leaves to extract water from fog to nourish my soul. For millennia. I am the mother of all Buddhist monks. I am aware of nothing other than this moment. Nothing exists outside my mind's eye, except a tinkling in my mycelium-laden roots – I am intimately connected to and dependent upon other Methuselahs. I am a 2000-year-old California Redwood. I have produced hundreds of millions of seeds; a few germinated and survived the ages. My seeds no longer germinate – the mists are vanishing. I am rare beyond imagination. I feel a chainsaw cutting into me. I feel the vibration of human screams. I feel the flow of my life force being severed, my red-sap-blood, my connection with my roots, my one-ness with all life. Severed. A human has lived for 700 days high up in my 1000-year-old tree-daughter across the stream. Protecting us. There are many. Now screaming. We have knowing beyond words. The tree human is Julia Butterfly Hill and hundreds of her companions are all screaming. It's late in a century called the 1900s, in an era selfishly named Anthropocene. As if it's all about them. I sense Earth-change. I am afraid. I am angry. I shatter into a million pieces as my skyscraper heft crashes to the ground. Fire erupts. Burning rainforests that have never witnessed fire. My flaming phoenix dust, swirling in distorted atmospheres of dystopia. I will re-emerge in a renewed world.

Parent:

I have resistance-to-change feelings in my body. I'm thinking about a conversation I had with my kids yesterday afternoon. It was 3pm, in the living room; my kids started talking about making signs and placards about the feelings of redwood trees, for upcoming Extinction Rebellion climate demonstrations. They were writing slogans about their feelings about their dystopian views that climate crisis, capitalism, all the -isms, will wreck everything; that our systems, our governments, our way of life, will collapse; that new, nature-centred systems will arise, but that dark times lie between here and there, showing the worst of humanity. I asked them about their utopia. Trying to stay positive and hopeful. I asked them to describe what a new sustainable world might look like. But they told me I couldn't understand utopia without understanding dystopia. They showed me a poem about the death of a grandmother tree. I just can't bear it. I shut it out. I can't imagine dystopia, utopia, or anything in between. I just want things to stay the same. I want hope. I told my kids that everything will be okay. Not to worry. Someone or something will solve this climate problem, save the grandmother trees, make our world fairer. And then the anger intensified. And I have this vivid image in my mind of the expressions on their faces – the anger, the rage, at me, at all adults. Feelings and imagery, fixed in my brain, that my kids may die trying to fix the crisis we created. But that some form of utopia will arise from the ashes. That's what they believe. It was a bright sunny day. We could have been outside playing. But we were inside a hot, stuffy, stagnant house, with this negative doom dripping down the walls like sticky oil. Kids shouldn't be burdened like this. It was dreadful. I felt sick to my stomach, sticky and sweaty. My hands were trembling, mind racing, heart pounding. And despite this, I kept arguing with my kids, as if by instinct. I couldn't stop myself. I acknowledge I have this resistance to change, resistance to name and explore my own feelings, to acknowledge my kids' feelings. How could I possibly acknowledge such dark feelings? Am I feeling grief or the eco-emotions we talked about earlier, Andy? I honestly couldn't tell you. It seems I have a resistance to feeling anything other than this vague sense of hope that somebody or something will solve the crises of humanity. I feel a resistance to acknowledging that the climate is my problem too. Resistance to accepting my children's conviction that humanity, as we know it, will end, and that species like the polar bear and redwood will go extinct. That our economy could collapse. It seems like a Mad Max movie. How the f##% could this possibly happen? I try to hide my fear, all these emotions swirling around in my body that I can't understand. I feel it in my body;, it's ravaging me. I can't sleep. I don't know what to do. I feel like it's all my fault. But I'm only a pawn in the system. My kids scoff at my recycling and bicycle riding. They want me to do so much more. But I have this ambivalent feeling about change. I'm just a drop in the bucket. A grain of sand on the beach. And the tears flow. I weep, for my kids, and for my family in Trinidad and Tobago, who feel climate even worse. I ignore them too. I feel this pressure crushing my body like I'm at the bottom of the sea. I can't protect my kids. And I feel this hopelessness deep in my heart. It's physically painful. In my heart, it feels like a bright red, pulsating, swirling little tornado, dragging me in, coalescing in an orb of solid heavy metal, like lead, sinking deeper and lodging itself in some recess of my heart.

Emotions, vivid imagery, somatic elements and stuck feelings are everywhere in this parental account of a troubling event with their children. There are so many coachable topics in this story, it's hard to know where to start, especially with all the conflict-oriented patterns of interaction. Our emotional language, however primitive, tells us what we value most, brings those values to life and identifies links between what we what we think and how we feel.

It starts with grief

Emotional validation is necessary in all relationships, but when our values, world views and climate narratives are mismatched, as they frequently are with our children, it can be hard to find common ground. My coaching focuses on exploration of inner emotional landscape and emotional validation, starting with grief. When we're vulnerable enough to unmask the grief we all hold and speak truth to it, what we are really expressing is the unfathomable love, courage and trust that we need in order to be able to feel what our amygdala – the part of the brain primarily concerned with processing emotions and memories associated with fear – keeps hidden. I help people figure out who they are by exploring ambivalence, overwhelm and scarcity through a systemic lens. We learn to overcome emotional denial and disavowal and to self-regulate our limbic and ventral vagal systems.

I examine why we (coaches and clients alike) subconsciously stuff troubling emotions into remote recesses of our bodies. Our emotional landscape is often so foreign we can't even name our big emotions, much less imagine being in relationship with them. We don't know whether our feelings are connected to our existential angst over the state of the world, to childhood incidents, to our children's grief, or to other external events. With the help of emotional clarity and vivid imagery, we can recharge biospheric values, re-story limiting beliefs, change mindset, and take action with conviction.

Creating a climate crisis mindset

We parents feel the pain of the world through our children's anguish. We don't know what to do. Our relationships suffer. We must learn how to talk about these issues openly and honestly with those we love most – our kids. Parents need to be agile, creative, resolute and resilient in the face of pervasive uncertainty. And we have so much to learn from our climate activist children.

Our children carry a heavy emotional toll. We have burdened them with our legacy. Our children feel that their own and the Earth's values have been debased, devalued and dismissed. They anticipate dystopia, yet find strength in imagining new worlds of possibility from being in community. Many kids are unhappy and unfulfilled at home. They need their parents to have their back. We all need to figure ourselves out, from the inside out. Why? Because emotions inform values and values inform behaviour. To change our behaviour, we must first change our relationship with and reconcile our grief, fear, sadness, anger, guilt and shame, among other negative emotions. The key to behaviour change is to use our emotions and values to visualise obstacles and vividly imagine what we can do about them.

Driven by vivid emotional imagery

The process of emotion coaching is simple and familiar: we precisely name our perspective, separate our mindset from fact, normalise experience and acknowledge difficulties and reframe them. We name and explore unacknowledged emotions, use them to activate and inform values, explore belief, change mindset and enable clients to act differently next time. We create autonomy, controllability, mastery, self-determination and motivation based on vivid imagery of what goal achievement looks and feels like. The premise is that emotions are connected to needs and that emotions have adaptive potential to make meaning and guide behaviour.

Emotion coaching is based on somatic experience in the present moment, reflection on past negative events and, ultimately, reconciling the mismatch between expected and experienced patterns of behaviour. But just talking about emotions is not enough. To dissolve their grip, we must also get to the other side by finding out why they gripped us in the first place and how deeply conditioned our response is. Our focus is not to rid ourselves of troubling emotions. Rather, we need to honour them and use them as a force for good, instead of paralysis. We start by revisiting recent troubling events, of small to moderate magnitude, and begin the unpacking there.

Blocked by untapped negative emotions

The method in parent-emotion coaching is deceptively simple: prevent our brains being hijacked by near-constant fear triggers. We do this by naming, acknowledging and understanding the meaning of emotions; focusing on parents' negative inner descriptions of troubling external events, and guiding parents through emotional processing, amygdala awareness, cortisol management and polyvagal health. As the existential increasingly holds our clients hostage from their emotions, coaches need to be intimately familiar with the functioning of the limbic system, polyvagal theory, how to make ventral vagal activation the default, attachment theory, and the functions of implicit and explicit memory, to name a few.

I blend tools from numerous disciplines and modalities, ranging from narrative coaching, emotional freedom techniques, emotion-focused therapy, motivational interviewing, EMDR, matrix reimprinting, compassionate inquiry and a plethora of emerging nature and climate coaching tools. It is my experience that traditional action-oriented goals flow freely from clients once they have truly tapped into their inner emotional landscape. For clients who are goal oriented, it's crucial to link goal-oriented behaviours with activation and reinforcement cues, rich in vivid imagery, to keep them on track through time.

Where big emotions live and what they look like

Most parent clients don't even know they harbour big eco-emotions, such is the grip of the fight-flight response. But with guidance, each and every parent can discover their own unique internal response to these challenging and troubling emotions – emotions that have been unconsciously tucked away in deep recesses of their bodies, often associated with pain, vivid images of shapes, colours and forms and, all too often, disturbing memories of childhood 'trauma' that also must be cleared of emotional baggage, to free up true emotional curiosity.

Expressing difficult emotions with words can be exceedingly difficult. Luckily, emotions show themselves in many ways: pain, colour, shapes, facial and postural expression, feeling, voice, dance, acting and role-playing, and through a plethora of other creative arts. Indirectly tapping into emotion can be a more user-friendly and safer way to increase intensity of awareness of emotional experience, enabling emotions to rapidly transition from unknown to known to de-triggered. The resulting emotional clarity brings new meaning-making and re-storying of troubling experience. Once our darkest emotions are repeatedly aroused and explored with gentle curiosity and love, they self-regulate. I have found no need to help clients regulate their emotions. Our bodies seem to know what to do. We need to re-train ourselves to trust our emotions, after centuries of analytical left-brain programming that started in ancient Greece and culminated in the Industrial Revolution.

I guide clients to where unknown-known emotions lurk, unconsciously causing havoc in their lives, damaging their relationships with their children, causing stress and dis-ease, blocking them from climate action and holding them hostage from themselves. Most of us are so fiercely protected by our unconscious, we skip through life, not even realising we have dark emotions that, when left unexplored, can have insidious effects on our health, wellness and identity.

Sifting through a lifetime of troubling emotion

We all have a lifetime of emotional exploration to catch up on, charged emotional incidents to reflect on and unhelpful childhood incidents and beliefs to clear, opening the road to behaviour change. Each big emotion needs to be explored, each bit of imagery reflected upon, each triggering event and somatic experience investigated with vivid imagery, each unhelpful belief explored with loving curiosity, with the goal of de-sensitising our conditioned responses of fight-flight and convincing the brain to let go of stress response. But this process can unfold very quickly with skilled emotion practitioners who can quickly identify and remove the legs of the table that is our dis-ease.

The trouble is that clients, when we first meet them, don't typically know their eco-emotions, or at best are vaguely aware of them. To find them, I mirror whatever words the client uses to describe the emotion around an event. With dads, it often starts with, 'I get this uncomfortable feeling in my gut when my kids get angry about climate crisis.' As we gently dialogue about the 'uncomfortable feeling in my gut', we peel the onion and go deeper and deeper until the client is able to name the emotion in their gut, attach meaning to it, link it to a belief, attach it to an event, and desensitise the emotional grip through statements of self-affirmation and acceptance. In this way, values are primed, beliefs re-storied, mindset shifts, and behaviour changes, so that parent and child no longer trigger each other.

It's a job of nuance and sensitivity, but once the client starts the journey, they are usually the one to tell me when they have landed on primary core emotions and when they are no longer gripped and paralysed by said emotions – they can feel it in their body. Then we test to ensure they are no longer triggered by the emotion, belief and event, and move on to the next.

Behaviour change: Emotional narrative unleashed

As with the above interview examples, I start by having parents tell me, using vivid imagery, incredibly specific sensory details about recent, top-of-mind events that symbolise how they are handling difficult conversations/events and managing difficult relationships with their kids. I talk with parents about how they reflect on and were affected by these events. Quite frankly, it's mostly learning how to get comfortable talking publicly about emotions and feelings around big taboo existential issues, like climate, that are centre-stage for many kids. I hear parents out, listen to their perspectives, witness, share my own vulnerabilities, and travel with them into the body, through pain points and discomfort that mask emotion. For those readers thinking 'What about purpose, doing and action?', all I have to say is that, in my experience, without sound emotional underpinning, purpose lacks clarity, behaviour change is fleeting and action fails.

We coaches are as triggered by and afraid of our big emotions as our clients are. We all have much work to do. There are many tension-filled steps between accepting that humans are killing the planet, acknowledging grief, finding gratitude and taking action, all of which require deep introspection. Most of us are taught to be wary of big emotion. But I have found that trauma-informed emotional deep dives are fun, meaningful and make us feel better about ourselves.

The commonality in my various emotional coaching methodologies is learning how to be accepting when there is no clear answer or solution. Through loosely structured processes of guided visual imagery, I work with parents and teens to uncover emotional contributing factors to problematic events. We discover internal strategies for self-discovery that help us stay with the tension of uncertainty. We expand our window of tolerance. We learn to recognise and respect our limits, gain confidence in self-expression and over-ride the amygdala-driven fight-or-flight response. I precisely mirror my clients' words, exploring each troubling event and layer after layer of triggering belief, exposing what our subconscious has worked so hard to keep hidden from us. We are all gripped by emotion, often connected to childhood events. We just don't know it. Exploring big emotion with loving curiosity brings emotional freedom, enabling relationship and re-connection to self, others and Earth.

The beauty of emotion coaching is that, once clients understand and lean into their emotions and feel heard and validated, they understand, hear and validate others, instead of letting difficult conversations paralyse and damage relationships. The magic lies in letting nature be the portal through which emotions can be safely accessed and the troubling events that surround them diffused.

Safety and connection: Identifying with nature

We start our coaching relationship by taking a walk in nature. We help each other find something important that we feel a connection with, like a tree or a rock or a stream, develop a relationship with it, and attribute its qualities to ourselves. We say, 'The trunk of the tree weathers the storm; I too can show the strength and resolve to live a lower carbon lifestyle. The seed holds all the potential to become a mighty tree, survive threats and thrive in adversity; so do my children. The water shapes the rock; negative or limiting beliefs I hold about myself can change and take on any shape I choose.'

We lean into the wisdom of nature to reveal the answers we have hidden in our bodies. We find our wellspring of strength from something in nature with which we connect. We travel there repeatedly, spiritually and/or physically, to that tree, rock or spring, throughout our coaching relationship, with simple guided visualisation, using talk therapy, until tensions in our bodies that protect us from our negative emotions, limiting beliefs and contradictions dissipate.

Many clients choose to embody a tree, imagining tree as self. It's often safer and easier to become embodied through imagining what our seeds, roots, trunk, branches, leaves, flowers and fruit symbolise and what they tell us about who we are. Tree work as parts work can be a comfortable way to safely access our contradictions and address our own parts-work paradox. We consist of many parts or sub-personalities that either complement or contradict our true self. The ideal is to acknowledge parts of self that cause us to be stuck, like those parts that underlie denial and disavowal, blocking us from accepting and coping with the fear, anxiety or dystopian feelings of our kids. The idea is to be in positive relationship with all our parts, understand the wounds and emotional underpinnings that hold them in place, and lovingly acknowledge and accept them. By bringing all our parts into alignment with self, we free ourselves to be in better relationship with our kids and take the dramatic action on climate that they demand of us.

Nature experience and nature metaphor work, whether through direct exposure or imagination, are central. We all know intuitively that we are one with nature and that we are in fact a mighty tree, but our reductionist, mechanistic, analytic, black-

and-white 'left' brain and our world now resemble each other too much. Coaches are accustomed to keeping clients out of their left hemisphere, but the imperative to do so in systems coaching is underscored by the fact that the left brain is incapable of seeing itself as connected to the world outside of ourselves (McGilchrist, 2022). Indeed, many of us have forgotten, de-prioritise, or argue against the notion that nature and self are indistinguishable. Connecting to our roots is key. No traditional indigenous/ Aboriginal language on Earth has a word for 'inanimate' (Little Bear, 2022). Thus, the distinction between nature and self is non-existent in traditional cultures and spiritual traditions, such as pantheism, and among modern-day romanticists. To this effect, we must respectfully take advantage of historic systems of knowledge that embody the concept of nature as self.

Emotional freedom

In climate coaching circles, I often hear people saying that climate is not an environmental problem; it's a behaviour problem. I agree, with a proviso: if you reduce behaviour to its lowest common denominator, what do you get? Emotion. Thus, climate is an emotion problem because our emotions and our relationship to them determine our values and behaviour. I have found that, without solid emotional underpinning, behaviour change is limited and fleeting. I have seen too many goal-based, value-oriented, behaviour-modification coaching efforts fail. Lack of attention to the mechanics of our client's inner emotional landscape is a contributing factor to that failure. I have found that behaviour change happens from an ability to observe ourselves emotionally and re-story and respond to external stimuli in a way that brings us joy.

My emotion coaching is about feeling our feelings, then talking about those feelings, and then using our heightened understanding of those feelings to unite families splintered by lack of ability to navigate difficult conversations. Once we coaches get familiar with our own emotions, working with client emotion is easy. I find that emotions are fluid; even grief can be reorganised, reprocessed and restructured into gratitude and joy. But a little grief always remains, keeping us honest with ourselves.

In my view, many coaches shy away from eco-emotions, especially big ones like grief, fear, sadness, anger, guilt and shame. It is my belief that, if we, as coaches and clients, can change our relationship to these core eco-emotions, we can change our relationship with climate and with Mother Earth herself. We can find true love for ourselves and create lasting connections. I believe that humanity knows exactly what to do to save ourselves from ourselves. We simply need to let ourselves find our map, locate our route and embark on a journey of understanding ourselves from the inside out, as one with nature. It is my premise that unlocking our emotions is key to re-locking the lid of Pandora's climate box.

The past: Wellspring of emotional wisdom

We know what to do: follow the wisdom of traditional cultures and others for whom meaning-making through emotional awareness and nature connection was never severed. The poet Keats (1817) knew it: the ability to be 'in uncertainties, mysteries, doubts, without any irritable reaching after fact and reason keeps the door open to wonder'. Maslow (1943) knew it: 'Never forget that our relationship to nature is equivalent to our relationship with self.' Jung (1964) knew it: 'Meaning makes a great many things endurable, perhaps everything.' The Dalai Lama (2016) knows it: 'To calm the mind, we map our emotions to make our awareness full of choices, compassion, meaning and purpose.'

I find great joy and practical coaching advantage in the universality of coaching with emotion. I coach indigenous/Aboriginal people in Canada and people of colour from across the globe from diverse socio-economic and educational experiences. I always find connection and coachable topics through emotion. Indeed, our universal experience of common emotion could be the great unifier of humanity. Those of us in the West could benefit from taking a back seat and learning from those in traditional cultures who never lost relationship with nature or emotion.

The need for emotional work around the climate crisis is great. One of the biggest coaching challenges I see is keeping clients out of their heads. Keeping clients from swinging back and forth between head and heart is tough, especially with emotions. We all have work to do. We are all guilty of shying away from troubling eco-emotions and jumping into 'potential and purpose' coaching. I have seen many coaches ignore troubling emotions like grief and shame, or prematurely rush clients through emotion work to focus on values and behaviour. My advice to coaches is to do whatever it takes to keep clients in their heart, delve deeply into shadow work, dive deeply into and step far beyond the body, use words rich in emotional imagery, avoid the brain completely, let the body talk, and free those eco-emotions from our subconscious.

The future: Dependent on vivid imagination

My coaching model is almost entirely based on the somatic emotional aspect of BEing. My observation is that DOing happens organically, as a result of a solid emotional foundation enabling re-imaginative mindset shift. To this effect, I recently heard David Drake, the founder of Narrative Coaching, speak in regard to goal setting and doing. He said:

> Clients are in a change process during coaching and it's about what the client is ready to do now, not later. Learning and development happen in the present. The future is not something that happens later. The future is just a new moment that hasn't arrived yet. We already have the clarity. We just need to open ourselves to it. (Drake, 2022)

Seeing the future in the present through imaginative mindsight enables heightened awareness to observe ourselves, to think differently about the world and to believe in the impossible. We need to re-birth the brave emotional insight we had as children. If difficult emotions can be tapped and plumbed with curiosity, reflection and love, they can be supplanted by, or supplemented with, other feelings. Emotions like grief can be supplanted or supplemented by gratitude. Sadness by joy. Shame by pride. Fear by courage. But let's keep that client anger close and use it to our advantage.

Resilience: Cultivating and redirecting righteous anger at home

I delicately cultivate anger as motivation for behaviour change. In all truth, I never advocate elimination of any emotions; they all have a positive role to play, but some need their intensity reduced, some need to be re-evaluated through reflection, and some that lead us into loops of repeating unhelpful behaviours need to be re-storied. The easiest way to tame emotional intensity and redirect emotional energy is by knowing them intimately, accepting them on a deeply spiritual level, learning how to be in relationship with them and re-channeling them to support behaviour change. How? By talking about them, befriending them and loving them. Going from a culture that does not talk about emotions to one that *loves* all of them, even the big eco-emotions, is, in my opinion, the greatest challenge facing Western humanity. And the best way to get in touch with our feelings is through nature connection and taking the lead from those who never forgot. Indigenous people in the Americas taught me much of what I know about practical coaching, ethics, morality and relationship.

We can only do so much as coaches. The holy grail is to un-attach from outcome and focus on what clients can do in the present by awakening clarity and sharing self-help tools to guide them forward. In my experience, the overwhelming majority of change happens outside the coaching relationship. I spend a lot of time giving clients the tools to do that. And it has the benefit of democratising what is otherwise an elite practice, unavailable to most of the world. And the rest of the world needs climate coaching as much as Western elites do. In fact, they often need it more. In my coaching work I've found that, although citizens outside the Western world have far greater resilience to change, they also feel the effects of climate crisis more acutely, and often feel eco-anxiety more intensely as a direct threat to life and health. So, as climate disasters increase, there will be massive need for coaching interventions outside the Western world, and particularly in the global south, where peoples will be most severely affected – and are already. My work has shown me that we all feel the same emotions and share a common emotional landscape. Emotion coaching is applicable globally, can yield results in only a few sessions, and can be self-applied. What better way to unite humanity?

Why parents? Why families?

Curiously, of all those I talk to about climate, I find parents are the group in greatest denial of eco-emotions. It's because parents care so much for their kids. Many parents actually come to coaching with physical illness and panic because they are repeatedly trigged by dire climate news; its cumulative stress literally becomes 'big T' trauma, causing divorce from self, damaging mental health, weakening the immune system and harming relationships with family.

I focus mostly on parents because their climate-activist children are often too exhausted to cope with coaching. Even when their emotions are embodied, their bodies tell me they can't go on much longer. They need love first. And for that, they need to be listened to. They need sensitive reciprocal communications to feel trusting security. And that is the work of the parent: just listening to kids' stories, starting with 'I want a world in which…', gently moving from dissonance to resonance, recreating that positive sense of self, dependent on awe and joy. Once their anxiety is tamed through vividly imagining what system collapse and deep adaptation (resilience, relinquishment, restoration, reconciliation) could look, feel, taste and smell like, the kids I see in my practice are often quite skilled at self-coaching. And their stories of deep adaptation are incredibly inspiring to parents, once they open themselves to their emotions and deliberatively use those emotions to inform core biospheric values.

Opposing narratives as drivers of disconnection

Parents and children in my climate coaching practice generally hold polar-opposite climate narratives and belief systems that are deeply in need of reflection and reconciliation. Activist kids often embrace a 'dystopian system change' or a 'dystopia to utopia' climate narrative in which many human systems – such as capitalism – collapse, humans tragically run amok, deep adaptation occurs, sometimes across multiple dimensions of time and space, and regenerative systems emerge like a phoenix, based on living systems and regenerative and ecological principles. The proximity of dystopia and speculative-future-fantasy keeps the kids in my practice light years ahead of their parents in embracing their complex eco-emotions. They just need their parents to start acting like adults and get on with addressing climate as crisis, within and without.

I have found that parents tend to have one of two dominant personal climate narratives. The first is positive future vision, characterised by doing without being, intense fear of uncertainty and fierce optimism that people and systems are capable of rapid change. The second is technocratic denial, characterised by disavowal, cynicism about real-time climate action and naïve optimism about future technological fixes. Surprisingly, the presenting conditions of both doing and denying climate-narrative parent groups are fear of uncertainty, denial of emotion and disavowal of negative future scenarios. Children's presenting conditions are fear, stress and burnout from activism, resulting in anger, grief and confusion about poor adult behaviour.

The seemingly paradoxical climate narratives held by many climate-activist teens can be challenging for many parents to understand, as are most things that are non-linear and non-binary! Sorry, Mum and Dad, you have some learning to do. But it's fun. I suggest starting with what your kids are reading. Futuristic and speculative climate fiction is all the rage among young people. Think of it as next-generation Gen-dread – sci-fi with surprisingly positive outcomes. Read these books, have crazy dreams, cry and mourn for all that has already been lost, hold close to your heart the billion climate refugees soon to be wandering the planet, imagine deep adaptation, and you'll understand so much more about your kids' climate narratives.

Family tribal connections

I'm often asked 'Why work with families?' The answer is, because we're tribal, because we make decisions based on the social norms of our people, because our response to climate crisis is a socially constructed silence, and because we can more easily break that silence by engaging with others in our tribe. Further, because our family tribes tend to have some common values and beliefs, and because values-based narratives drive our response to climate, there is much to be gained from working with family units to help get everyone on the same page.

Emotion, connection, trust and intimacy are closely related: when the parents I coach feel emotional availability, they report a marked increase in their ability to connect with their children over climate – to listen, accept their kids' feelings, not try to fix anything, and simply BE in relationship with self and family. Once parents and children accept that the world is going to change dramatically, cease being gripped by uncertainty and control and figure out their own way to make meaning and contribute to creating a vibrant new world, we're off to the races. In the words of EFT coach and psychotherapist Leslie S. Greenberg, 'It is possible to facilitate change in the most complex domain of human experience, the domain of emotions, in our inner realms, beyond reason, beyond words' (Greenberg, 2015).

Returning to the two intake interviews I reported at the beginning of this chapter, Leslie Greenberg's words ring clear. Both parent and child are initially operating from a place beyond reason, beyond words, from an inner realm that nobody but they can tap into. For the parent at least, their inner emotional realm is unavailable, unknown, unheard and unseen. Once we 'daylight' our feelings, make sense of, de-trigger and share our inner emotional experience with those we love most, our kids, we can make huge leaps forward.

The simple act of a mother reading her 'letter to self', first to a tree, then to her children, enabled a much deeper discussion than they had had in years. As a coach, I ensured they emerged from that deep dive in a grove of ancient trees. They found room to let nature hold the space, to hold one another, have tolerance, practise love and embrace radical self-acceptance. In the initial series of five coaching sessions with parent and kids, doing was absent; it was all about being. That was enough. They went home with the tools and self-coaching skills they needed to go deeper. They consulted with me occasionally. When they were ready to DO, about a year later, they got in touch and we coached DOing. Within five sessions, they dealt with their overwhelm (it's too big a problem) and scarcity (there is not enough time to solve the problem), found a tribe, and took action of far more consequence than they ever dreamed possible. They did it together, from a place of love. And it was all because we spent so much time on emotions, informing values, clearing limiting beliefs and enabling cortisol reduction and ventral vagal recalibration, so the prefrontal cortex could resume duty and help them fight climate crisis.

Tapping into biospheric emotions and values

The following lists are of emotions and values that I find particularly useful in guiding pro-environmental/social behaviour:

> *Emotions*: hopeless, powerless, shocked, worried, overwhelmed, disgusted, stressed, ashamed, frustrated, mad, sad, grief, guilt, denial, optimism, confusion, scepticism, anger, resignation.

> *Values*: reciprocity, harmony, adaptability, determination, awareness, curiosity, compassion, connection, empathy, sustainability, discovery, innovation, intuition, community, autonomy, belonging, appreciation, reflection, empowerment, humility, engagement, making a difference.

I start many climate-coaching relationships with nature-based, guided visual imagery featuring a 10–20-minute clip from a visual tone poem film such as *Koyaanisqatsi* (1982),[1] *Baraka* (1992),[2] *Samsara* (2011),[3] or *One Earth* (2020),[4] with abundant vivid images, sharply contrasting nature and traditional people with the effects of capitalism and colonialism. This gets clients out of their heads and into their hearts. This is followed by having clients select top-of-mind emotions and values from the above lists that have been awakened by the film clip, followed by storytelling about recent troubling events connected to those emotions and values. This quickly opens the vulnerability door, enabling an ordinary coaching session to be extraordinary. Once big emotions are acknowledged and greeted with curious exploration, their grip is lessened and they can strengthen biospheric and humanistic values, which in turn can be used to change belief, mindset and behaviour.

Further reading

Brosch, T. (2021). Affect and emotions as drivers of climate change perception and action: A review. *Current Opinion in Behavioral Sciences, 42*, 15–21.

Dana, D. (2020). *Polyvagal exercises for safety and connection.* W.W. Norton & Co.

Dodds J. (2021). The psychology of climate anxiety. *BJPsych Bulletin, 45*(4), 222–226.

Harvard Health Publishing. (2020, July 6). *Understanding the stress response: Chronic activation of the survival mechanism impairs health.* [Online.] www.health.harvard.edu/staying-healthy/understanding-the-stress-response

McGilchrist, I. (2019). *Ways of attending: How our divided brain constructs the world.* Routledge. (See also https://channelmcgilchrist.com).

Murtugudde, R. (2014, April 25). *Climate change response: Fight or flight? Rest or digest?* Earth System Science Interdisciplinary Center. University of Maryland. https://essic.umd.edu/joom2/index.php/blogs-main/researcher-blogs/gudde-blog/1621-climate-change-response-fight-or-flight-or-rest-and-digest

Porges, S.W. (2009). The polyvagal theory: New insights into adaptive reactions of the autonomous nervous system. *Cleveland Clinic Journal of Medicine, 76*(S2), S86–90.

1. *Koyaanisqatsi: Life out of balance.* (1982). Godfrey Reggio (Dir.). Qatsi Productions.
2. *Baraka.* (1992). Ron Fricke (Dir.). Magidson Films.
3. *Samsara.* (2011). Ron Fricke (Dir.). Magidson Films.
4. *One Earth.* (2020). Romain Pennes. YouTube. www.youtube.com/watch?v=QQYgCxu988s

References

Dalai Lama. (2016, May). The Dalai Lama and the Atlas of Emotions. *Science and Non-Duality*. www.scienceandnonduality.com/article/atlas-of-emotions-dalai-lama-in-the-fields-of-emotion

Drake, D.S. (2022). *Living liminal lives: Creating new stories for new times.* Climate Coaching Alliance Annual Conference, March 5.

Greenberg, L.S. (2015). *Emotion-focused therapy: Coaching clients to work through their feelings.* American Psychology Association.

Jung C.G. (1964). *Man and his symbols.* Doubleday.

Keats, J. (1817, December 21). *Letter to his younger brothers, George and Thomas.* http://mason.gmu.edu/~rnanian/Keats-NegativeCapability.html

Little Bear, L. (2022, March 30). *Environment and sustainability from a metaphysical Blackfoot perspective.* YouTube. www.youtube.com/watch?v=FMyfvA7N5Eg

Maslow, A.H. (1943). A theory of human motivation. *Psychological Review, 50*(4), 370–396.

McGilchrist, I. (2022). *The matter with things: Our brains, our delusions, and the unmaking of the world.* Perspectiva Press.

About the contributors

Bayo Akomolafe, rooted with the Yorùbá people in a more-than-human world, is the father to Alethea and Kyah, the grateful life-partner to Ije, and son and brother. An international speaker, posthumanist thinker, poet, teacher, public intellectual, essayist, author of *These Wilds Beyond our Fences: Letters to my daughter on humanity's search for home* and co-editor of *We Will Tell our Own Story: The lions of Africa speak*, Bayo is the founder of The Emergence Network and host of the online post-activist course 'We Will Dance with Mountains'. He currently lectures at Pacifica Graduate Institute, California, and University of Vermont, Burlington. He sits on the boards of many organisations, including Science and Non-Duality (US) and Local Futures (Australia). In July 2022, he was appointed the inaugural Global Senior Fellow of the University of California's (Berkeley) Othering and Belonging Institute. He has also been appointed Senior Fellow for The New Institute in Hamburg, Germany. www.bayoakomolafe.net; www.emergencenetwork.org

Roger Duncan is a registered systemic family therapist, systemic supervisor and author, and writes and lectures on systemic psychotherapy and the epistemology and practice of ecosystemic psychotherapy. He originally studied biology and has been involved in working with adolescents and nature-based practice for more than 30 years. He was one of the pioneer tutors of the Ruskin Mill Education Trust, where he was involved in the development of innovative therapeutic education programmes for adolescents with complex and challenging behaviour in the woodlands and wilderness settings, and had a leadership role in senior management. Roger was a visiting lecturer in psychological therapies for the Tavistock and Portman NHS Trust and course director of the Confer diploma on 'Eco-psychotherapy and the Emerging Adolescent Mind: A systemic integration of our relationship with nature into child and adolescent psychotherapy practice'. His book, *Nature in Mind: Systemic thinking and imagination in ecopsychology and mental health*, was published in 2018. Roger has worked for more than 10 years in the NHS Child and Adolescent Mental Health Service (CAMHS) with adolescents who have experienced complex trauma, including unaccompanied asylum-seeking children, and in private practice with individuals, families and organisations.

Fred Ehresmann is a piano and Hammond organ player with a degree in music who somehow found himself qualifying as a registered mental health nurse specialising in working with children, young people and their families. In a career spanning some 30 years, his work has taken him into a wide variety of settings across health, social care and education, encompassing everything from secure units through to GP practice. He trained in solution-focused practice with Brief in London, specialising in working with parents and groups with Parents Plus in Dublin. He works at the University of the West of England as a senior lecturer in mental health, where he has designed and leads an undergraduate module in solution-focused practice.

Hetty Einzig works globally in leadership development, with individuals, teams and organisations, designing and delivering programmes in the corporate and public sectors. She is also a coaching supervisor and fully trained psychotherapist. This deeper understanding and experience underpins her coaching. Her roots lie in psychosynthesis, a transpersonal psychology. Hetty's approach is holistic and systemic. A partner with selected coaching leadership providers and a senior associate with Common Purpose (building social and environmental awareness and responsibility in organisations), she teaches on the diploma in executive coaching at the Irish Management Institute (IMI), and (in French) on the coaching diploma at BMH Coach in Casablanca. Hetty is Publications Strategy Director with the Association for Coaching and Executive Editor of *Coaching Perspectives*, the AC global magazine. Hetty's career has spanned the arts, journalism and television, psychology, health, environmental awareness and culture change. She was a founder member of Be the Change, the social change organisation. With the Pachamama Alliance, she facilitated train-the-trainer programmes to deliver their ground-breaking symposium, 'Awakening the Dreamer, Changing the Dream'. She is also a facilitator with Analytic-Network Coaching and a member of the Eco-Leadership Institute. Her latest book, *The Future of Coaching: Vision, leadership and responsibility in a transformed world,* was published in 2017.

Caroline Frizell is senior lecturer on the MA Dance Movement Psychotherapy at Goldsmiths, where she has worked since 2007. Caroline holds a PhD in posthuman, eco-feminist research and this inquiry informs her practice as a dance movement psychotherapist and supervisor (UKCP, ADMP), working indoors as well as on the wilds of Dartmoor. Caroline's extensive publications intersect dance movement psychotherapy, eco-psychotherapy, supervision and critical disability studies.

Niki Harré is a professor at the University of Auckland, specialising in community psychology and the psychology of sustainability. Her research addresses issues of environmental sustainability, citizenship, values and political activism. In 2007 she co-edited the book *Carbon Neutral by 2020: How New Zealanders can tackle climate change.* Her two latest books are *Psychology for a Better World: Strategies to inspire sustainability* and *The Infinite Game: How to live well together.*

Caroline Hickman is a psychotherapist and lecturer at the University of Bath. She has researched children and young people's emotional responses to climate change around the world for 10 years, examining eco-anxiety and distress, eco-empathy, trauma, moral injury and intergenerational stresses. She is co-lead author on a 2021 quantitative global study into children and young people's emotions and thoughts about climate change published in *The Lancet Planetary Health*. She has been developing a range of therapeutic and psychoeducational tools for ecological distress and a psychological assessment model for eco-anxiety, and delivers workshops in climate psychology, emotional resilience and mental health internationally. http://caroline-hickman.com/index.html

Chris Johnstone is one of the UK's leading resilience trainers, with a background in medicine, psychological therapies, groupwork and coaching, His work explores what helps us face disturbing situations (whether in our own lives or the world) and respond in ways that nourish resilience and wellbeing. His books include *Active Hope* (co-authored with Joanna Macy, published in 14 languages and significantly revised in 2022) and *Seven Ways to Build Resilience*. His online courses in resilience and active hope have attracted many thousands of participants. He has websites at ChrisJohnstone. info, CollegeOfWellbeing.com and ActiveHope.Training.

Yasmin Kapadia is a Re-Vision trained transpersonal integrative counsellor and eco-therapist based in Brighton. She has a particular interest in working with issues of difference, diversity and social-ecological injustice.

Jo McAndrews is an experienced training consultant, facilitator and qualified psychotherapist. She specialises in working with young people, parents and professionals who work with children, particularly around growing resilience in the face of crisis. Her work is informed by current research into interpersonal neurobiology and polyvagal theory, which offer fantastic insight into the needs of children as they develop and also into human thriving. She is particularly interested in the impact of trauma on child development, what the conditions for recovery are and how to grow resilience in children, adults and communities. In the past few years she has become more strongly involved in the field of climate crisis action with a systemic and global justice approach. She gives talks and trainings on supporting children in the face of climate and social crisis, eco-anxiety and resilience. She now runs LifeKind, a training organisation dedicated to this work.

Andy Miller is a climate coach in Vancouver, Canada, the greenest city in the world. He was the lead scientist and Aboriginal liaison at Canada's largest environmental group for 20 years. He has an MSc in the business psychology of sustainable development. He is a certified EFT coach. He is the devoted father of an indigenous, transgender, two-spirit youth activist, who taught him much about navigating difficult conversations, emotional validation and sharing our truth. He explores human potential at difficult crossroads. He finds growth spending time in uncomfortable, in-between, liminal spaces. Andy is particularly fond of the broad range of facilitation tools that encompass The Work That Reconnects.

Pedro Oliveira completed a five-year training at the University of Coimbra (Clinical Psychology branch), and a master's in child development (MSc) and a doctorate in cultural diversity, both at Brunel University, London. His doctorate was followed by further clinical training at the Tavistock Institute and West London Mental Health Trust, and a post-doctorate position at the Institute of Family Therapy. He currently runs an English-speaking therapy service in Lisbon for international clients. Simultaneously, he has founded a collective of eco-aware psychologists (ecopsi.org) in Portugal, working similarly to the Climate Psychology Alliance. He is currently finishing a five-year training programme as a systemic couples and family therapist.

Born in the late 1960s in the UK, **Matthew Painton** has made the most of the privileges and advantages of peak-civilisation and a British passport all his life, having enjoyed the freedom to live, study and work in many countries throughout the world. His early student activism against social injustice gave way to a varied career: teaching English, then environmental conservation, countryside access, land estate management and, for the past decade, coaching and group facilitation. He is a certified co-active coach and has a BA in philosophy and religion and a masters' in agroforestry. Currently living in Brighton with his boyfriend, after being abruptly Brexited from Bulgaria, he is now looking at co-housing as the optimal way to reduce his enormous footprint and to weather the unfolding planetary meta-crisis in community. He is a co-founder of the Deep Adaptation Guides community.

Emma Palmer lives in Bristol, south-west England, wandering in the tracks of many of her ancestors. Working as a therapist since 2003, she is fascinated by the eco-psychological play between the present moment, the emergent and the liminal. A long-term apprentice of the Buddha, Emma appreciates the insight of age-old traditions and practices in the chaos of 2022. She has written four books under her former name – Kamalamani. With Deborah A. Lee, she co-edited *#MeToo: Counsellors and psychotherapists speak about sexual violence and abuse*, published by PCCS Books in 2022. www.kamalamani.co.uk

Robin Shohet has written extensively on supervision. His latest book, *In Love with Supervision*, was co-written with Joan Shohet and published by PCCS Books. His approach to tackling climate change is a deep inquiry into our thinking and our 'polluting' thoughts. This approach has led him to study first revenge and then forgiveness. He has organised two international conferences on this topic and plans another. He is a student of 'A Course in Miracles'.

Nick Totton is a body psychotherapist, supervisor and trainer, in practice for more than 40 years. He founded and for some years taught training in embodied-relational therapy and in wild therapy, which seeks to bring therapy into the wild and wildness into therapy. He is the author of a number of books, including *Wild Therapy* (PCCS Books), now in a second edition, and editor of several others. Nick lives in Sheffield with his partner. He has a daughter and two grandchildren. www.nicktotton.net

Maggie Turp is a psychotherapist whose practice is somewhere on an arc between psychoanalytic and narrative approaches. Her previous publications include two books, *Psychosomatic Health: The body and the word* (2002) and *Hidden Self-Harm: Narratives from psychotherapy* (2002), and a number of journal papers. In recent years she has focused on climate and ecological issues. She is a member of the editorial team of the Climate Psychology Alliance (CPA) journal *Explorations*, and its 'Cli-Fi Corner' section reflects her special interest in the ways in which fiction might help us to imagine and think through possible future scenarios. She is also part of the CPA therapeutic support team, offering a limited number of *pro bono* sessions to climate activists. Her desk-based work is complemented by time spent on the allotment, in the community garden and on long country walks.

Name index

Subject index